PRAISE FOR THE AUTHOR'S 'V2V' SERIES

Mary Anne Yarde – Author of the Du Lac Series

"These are not dry dusty books whose historical characters are one dimensional. Hughes has brought these men and women back to life with her quick wit and beautiful prose. The stories she tells are fabulously descriptive, as well as at times profoundly moving. She pulled it off beautifully."

D.K. Marley – Historical Fiction author of *Blood and Ink*

"What an incredibly fascinating walk through history with such in-depth historical research. I applaud Trisha Hughes for this immense undertaking, as well as the beautiful imagery and story-telling quality of her voice. I highly recommend taking this ambling journey into the pages of this historical series"

David Baird – David's Book Blurg

"Trisha Hughes did a great job of bringing each of these Kings and Queens to life. This is the kind of book that gives you the juicy, interesting facts and ignites the flames of passion for history"

Tony Riches – Historical Author of the *Tudor Trilogy*

"I wasn't disappointed as Trisha's lively and engaging style takes us on a grand tour of those who enjoyed wearing the crown. As Trisha Hughes says 'these stories span hundreds of years of lust, betrayal, heroism, murder, cruelties and mysteries.
What more could you ask for?"

Lyn Horner – Author

"Written in a lively, never boring style, I thoroughly enjoyed this historical epic. A definite 5 stars."

Paul Bennett – Author and Book Reviewer:

"Detailed research is evident throughout the book giving the reader a full picture of the events and the larger than life people who sought for the crown of a kingdom seemingly in constant turmoil and uncertainty. A fascinating tutorial of the
period of Canute to Elizabeth,
I'm looking forward to the next book.
5 stars"

PREVIOUSLY BY THE AUTHOR

Autobiography

Daughters of Nazareth

Historical Fiction

Book 1

Vikings to Virgin – *England's story from*
The Vikings to the Virgin Queen

Book 3

Victoria to Vikings – *England's story from*
Queen Victoria to The Vikings

'The Circle of Blood'

The Tartan Kings - *A Powerful & Rich Story of Scotland*

Crime/Mystery

Dragonfly

Chameleon

Scorpion

VIRGIN TO VICTORIA
ENGLAND'S STORY FROM THE VIRGIN QUEEN TO QUEEN VICTORIA

SECOND EDITION
BOOK TWO

TRISHA HUGHES

First published in Great Britain 2018 by
The Book Guild Ltd

Copyright © 2024 Trisha Hughes

The right of Trisha Hughes to be identified as the author of this work has been asserted by her in accordance with the Copyright, Design and Patents Act 1988.

All rights reserved. No part of this publication may be reproduced, transmitted, or stored in a retrieval system, in any form or by any means, without permission in writing from the publisher, nor be otherwise circulated in any form of binding or
cover other than that in which it is published and without a similar condition being imposed on the subsequent purchaser.

This work is fiction based on real events in history.

Typeset in Garamond

Cover by Ashley Risk

FOREWORD

To the victor goes the spoils and nowhere is this truer than in British monarchy history. Many of the early British kings are hidden in the mists of time while some, the ones who lost crucial battles, have almost completely disappeared when the victors erased their rivals from all surviving records. The men, and a couple of women, who triumphed made sure that the records showed their better claim to the throne, their better prowess in battle, and their greater benevolence and consequently love and support of their people. There was always someone in power who wanted to hide or obscure the truth.

Sources of those early years rely on fragments of information from various documents: the most notable the Anglo-Saxon Chronicle. It is partial and not always correct but it is invaluable as a guide to show us people and events that shaped British history. They were often written quite a while after the event, based on hearsay, and therefore it leaves room for historians to debate about what is correct and what is not. As well as this, only fragments of the original documents have survived through the centuries so early historical events are often circumstantial and some of the chroniclers had axes to grind which means their information is sometimes not entirely accurate. One of the most obvious chroniclers is William Shakespeare who needed to support Elizabeth 1 and the Tudors to earn a living.

FOREWORD

Many of his plays reinforce the Tudor claim to the throne when in actual fact, it was very tenuous. But it was a brave subject who went against the monarch.

By and large, unless a monarch was truly treacherous, his subjects could be depended on to support him. Even Charles 1 believed in that support and never considered that he would be executed.

In early Britain, the crown did not necessarily pass from father to son (primogeniture) as it does now and the question of succession was always difficult and in jeopardy. Among the Anglo-Saxon kings, it was sometimes from brother to brother due to the youth of the new monarch. This was the age when a king proved his strength in battle, and they almost never reached middle age, so a young boy was often left as their heir who could not possibly hold his own against rival family members. Inevitably, such a choice would lead to numerous rivalries between family members and, more often than not, resulted in invading armies.

Thanks to dynastic marriages, most rulers had foreign mothers and foreign wives and produced foreign children. The end result of this was many ruling families in Europe were closely related by blood and birth. This is certainly true when looking at the Normans, the Plantagenets and the first few Hanoverian kings who did not speak or even understand English. As with Queen Victoria, she was a predecessor of virtually every ruling house in Europe at the outbreak of World War I.

After having travelled through time in my first book 'Vikings to Virgin – The Hazards of being King', this second part in my 'V 2 V' series covers British monarchs beginning with Queen Elizabeth I and ends with Queen Victoria. It's a story of those bloodlines and I'm hoping you find it as incredibly interesting, sometimes amazing, as I do, and a wonderful drama.

They include, among their number, the vain, the greedy and the downright corrupt. There are adulterers, swindlers and cowards. Yet this group also shares one thing in common. In their own lifetimes, they were the most powerful individuals in the land. Their stories are full of lust, betrayal, heroism, murder, cruelty and mysteries.

Times were brutal and many saw the only option to gain the throne was to snatch it. As dangerous and fierce as that sounds, keeping it was even more difficult.

PART I

DAWN OF THE ELIZABETHAN ERA

When we wander through art galleries, pictures of a 16th-century English countryside are full of flowers and golden sunshine. We see cows grazing lazily on grassy hilltops with dappled light drifting softly through the trees and we see colourful butterflies floating languidly among the flowers. It all looks wonderfully peaceful and idyllic. But don't be misled. For most, it was anything but peaceful.

In those same pictures, if you look a little closer, you will see quaint thatched cottages dotted here and there and you will notice they are basic dwellings that would have housed poor families. Times were hard, jobs were few and their worldly possessions were a few pots, a ladle, some plates and if they were lucky, some mats to sleep on at night. Few people could afford candles and the only sounds at night would have been the soft raindrops on the thatched rooves, children tossing fitfully in front of a meagre fire and the rustle of vermin in the dark corners. And they would have known that with vermin came disease. The threat of catching typhoid, dysentery or the plague was an everyday terror that would have affected their whole way of life. It was an unbelievably harsh time for some but not everyone was at the bottom of the ladder.

In those same art galleries, we also see men and women in extravagant clothes wearing magnificent jewellery. Unlike the other paintings, these people look well fed, clean and privileged. But again, if you look closer still, you will also see a little doubt and uncertainty lurking in their watchful eyes. Don't forget, the more you had, the more you could lose and you had to be very particular who you spoke to over a glass or two of wine and you knew you had to choose your words very carefully.

These people lived in houses that looked more like palaces than the squalid homes of the poor. They had silverware, carpets, servants and maybe even a mirror. The appetite for luxuries was endless for those who could afford them. It was a time when Tudor architecture blossomed and companies began setting up shops full of crystal, tapestries, oak furniture and curtains and it was a time when lace was all the craze for both sexes.

But whether you were rich or poor, it was a time when you knew to abide by the law. In any society, laws are meant to give people security and with that security, farmers can farm, artists can paint and writers can write. This was Queen Mary's era and security was only available if people accepted basic laws... *her* basic laws... stating Catholicism was the one and only true religion. If you didn't agree with her, you would have been one of the hundreds of people burned at the stake, hung or beheaded because of your religious belief. But if Queen Mary thought that heretics would eventually convert to Catholicism, she was being very optimistic.

Between 1553 and 1558, England had suffered under the iron rule of Bloody Mary. Before Mary, her father Henry VIII had ruled and before him, his father Henry VII. None of them could be called shrinking violets when it came to chopping off people's heads and dishing out punishments. Before them even, England had survived the unrelenting Lancasters and Yorks and the War of the Roses. They had survived during the brutal reign of the Plantagenets and the invasion by the Normans. Before all of them, stood the Vikings. For 1500 years, they had endured wars, battles, rebellions, plagues and famines. They had been taxed so harshly that survival was a daily problem and their mortality rate was one of the worst in Europe. But as difficult as it all was, they had endured. Better than that, they had *survived*. As a race of people, the English are not ones to just throw their hands in the air and give up. That they will *never* do.

Two months before Mary died, a comet blazed across the London skies. It was half the size of the moon and fire streaked behind it in the glorious Tudor colours of red, white and gold for seven days and nights. In a time when superstition was rife, it was a sure sign to the English people that a change was about to happen and hope resurfaced. And heaven knows, they needed every scrap of hope they could find.

The comet was what England had been waiting for – a sign of better times. A new beginning even. They had suffered so much persecution during Mary's reign that they believed things could not get any worse. This comet, this *sign*, meant it was all coming to an end at last. Surely, that's what it meant, they prayed.

And they waited. And waited. Then in November of 1558, after a lengthy sickness, Queen Mary died and a new queen came to the throne with promises of reformation and a brighter, fresh England. Their new queen, Elizabeth, had a swarthy complexion like her mother and despite her slightly hooked nose and long face, her bright, expressive eyes softened her sharp features and made her look almost attractive.

Ironically, Queen Elizabeth's birthdate was 7th September, the feast day of the Nativity of the Virgin Mary.

ELIZABETH I

Born 1533
Reign 1558 – 1603

Elizabeth's life was troubled from the moment she was born. Despite the challenge of being Henry VIII's daughter, or perhaps *because* of it, she was a quiet and studious girl who could write English, speak Latin and Italian before progressing further on to French and Greek. By the time her formal education ended, she was the best-educated woman of her generation quietly living in the shadow of her father. When he died, everything suddenly and irrevocably changed.

This is when we have to let our imagination take over for a little while. Imagine being a quiet 13-year-old who hears that her father is dead and she is to be packed up from her home and sent to live with her stepmother, her father's sixth and last wife. Don't let your imagination go too far though because Kateryn Parr was nothing like Queen Grimhilde from the Snow White story. Kateryn was always kind and gentle, but Elizabeth was just a little girl who had been protected and secluded for most of her life and she was understandably nervous at this latest big change in her life. She'd lost her mother Anne Boleyn years before and now her father was dead and her nine-year-old half-brother Edward was about to be crowned king. To top it off, she had an elder half-sister who was cold, sometimes erratic, and who scared the life out of her most of the time.

As Elizabeth settled in with Kateryn, her younger brother was settling onto his throne. Being nine years old and the King of England was not what he had expected either. Like his sister, when their father died everything changed for him as well. Before he knew it, his uncle, Edward Seymour Duke of Somerset, had stepped in with the backing of thirteen of the sixteen council members and had declared that he would act as the Regent until the young king came of age. Being king would have been very daunting for the young boy and he was probably very grateful to have a familiar figure by his side.

For Elizabeth, living with Kateryn was a strange new world and there was a lot to take in. She was more than a little confused with the changes and the suddenness of everything, despite her father's lengthy ill-health. What was perhaps even more confusing to Elizabeth was that there seemed to be a lot of comings and goings in her stepmother's house by the Duke of Somerset's younger brother, Thomas Seymour, at all hours of the day and night. This is where our story gets juicy. But to tell it, you need a little background first.

From a very young age, both Seymour brothers were gifted with lands and titles. Then to add to those titles, the elder brother Edward was given the title of Viscount Beauchamp of Hache in Somerset after their younger sister Jane married Henry VIII. A year later, Thomas was also granted the castle of Holt in Cheshire prior to the christening of his nephew Prince Edward while Edward was elevated to the earldom of Hertford. Although Thomas continued to be the recipient of lands and manors, no further titles came his way. The titles were all reserved for his elder brother Edward.

To say the least, Thomas felt 'hard done by' which goes a long way to explaining the tenseness between the two brothers. It didn't improve at all when Henry VIII died and his elder brother took over the regency as Lord Protector for young Edward. Wanting a piece of the action as well, Thomas demanded to be named as governor to the young king; after all, Edward was *his* nephew as well.

Edward Seymour, now Duke of Somerset, tried to buy his brother off with the title of Baron of Sudeley and the appointment of Lord Admiral, as well as granting him several pieces of land and a seat on the Privy Council.

But Thomas wasn't having anything to do with it. As uncle to the king, he felt he should receive more, at the very least an earldom. It was even hinted that Edward was the one behind the lack of titles coming his way.

When looking back in history, Thomas' demands seem understandable. When kings were in their 'minority', it was common that any remaining uncles were given much greater titles than what Thomas received. And with his brother as Lord Protector of the Realm, Somerset had the power to recommend that his brother be granted a greater title than just baron. But for some reason, it seems he didn't. If you were a suspicious sort of person you may think that Somerset had the notion that his brother would attempt to over-throw him at some time in the future if he had too much power in his hands. It wasn't such and outrageous thought when you think about it, considering the antics of past generations.

So Thomas never received what he felt he truly deserved and he never believed he'd been given his fair share. Wanting a far greater portion of power than the two titles gave him, his plotting began in earnest.

And that was his greatest weakness. Although seen as a greedy villain in history books, it's easy to see that he was also a victim of his elder brother's ambitions. Imagine seeing his younger sister married to Henry VIII, getting everything her heart desired, then seeing his elder brother as the King's Protector, gathering titles, land and power, and then there he was, stuck in the middle, feeling left out and forgotten.

Thomas was nearly 40 years old when Henry VIII died and there's no doubt he could have married any noble woman he wished. But his ambitions were always greater and higher than most. What Thomas wanted was a marriage that would give him money, property and political standing that would rival his brother. And this is where Kateryn Parr enters the scene.

Before Kateryn and Henry had married, she and Seymour had hoped to marry after the death of her third husband, Lord Latimer. But there was a necessary mourning period involved for grieving widows and this delayed their marriage request to Henry and their subsequent and hopeful wedding announcement. And so they waited. Then, only a couple of months after Latimer's death and while still in mourning, Henry asked Kateryn to marry *him* and of course, who would have been brave enough to turn down Henry VIII?

By then, Henry was a massive sallow-looking 51-year-old man with thinning hair, a huge ego and a terrible disposition. No doubt Kateryn was comparing the handsome Thomas to the not-so-fetching Henry as he watched her with sharp little eyes behind fat eyelids and smiled down at her with his moist, swollen lips that didn't quite hide the decaying teeth and foul breath. She would have smelt the horrible odour from the yellow pus bubbling up into the dressing on his bandaged leg and she would have been dreading the moment he would bend down to kiss her wetly. She would have wished she could escape to any place on earth instead of gambling with her life with Henry.

That was never going to be the case. Henry did *not* have to follow the same rules as everyone else and all preparations were made for the happy nuptials. Subsequently, and perhaps shrewdly, after their marriage, Henry sent Thomas abroad several times to battles and embassies, which sufficiently kept him well away from Kateryn.

This probably fuelled Thomas' internal fire to strive for what he thought he justly deserved and should have been his. With his nephew Edward on the throne, it opened a new door of opportunity for Thomas.

Thomas' next step was to write a letter to the young king, via an advisor John Fowler, requesting permission to marry Kateryn Parr.

It was a clever, conniving plan since Kateryn's household also included 11-year-old Lady Jane Grey and the 13-year-old Lady Elizabeth, which meant wealth and a certain degree of power would be at his disposal. The letter was secretly given to young Edward for his signature and when Somerset found out about it, he went ballistic.

But by then, it was already too late. The letter had been signed, sealed and delivered and the couple had not wasted any time with a lengthy courtship. They'd headed straight to the altar. The happy couple then took Elizabeth and Jane into their household at Chelsea.

There's no doubt that Thomas Seymour was a handsome, charismatic man. All the women at court agreed on that fact. And at 14 years old, Elizabeth was no different. She was young, hormonal and impressionable and she was clearly smitten. Happy evenings, full of romps and horseplay, soon escalated when he began to enter her bedroom in his nightgown and tickle her, sometimes spanking her. Rather than confronting her husband over his inappropriate activities, the heavily pregnant Kateryn passively watched. These frolics abruptly ended one night when Kateryn discovered her husband and Elizabeth in a tight embrace. It was probably then that she would have remembered that Elizabeth was, after all, the daughter of Anne Boleyn. Before she knew it, Elizabeth was unceremoniously removed to Waltham Abbey and later on, reportedly moved further away to Hatfield House.

As final as that sounds, things changed dramatically months later on 30th August. In the middle of the night and after a long and difficult delivery, Kateryn delivered a baby girl at Thomas' county seat, Sudeley Castle in Gloucestershire.

Kateryn was 36 years old and the pregnancy, as far as we know, was her first. For Tudor times this was very late to be embarking on motherhood and Kateryn, plagued by morning sickness and general discomfort, found the experience draining and difficult. Perhaps her general condition had even been compounded by the realisation that her husband had been openly flirting with Elizabeth. Because of this, it was Lady Jane Grey who had accompanied Kateryn to the Cotswolds for her confinement. It is there that Thomas and Kateryn seem to have repaired their marriage while waiting with mounting excitement for the birth of the child whom Thomas was confident would be a boy.

To his credit, Thomas seems to have been delighted that the new arrival was a girl. She was christened Mary and the healthy child entered life with two doting parents. The happiness did not last long. Six days later, Kateryn was dead from complications, unable to withstand the dangers of bacterial infection any more than a woman of much more humble origins.

Almost immediately, Thomas renewed his attentions towards Elizabeth. Rumours abounded that he even had full intentions of marrying her and for a short time his brother ignored the court gossip. Until the day Thomas came to see him and asked for permission to marry Elizabeth immediately.

Once again Somerset exploded. This, added to Thomas' last escapade, was the last straw. Only days after Kateryn died, Thomas had been caught trying to break into Edward's apartments at Hampton Court Palace, perhaps with thoughts of gaining permission from Edward to marry Elizabeth. He'd entered through the privy garden and in the process, he'd woken one of Edward's pet spaniels, setting it off into a frenzy of barking.

I'm sure, in hindsight, Thomas would have preferred that he hadn't shot and killed the animal. But hindsight is a wonderful thing and Thomas' only instinct at the time was to shut it up. So he shot it. A drastic move in the heat of the moment, but there you have it. The next day, he was arrested and sent to the Tower of London. The incident, being caught outside the king's bedroom, at night, with a loaded pistol, was interpreted in the most threatening light, even casting suspicion on Elizabeth's involvement in the incident. Thomas was eventually released but the case was still pending while an investigation was being held.

Perhaps we should give Somerset a little credit because it seems he tried to save his brother from ruin, calling a council meeting so that Thomas might explain himself. Rather stupidly, Thomas did not show.

When realising that Thomas would probably be executed, Elizabeth was noticeably distressed. For weeks she was interrogated and the council found itself engaged in a sharply defined game of wits with the 15-year-old girl. She answered all the questions shrewdly but eventually the embarrassing details of the flirtatious romps with Thomas came to light. Humiliating as this must have been for Elizabeth, her relief would have been obvious when the council stated that they believed her to be innocent of any part in the plot. Thomas was not so lucky.

On 22nd February, the council officially accused Thomas of 33 charges of treason. He was convicted and condemned to death and finally beheaded one month later.

From this difficult experience, Elizabeth seems, for the first time in her young life, to have become fully aware of the serious, even deadly, nature of things. When she made her next very public appearance at court, she was just turning 16 and this new Elizabeth was a very different person from the one they had seen more than two years before. Subdued and silent, she was dressed in a simple, drab dress with plain and unadorned hair, contrasting sharply with the other ladies who dressed in bright showy splendour. It was an amazing transformation, almost as if she was trying to live something down. Something to keep in mind for later on.

In this supposed show of self-rehabilitation to restore her good name and reputation, she was largely successful. In the short span of 22 months, from May 1547 until March 1549, when she was just 13, 14, and 15 years old, she had experienced the sexually charged flirtation with Thomas (her sometimes 'uncle,' sometimes 'stepfather'), the unexpected death of her stepmother in childbirth, Thomas's sudden arrest and execution, even herself accused of treason through association with him. There can be no doubt that these experiences made a lasting impression on Elizabeth, and affected her personally. Don't forget, her mother Anne Boleyn was beheaded years before at her father's order. Some things you just don't get over.

The age of 16 seems to have been a dangerous age if you were a Tudor. Elizabeth's uncle Arthur had died at almost 16 and her illegitimate half-brother Henry Fitzroy had died at almost 17. 16th century illness was a terrifying thing and even a king was prone. The cold that her brother Edward caught almost four years later in 1552 gave way to a string of serious ailments from measles to smallpox then tuberculosis. The medical treatments subjected to him had caused his skin to deform and blacken, whilst his limbs swelled and his hair began to fall out. He was moved from palace to palace, trying the cleaner air away from the dust of London and subjected to increasingly desperate 'remedies'. Nothing worked. Emaciated, ravaged by illness and in constant physical agony, Edward was clearly dying and months later, he was dead.

Charming, brilliant, athletic, handsome and musically gifted, Edward could, and did, show himself to be ruthless and cold, just like his father. In his attempt to create a Protestant monarchy in Britain, he had named his cousin Lady Jane Grey as his successor and not his Catholic sister, Mary. Both sisters, Mary and Elizabeth, were disinherited. As his disfigured corpse was prepared for burial in the Henry VII Chapel at Westminster Abbey, the great crisis of 'The Nine Days' Queen' and Mary Tudor's improbable, but heroic, triumph was about to begin.

In history, Lady Jane Grey has become an iconic Tudor victim: virginal and sweet. Jane was a tiny, red-haired, red-lipped young girl who accepted her new role as queen tentatively wearing platform shoes to give her more height. As Jane struggled to hold on to the throne, Elizabeth was smart enough to remain quiet in the countryside, unwilling to come out into the limelight. She'd already had her fair share of trouble and she had no need to go through the horror of suspicion and rumours again. Although she was not keen on her half-sister Mary, she knew that if Jane were recognised as the queen, her own claim to the crown would be gone as well. So she chose the safe course: she remained quiet. Like all England and most of Europe, she was watching and waiting.

She did not have to wait long After only nine days, Mary had arrived in

London with an army and imprisoned Jane. She was tried and convicted of treason, and at only 16 years old, her cousin Jane was beheaded on February 12th 1554. On that day, Elizabeth's elder half-sister, Mary Tudor, became Queen of England.

At first, Mary was magnanimous towards Elizabeth and I can only imagine that this was due to relief that after so many uncertain years, her dream had finally come true and she was, in fact, the queen. But even then, doubt and suspicion began creeping in. Mary would have known full well that *being* the queen and *staying* the queen were two different issues. Doubt would have hit her like a lightning bolt when she rode into London with Elizabeth riding in place of honour by her side as the jubilant crowds cheered, not just for her, but also for her young sister who waved and smiled back at them. Mary would have suddenly been aware that she was 37 years old, tending to plumpness, with a small mouth and piercing eyes. Worse still, she was unmarried and childless. Beside her was the quietly confident 20-year-old glowing Elizabeth, who had youth and looks on her side, carefully playing the obedient sister. Up until then, Mary had openly held Elizabeth's hand at public ceremonies. It was never to happen again.

Mary Tudor's reign was not good and many remember her as simply 'Bloody Mary' because of the number of religious executions she ordered. All told, 300 were executed, most by burning, and all in the name of religion. Five years after her coronation, still childless, Mary was dead of ovarian cancer and Elizabeth had ascended to the throne of England as the third queen to rule in her own right. She would inherit a bankrupt nation where English credit had been at 14% for its loans since her father's reign. It had worsened during Edward's reign and by the time Elizabeth came to the throne, she was to find that the Tudor fortune had simply gone missing. She would also inherit a nation torn apart by religious discord. It was chaotic.

After Bloody Mary, England had high hopes for Elizabeth when she came to the throne. But they also had a deep anxiety. The coronation was carefully designed to show Elizabeth as a paragon of virtue but her charade of piety was not enough to cover what the population saw as their bad luck at having yet another woman on the throne. As it turned out, the sceptics were pleased at her first council when she did not exude an air of girlishness as they had expected. Instead, she stood confidently before them with an air of dignity and authority.

To be the daughter of Henry VIII and unmarried at 25 years of age was incredible and Elizabeth would have been very well aware of her responsibilities. Without a doubt, she was expected to marry and produce an heir very quickly to continue the Tudor line. If her father had taught her anything at all, it had been that. And as you can imagine, there was no lack of suitors. She was flooded with offers from Philip II of Spain, Erik XIV of Sweden and the Archdukes Ferdinand and Charles of Austria.

But with these offers, other problems surfaced. Apart from the intense rivalry as English suitors put their hands up as well, the question on everyone's lips was which one would be the most advantageous and profitable for England. For some reason, the more council pushed her for a decision, the angrier Elizabeth became and resisted.

Then the spring of 1559 came and council knew why Elizabeth had been acting cagey. It had become pretty evident that Elizabeth was in love with her childhood friend, Lord Robert Dudley.

To explain fully how Robert Dudley comes into the picture, we need to retrace his part of the story a little as well. Robert Dudley was the 5th son of John Dudley, the Duke of Northumberland who had been a trusted friend of Henry VIII and nominated as one of the sixteen executors of Henry's will. As such, he had considerable power over young Edward during his reign and everyone was very wary of him. John Dudley organised Edward's education, chose his friends and influenced him in many ways that made most of the nobles sit up nervously and take notice.

Things were going well during Edward's reign but undoubtedly, Northumberland wanted to be rid of the Duke of Somerset, Edward's Protector. Somerset was a man who was equally ambitious and who was not afraid to use underhand methods to achieve his agenda. There is good reason to believe that through Northumberland's influence, the 14-year-old king was persuaded to sign his uncle, Duke of Somerset's, death warrant. Many were sure he had also coerced Edward to nominate Lady Jane Grey as his successor instead of Mary. You see he had a very good reason to influence Edward.

His son, Guildford Dudley, had hurriedly married Lady Jane Grey just a few months before Edward died. Once again, John Dudley had been the pushy one by pointing out to his son the benefits of being married to a future queen. Insider information you might say. All he had to do was hint to Jane's mother, Lady Frances Brandon, the greedy, stout bejewelled daughter of Henry VIII's youngest sister Mary, that her daughter could possibly be the first eligible female in the line of succession to the throne. Then, if Jane married his son Guildford, there would be no end to the power both their families would have. And of course it didn't take too much convincing for Frances to agree wholeheartedly. John Dudley knew full well that with his son by Lady Jane's side during her reign, the status he currently enjoyed would improve even more dramatically. Remember, the royal court was all about power and position and there were few more powerful than John Dudley. And he hadn't stopped there.

While Mary Tudor was assembling her supporters in Norfolk, his son Robert Dudley was leading a small force of 300 men at his father's insistence to stop her. After securing several towns for his sister-in-law Jane, Robert Dudley took King's Lynn and proclaimed her the new queen. What he didn't know was that in London, Jane's reign was basically already over. Only days before, as Jane's barge had sailed down the Thames, people lining the shores straining to catch a glimpse of her were absolutely silent. They had only just learned that Edward had died and there she was, a young unknown cousin claiming the throne for herself. No one was aware that Jane was just another pawn in the deadly game John Dudley was playing.

The fear of yet another fearsome family war about to be unleashed on Britain would have been evident in their wary eyes as they watched Jane sail past and in their ominous silence, she would have suddenly known that nine-tenths of the population were in Mary's favour.

Mary Tudor was not stupid. She knew exactly what had been happening and as soon as she was on the throne, Robert and the rest of his small troop, along with his father and four brothers, were sent to the Tower of London where they waited nervously for sentencing. There was never a chance in heaven that John Dudley and Guildford would ever be pardoned for their part in the attempt to gain the throne for Jane, but the rest were crossing their fingers and hoping for a lucky break.

As expected, both men were executed. But thanks to a family member who knew Mary's new husband, Philip of Spain, Robert and his other brothers were eventually released. It was during Robert's stay in the Tower that he became reacquainted with his childhood friend, Elizabeth, who had also been imprisoned in the Tower at the same time by her sister Mary. It was a much younger Dudley who the eight-year-old Elizabeth had confided in at the execution of her third stepmother, Catherine Howard, in 1541, vowing, "*I will never marry.*"

The years of uncertainty during Mary's reign left Elizabeth constantly fearing for her life and this fear brought her even closer to Robert Dudley. Mary was suspicious of everyone and she trusted no one, especially her popular sister, Elizabeth, who was next in line for the throne if Mary didn't produce an heir. Mary jumped at shadows and watched her back constantly. As a consequence, after a failed rebellion led by Thomas Wyatt, a man who had professed his love for Elizabeth's mother, Anne Boleyn, Mary was instantly suspicious of Elizabeth's involvement. Without any proof at all, Mary imprisoned Elizabeth in the Tower until evidence of a conspiracy was found. It was there that Elizabeth and Robert became reunited and even more devoted to each other.

During the subsequent 90 beheadings of Wyatt's supporters, Elizabeth constantly protested her innocence. But it would be months before Mary was forced to admit that Elizabeth had not been a part of the rebellion and release her from the Tower.

Over the years, through Mary's reign and after her death, then through her own early years as queen, the friendship between Robert and Elizabeth grew until she could barely stand to have him leave her side. She appointed him to be her Master of Horse, which involved regular attendance at her side.

Unfortunately, there were a couple of things that stood in the way of their marriage. Firstly, the nobles disliked and distrusted the Dudley family intensely. And secondly, Robert was already married.

Despite this, they remained close. Very close. Letters were sent to each other and the symbol they used was 'ôô' as a code for the nickname 'Eyes' she gave him. She even had his bedchamber moved next to her personal apartments, further igniting rumours of sexual liaisons. As his influence grew, so did Elizabeth's possessiveness and jealousy.

To say their relationship was platonic is naïve. In the 16th century, sex was seen as an expression of love and I don't believe Elizabeth was against it. She had already declared that she was 'fond' of Robert and she even called him her *'sweet Robin'*. While foreign suitors vied for her hand, everyone was gossiping about the scandal between Elizabeth and Robert Dudley and their flirtatious behaviour. Catholics challenged her virtue and accused her of 'filthy lust' and the courts of Europe were abuzz with gossip about the Queen of England's sexual behaviour. Talk was that she was not considering any of their offers because she wanted to marry her favourite, but was unable to do so.

The last time Robert saw his wife, Amy Robsart, was four days over Easter and once during the summer of 1559 when she visited London. Apparently, they never saw each other afterwards. Then one year later, on 8th September 1560, one day after Elizabeth's birthday which she celebrated with Robert, Amy sent all the servants out for the day to a local fair and shortly afterwards, she was found dead at the bottom of a flight of stairs with head injuries and a broken neck.

As you can imagine, the gossip went berserk.

To say the very least, Robert Dudley's reputation was tarnished. The story grew more scandalous by the day until eventually he was being accused of arranging his wife's death so that he would be able to marry Elizabeth. And the scandal played into the hands of many nobles and politicians who were desperately trying to stop Elizabeth from marrying him. Warning bells were clanging loudly in their heads when they remembered stories of his father and his brother Guildford. Many of them were desperately trying to remind England about the similarity of circumstances in Robert's family members. His father, John Dudley, had wielded considerable control over both Henry VIII and young King Edward. Robert's brother Guildford Dudley had married Lady Jane Grey two weeks before she became queen as a stepping-stone to the throne and Robert Dudley was trying to do the exact same thing by getting rid of his wife so he could marry Elizabeth. They were frantic to make it look like the Dudley family had a predisposition for this sort of behaviour.

At the end of the inquest, the verdict came back as an unfortunate accident, perhaps even suicide, but in the end, it didn't matter. The rumours had done their work, not just in the kingdom but also across the courts of Europe, and the implications of his wife's death affected him for the rest of his life. Even if Elizabeth had seriously considered marrying Dudley at some time, there was no way she could marry him after that. Dudley suggested that he leave England for a while but Elizabeth would have none of it and everything remained the same.

While Elizabeth dithered over suitors, many nobles remembered full well the contents of Henry VIII's will. Without any doubt, he had stated, Edward was to be regarded as the only legitimate child and both Mary and Elizabeth were to be regarded as illegitimate. Most nobles also knew that in France, there was a 17-year-old girl married to the French King who was also the Queen of Scotland with Tudor blood coursing through her veins.

Even before Henry VIII's sister Margaret had her sixth birthday, their father, Henry VII, had thought that a marriage between his eldest daughter and James IV of Scotland was a way to end Scottish uprisings. James V of Scotland had been their only surviving legitimate heir and he in turn had married Mary of Guise, from France. Their daughter Mary was born on 8th December 1542 and six days later, she had become the Queen of the Scots on the death of her father. At five years old, Mary had been betrothed to the infant French dauphin, Francis, and with the agreement in place, she was sent to France to spend the next eleven years of her life in readiness to enter the French Court as queen consort.

Vivacious and beautiful, Mary had a wonderful childhood with the best available education in languages, poetry, horsemanship, needlework and music. By 16, she was a cultured married woman with the world at her feet.

Despite Mary being quite tall for her age at 5 feet 11 inches and her husband quite short at 5 feet 3 inches, the two seemed happy enough. One year later, the French king was dead and her husband Francis was crowned King of France. At 17, Mary had become Queen Consort of France and Queen of Scotland and she was more importantly, legitimate. It was a far cry from Elizabeth's circumstances where her father had declared his marriage to Elizabeth's mother, Anne Boleyn, as null and void, effectively making her illegitimate.

With Mary Tudor dead, Mary Queen of Scots watched England with mounting interest. In those brutal and uncertain days, we can only assume she was waiting for the right moment to step forward and stake her claim. As Elizabeth took the throne of England, the eyes of Europe were also watching and waiting. Everyone knew that Mary Queen of Scots had a far better right to the throne than Elizabeth.

At this time in history, there were three women who held power in England, Scotland and France: Elizabeth in England, Mary in France and

Mary of Guise, her mother, in Scotland. And with the force of France behind her, Mary stood a good chance of gaining it.

Despite both being so closely related to Henry VII, the two cousins were nothing alike. Mary was unable to separate emotions from politics while Elizabeth had learnt from her bitter childhood to be vigilant at all times. With her auburn hair, fiery temper and almost inexhaustible energy, there was never any doubt who Elizabeth's father was. Unfortunately, like her father, there were also fits of melancholy followed by buoyant cheerfulness and then sudden, convulsive rage.

Elizabeth also had her own definite ideas about religion and everything that her sister Mary had worked hard to accomplish, she swiftly undid with the help of her trusted adviser William Cecil. Together, the two were determined to return England to its former Protestant-friendly environment. Her wish was to reign justly and in all fairness, she did exactly that. In history, she is widely acknowledged as being a charismatic survivor in an age when government was ramshackle, money was tight and monarchs in neighbouring countries faced internal conflicts of their own.

But the question on everyone's lips was always *"When will she marry?"* The unspoken truth was that if she died without an heir, all would revert to the Catholic Mary Stuart, Queen of Scots, living in France. If the Scottish queen came to the throne, all would revert yet again to Catholicism and after what England had already suffered with Bloody Mary, it was a frightening thought.

If Elizabeth's sister Mary had been considered a suspicious queen, Elizabeth surpassed her hands down. News was arriving daily in England that the French were plotting to assassinate her and Elizabeth began taking every precaution. Around her, she gathered Protestant supporters who would rather die than let any harm come her way and she hired bodyguards as food tasters where everything was fully examined and tasted before she would even lift it to her mouth.

Safety wasn't the only problem Elizabeth was facing. The idea that a person could pick and choose his own religion had been as alien as the idea of whether he should obey the law or not. Through Edward's reign and then especially through Mary's, people were scared to voice their opinions for fear of losing their heads. The safest thing for anyone to do was to keep quiet about their beliefs.

But Europe had been restless with religious turmoil. Men talked and they wrote and they printed thousands of copies of their own writings and beliefs. In this culture, the discordant Puritans thrived. Elizabeth soon realised that not only did she have to face the Roman Catholics but she also had to face the Puritans led by the exiles of Mary's reign. England seemed divided between those who thought things had gone too far and those who wanted to go a step further. Silence had become impossible.

Elizabeth was in a dilemma. As a staunch Protestant, she could not allow Catholicism to gain any more favour than it already had. But as a fair monarch, she wanted to look as if she was giving her people a choice. Whatever she did, she had to do something that would keep her in favour. Eventually, she came up with a solution. People should outwardly conform, but they were to keep quiet if their opinions differed from hers. They could think what they liked in private as long as they followed the rules in public. At the risk of the whole world regarding her as disgustingly permissive and completely mad, *that*, she stated, was the most she would grant them.

Without a doubt, she was suspicious of everyone but her greatest concern was always Scotland. The danger from Scotland loomed even more threateningly as France declared their support for the French Queen and her French mother. As Elizabeth watched anxiously, it looked definite that French troops would land in Scotland at any time. If the French gained control of Scotland, their next move would certainly be to move south and attack her in England.

As always, a lack of money was the big issue for Elizabeth. With very little money in the treasury, it was a scant fleet that was hurriedly put together to try and blockade ports against French reinforcements. At that very moment, as the French were planning an imminent attack, Mary of Guise, the Queen of Scot's mother, suddenly died.

For over a week, Mary of Guise had been seriously ill. Her mind had begun to wander and on some days, she could not speak at all. On the 8th June 1560, she made a will and three days later, she was dead. On that day, everything changed. At the news of her death, France instantly withdrew their troops from Scotland and Elizabeth was let off the hook.

In modern times, Hollywood has speculated that she died of poisoning because of the suddenness of her death, perhaps even on the order of Elizabeth herself. But at the time, in a paranoid political climate when many royal deaths were suspected to have been murders, none saw her death as 'foul play.' It was diagnosed as dropsy, a swelling from fluid accumulation in body tissues. It most commonly occurs in the feet and legs but as the body is primarily made up of water, excess fluid sometimes collects in the lungs and the heart tissues, which can cause a heart attack or the brain to swell.

As the *legitimate* great grandniece of Henry VIII, Mary Queen of Scots could be forgiven for thinking she had been robbed of the throne of England. Three months later after the death of her husband Francis from an ear infection, she could also be forgiven for thinking that France had turned its back on her as well. With her husband Francis dead, his younger ten-year-old brother Charles had become King of France and their mother, Catherine de Medici, had managed to craftily outwit other members of the family and was now effectively ruling France as his Regent. It effectively meant that Mary was expected to leave France immediately.

She could also be forgiven for thinking that England had gone too far when they refused her request to dock in London on her way to Scotland from France.

Mary was furious at the insult. Putting aside the fact that she had a legitimate right to *contest* the English throne, and some would have stated that her claim was an even *better* one than Elizabeth's claim, her cousin should have at least awarded her a certain level of courtesy, given her plight and predicament. Inevitably, with the snub, Mary had no choice but to return to Scotland by another longer and more dangerous route. And England fervently prayed that danger stepped in quickly. Elizabeth didn't want her in England but she certainly had no want for her to return to Scotland either. The religious balance in Scotland was already delicate and a strongly Catholic monarch would probably start a civil war with the Protestants. If Mary won that civil war, she would probably turn her attention back to England again since she was regarded as the rightful queen in the eyes of many European leaders.

Before Mary left, dark storm clouds began to gather menacingly in the distance as she stood on the bow of the ship cursing Elizabeth profusely and praying that all the power of God would reap vengeance on her cousin. Later that night, it seemed that God had been listening to her prayers.

It was the summer of 1560 on the evening that Elizabeth had sent the letter to Mary refusing her permission to enter London. She had watched as

Mary's ship left the harbour, growing smaller and smaller until it had become just a tiny black spot on the horizon. She would have been imagining it was Mary's red cloak that she saw fluttering wildly in the breeze. As she watched, storm clouds gathered menacingly in the distance.

As dusk fell, a vicious storm broke over London sending everyone scurrying through the flooding streets to escape the raging torrent of rain. As the temperature dropped dramatically, winds howled and trees were blown almost horizontally. Then at midnight, a lightning bolt struck the highest point of St Paul's Cathedral, sending it up in flames. An hour later, the steeple had been destroyed and the spire had fallen through the nave roof. The fire was hot enough to melt the cathedral bells, and lead that covered the wooden spire poured like lava through the burning roof. It was only at two in the morning that the fire was finally extinguished.

As Elizabeth stared in shock at the blackened ruin of St Paul's Cathedral, had she been wondering if she was being punished for refusing Mary to enter the harbour? Had she been too hasty in that refusal?

No doubt, it was an evening Elizabeth would never forget, especially with certain events not too far in the future.

From here on, England and Scotland's history is closely intertwined.

Elizabeth was not only very aware of Mary's legitimate claim to the throne but also her capability to gather Catholic supporters in Scotland, England and Ireland. And if Mary had been smart, she would have used that incredible opportunity to her utmost advantage. But despite Mary's meticulous education, you can't teach someone how to cope with dangerous and complex situations. Trouble was never far away from Mary.

As in England, Scotland was torn between Catholics and Protestants and many different religious groups had established themselves throughout the countryside. With news that Mary was on her way home, Catholics were rejoicing that their ruler, who had declared herself a fervent Catholic, would soon be back in Scotland to take matters in hand. While Mary had been in France and after her mother's death, Scotland had been under the control of her illegitimate half-brother James Stewart, who was also the leader of the local Protestant group. Local sporadic fighting had broken out but things had settled down a little with news of Mary's imminent arrival. Within weeks, she'd made her first mistake.

It's true James Stewart said all the right things to Mary. He offered his undying support and he gave the appearance of steadfast loyalty. But words are just words and appearances can be deceptive. Unfortunately for Mary, she would find that out the hard way. So instead of dismissing James, she kept him on as her chief advisor. Not only that, she made him the 1st Earl of Moray. Sometimes your worst enemies come disguised as family members.

While Mary settled in to life in Scotland in 1561, Elizabeth kept a low profile. Her movements during this time are somewhat scarce in history books until 1562 when it's known she contracted smallpox. With no heir apparent apart from her cousin Mary Queen of Scots, England waited in abject horror to see if Elizabeth would pull through. To add to that fear, she made several unusual demands while she was delirious with fever, including requests to her advisers that Lord Robert Dudley be made Protector of the Realm. He was also to have a pension of £20,000 a year and an income was arranged for a servant of Dudley's, a man called John Tamworth. *'Which one was worse,'* the nobles were thinking, *'a Catholic barbarian queen from Scotland or a wolf in sheep's clothing scheming to snatch the throne for himself?'* And then miraculously, Elizabeth showed signs of recovery and England let out an almost audible sigh of relief.

While Elizabeth was recuperating from her bout of smallpox, back in Scotland, Mary was having second thoughts of the wisdom of crossing Elizabeth years before. To make up for the breach, she invited Elizabeth to visit her in Scotland and of course, Elizabeth refused. A year later, arrangements were again made for the two queens to meet, this time fixed for York. Once more, Elizabeth's caution took over and she cancelled at the last minute. Then in 1563, Elizabeth made an extraordinary proposal.

When we consider her 'affection' for Robert Dudley, the proposal seems laughable in so many ways. Elizabeth's solution to the growing problem was that Robert Dudley should marry Mary and they should all live happily together as a family at the English court, so that she would not have to lose her favourite's company. Stunned, Mary asked Elizabeth if she was serious (a thought that crossed my mind as well). Elizabeth countered that she would only be prepared to acknowledge Mary as her heir on the condition that she do as she was requested and marry Robert.

To Mary's utter surprise, her Scottish advisors warmed to the prospect of having Robert as her consort and in September 1564, Elizabeth gave him the title of Earl of Leicester to make the offer even more tempting and acceptable. Despite what Elizabeth or Mary's advisors thought, both Mary and Robert proved very unenthusiastic about her arrangement for a happy threesome and on 29th July 1565 Mary put paid to the suggestion and married her cousin Henry Stuart Lord Darnley, instead.

Henry Stuart carried his own claim to the English throne through Margaret Tudor, Henry VIII's elder sister. After the death of Margaret's first husband James IV, she had married Archibald Douglas, Earl of Angus. From that marriage, there was one surviving daughter who in turn delivered a baby boy. Henry Stuart Lord Darnley. As a descendant of a daughter of James II of Scotland as well, Henry was in the front of the line for the throne of Scotland and a good chance for the English throne to boot, which is more than likely what he had in mind in the first place.

Mary had briefly met her cousin in February 1561 when she was still mourning her husband Francis. Darnley's parents, the Earl and Countess of Lennox, had sent him to France to ostensibly extend their condolences but in the back of their minds there was hope that a potential match could be arranged between their son and Mary. Nothing came of the visit but the seed had been planted. When the two met again in February of 1565, Mary fell in love with him.

And Darnley had plenty to offer. Three years younger than her, he was brought up conscious of his status and inheritance. He was well educated speaking Latin, Scottish Gaelic, English and French and he excelled in singing, lute playing and dancing. He was strong, virile and athletic, a good horseman with a passion for hawking and hunting and he had a sound knowledge of weapons. Who could forgive Mary for snapping him up?

If ever there was a whirlwind romance, this was it. On 22nd July, Darnley was made Duke of Albany in Holyrood Abbey and the banns of marriage were called. A proclamation was made in Edinburgh that government would be in the joint names of the King and Queen of Scots, giving Darnley equality and precedence over Mary and a silver coin was circulated in the names of Darnley and Mary. On the 29th, they made it official without the papal dispensation for the marriage between first cousins.

The marriage both infuriated Elizabeth and made her very nervous. It was, after all, the marriage between her two strongest claimants to the English throne and Darnley was the natural choice for many of Elizabeth's enemies because he was male, English born and a Catholic. But to do it without her permission, (he was after all an English subject), was unforgivable.

But Elizabeth need not have worried. With all of Darnley's accomplishments, he would have been a real catch except for one major flaw. He had a mean, violent streak in him, which was aggravated by his drinking problem.

It's no wonder this impulsive marriage was a disaster from the beginning. With literally a world of choices at Mary's feet, Mary had chosen to marry an arrogant man with a drinking problem who soon began making demands to be recognised as the co-sovereign of Scotland as well as having the right to keep the Scottish throne for himself... if he outlived her.

Mary must have had an inkling of the significance of the suggestion and the ominous overtones because she adamantly and constantly refused his request. Apparently, she was smarter than she was given credit for. But her refusals put great strains on the already unsteady marriage and all too soon, Mary realised she was pregnant.

With news of her pregnancy, Darnley decided the honeymoon was definitely over. It meant the child would be in front of him in the queue to the throne and more than likely, he would never become the king. And now for the magic words: *as long as the child was his and as long as the child lived.*

It's pretty safe to consider the possibility that the throne was all he ever wanted from the beginning. But with that option taken away from him, he had to come up with an alternative plan.

Months before, Mary had employed a secretary by the name of David Rizzio, who was himself a descendent of a noble Italian family. As her secretary, David was in close and regular contact with Mary, which must have sparked the idea into Darnley's head. What if he could convince everyone that Rizzio was really the father of Mary's child?

Over the ensuing months, the thought grew and festered in Darnley's head until it all came to a head when Mary was seven months pregnant.

The plan to murder Rizzo and potentially harm Mary was a complex one full of 'ifs' but Darnley decided to put it into action on 9th March 1566 anyway. Together with some of his supporters, Darnley was hoping that *if* Rizzio died, it would have such a traumatic impact on Mary and that it would result in a miscarriage and would ultimately damage her health permanently. *If* she became ill and *if* that illness resulted in her slow death before the baby was born, and *if* the baby died as well, then Scotland would be forced to hand the crown over to him as her husband. As I said, complex and iffy.

It would seem Mary had no idea of the ideas running through her husband's mind. On 9th March, as she and her secretary were bent over, intent on a document, Darnley, Lord Ruthven and her half-brother Earl of Moray burst into the room demanding that Rizzio leave immediately with them under arrest. There was very little she could do at seven months into her pregnancy but she valiantly stood her ground at gunpoint with Rizzio cowardly hiding behind her skirts as she tried to protect him.

The hysterical screams of both Mary and Rizzio echoed through the palace and into the dark streets of Edinburgh. Many of the locals were warming themselves in the taverns when they heard bloodcurdling screams coming from Holyrood Castle. It was enough to send most of them pouring out of taverns with makeshift weapons and running to the castle. With a gun held to her side, Mary was told to go to the window and dismiss them. In the uproar, Rizzio was stabbed an alleged 56 times and then thrown down the main staircase and stripped of his jewels before people were able to crash through the main door to help them.

Needless to say, the marriage was over. After the rather botched attempt on his wife's life, Darnley knew he'd have to suffer the consequences of the fiasco sooner or later, so before they could relieve him of his head, he fled.

In England, Elizabeth was horrified by the news filtering back from Scotland. When Mary delivered a baby boy two months later, naming him James in memory of her father, Elizabeth's horror turned to resignation. One year after that, when Elizabeth heard that Darnley had suffered a rather sudden, unfortunate death, resignation turned to suspicion. And then she heard the rest of the story.

We know that Mary was prone to making mistakes but this one was the worst one of all. The scandalous story was that Darnley had been recovering from a bout of smallpox when two explosions rocked the foundation of Kirk O'Field where he was staying. Later on, the explosions were attributed to two barrels of gunpowder placed in the small room under his sleeping quarters. Dressed only in his nightshirt, Darnley had fled from his bedchamber but was later found dead outside, murdered, not from the explosions as originally suspected, but apparently smothered since there were no visible signs of violence on his body. Suspicion quickly fell on a rather *close* friend of Mary, the Earl of Bothwell, whose shoes had been discovered at the scene of the crime.

Now you don't have to be a rocket scientist to join the dots together here when, only three months later, Mary made another serious mistake and announced their marriage. Bothwell had obtained a quickie divorce from his first wife twelve days beforehand (she was obviously fed up with him by then) and the happy twosome had married in secret. Put that with the shoes left rather stupidly near the crime scene and you have no doubt in anyone's mind who had planted the gunpowder and killed Darnley.

An unpopular and quarrelsome man, the Orkney-born nobleman, Bothwell, seems to have appeared when he visited Mary at the French Court in the autumn of 1560. He supported Mary's mother, Mary of Guise, in Scotland and together with 24 followers, he took 6000 crowns of English money destined to be used against Mary of Guise at an ambush near Haddington on Halloween 1559. After her death, he appears to be no more than a troublesome nobleman at court, although he was obviously smitten with Mary.

He was acquitted of any wrong doing in a trial on 12th April 1567 and the rumour was he would marry Mary. That is until eight bishops, nine earls, and seven Lords of Parliament put their signatures to what became known as the Ainslie Tavern Bond, declaring that Mary should marry a native-born subject and handed it confidently to Bothwell.

Four days later, while Mary was on the road from Linlithgow Palace to Edinburgh, Bothwell suddenly appeared with 800 men and assured her that danger awaited her in Edinburgh. She was to come with him to his castle at Dunbar, out of harm's way. It appears Mary agreed to accompany him and arrived at Dunbar at midnight where she was taken prisoner by Bothwell and allegedly raped. Bothwell's reasoning was that this would secure his marriage to her (although whether she was a willing accomplice or an unwilling victim remains a controversial issue). On 12th May, Mary created him Duke of Orkney and Marquess of Fife and three days later they were married at Holyrood.

In England, Elizabeth was livid as the updates filtered back to her.

It wasn't just Elizabeth who was adding two and two together, the Scottish nobles were doing the same thing as well. As the realisation suddenly hit them that Mary was probably involved in Darnley's murder, they knew a decision had to be made. And you can believe that her half-brother, the Earl of Moray, played a major part in making that momentous decision. Without too much delay, a council informed Mary that she would have to abdicate in favour of her one-year-old son James. Coincidently, they said, her half-brother had helpfully and willingly stepped forward and nominated himself as Regent and the nobles had already accepted his generous offer. As a finishing touch, they informed Mary that after she abdicated, she was then to be imprisoned in Loch Leven Castle ready for the charge of murder to be heard in a court of law. There was nothing she could do, they informed her. It was a done deal.

By this time, Bothwell had seen the writing on the wall. He'd fled after one final embrace from Mary, leaving her to face the music alone. Bothwell was never seen again but reports filtered back over the years that he had been captured without proper papers off the coast of Norway and when King Frederick of Denmark heard that the English Crown was seeking Bothwell, he had him imprisoned in Dragsholm Castle near Copenhagen where he was slowly going insane in appalling conditions. Still reeling from the desertion of her new husband, Mary miscarried a set of twins.

From somewhere deep in her soul, despite her immense grief, Mary must have been determined that her rights as queen should, and would, be restored. Inside a month, she had lost a husband and a set of twins, she was not about to lose her throne as well.

Loch Leven Castle was actually a grey stone house with small windows that barely kept out the cold winds that blew across the water. Outside was a narrow strip of scrubland and further still was the lake that took half an hour for a strong man to row to the mainland. When the weather turned foul, the strip submerged and the waves lashed the stones of the perimeter wall.

It was a hard prison from which escape and endurance seemed impossible. For someone like Mary who had been raised in a glittering court in France surrounded by priceless jewels and gorgeous clothes, attending banquets and plays, it was beyond hell to endure. The boredom would have driven her almost insane. During her time in the prison, she constantly declared that her abdication had been forced upon her under the threat of death and most of Scotland believed her. And she continually plotted her escape.

It took Mary almost a year to accomplish, but on 2nd May 1568, with the help of George Douglas, the handsome half-brother of Sir William Douglas, owner of Loch Leven, she escaped. Whether she granted George certain 'favours' more than mere kisses, (if you know what I mean), is unknown but I would assume that anything more would have been risky with her already besmirched reputation. But then again, she had made some terrible blunders up until then. In any case, Mary's supporters smuggled her out and whisked her away, hoping to reach the safety of Dumbarton Castle.

News of Mary's imprisonment had not been popular with the Scots in the first place so when word circulated that she had escaped, the news was widely welcomed. With an escort of 50 supporters led by Lord Hamilton, she rode in to Lanarkshire to join up with many more nobles who were willing to take up the fight with her and within a few days; she had managed to gather 6,000 men. With this sizeable army standing at the ready behind her, plus the assistance of eight earls, nine bishops, eighteen lords, twelve abbots and nearly one hundred barons, the council was more than willing to pass a ruling that the Earl of Moray's actions had indeed been treasonable.

They say the road to death is a long march full of terrors and Mary had every intention of dodging that horrific end to her story. One of the ways to do that was to avoid battle at all cost. Her plan was to retire to Dumbarton Castle while expected reinforcements came from the north to help and with this added strength, she was certain she could take back the country by degrees from her half-brother.

With the full intention of temporarily bypassing Moray, Mary rode to Rutherglen Castle intending to pass on the north side of the Clyde estuary to avoid a direct confrontation with him. She had no wish to ride into a trap so until she had a full army at her disposal, she had to err on the side of caution.

Unlike Mary, Moray wasn't about to give up without a serious fight. His plan was to draw up his army close to the village several miles south of Glasgow, well within the city limits, and attack at the moment when Mary would least expect it. One of his commanders noted Mary's movements and he ordered his musketeers to stand ready behind each of the horsemen hiding among some cottages, hedges and gardens bordering a narrow lane through which Mary's army needed to pass. Moray would lead the rest of the army across a nearby bridge.

Moray's army had only just established themselves when Mary's army advanced through the village. The battle was on.

Mary's commander, Lord Argyll, had very little military skills so he hoped to simply push Moray aside by sheer force of numbers. As Lord Hamilton advanced slowly, Mary remained safe and secure at the rear. All was going to plan until Hamilton was met with fire from the musketeers and it was as if the world exploded in an almighty crash of metal. Many in the front were killed but Hamilton determinedly pushed on through the mayhem, finally reaching the top of a hill.

What he saw frightened him. The enemy had totally blocked them off and they were advancing quickly.

What happened next has happened many times throughout history. Both armies collided in a forest of spears so thick, it is said that if anyone had thrown their discharged pistols at the enemy, the weapons would have come to rest on top of the shafts rather than falling to the ground. Forty-five minutes later, the Battle of Langside was over.

As the cries of screaming men and horses reached her, Mary watched in abject horror as over 300 of her men were slaughtered. Feathered shafts protruded from bodies, limbs had been hacked off and the smell of blood hung heavily in the air.

As dreadful as it was, if Moray had not called a halt to the fighting, it was certain the count would have been much higher. But if Mary had been in danger before, her capture at this crucial moment would certainly have been her final chapter. In a panic and with an escort, Mary fled across bleak windswept moorland, burning bridges behind her to slow pursuit, in an attempt to reach Dumbarton Castle. But then suddenly, she changed direction and turned south, heading towards a magnificent Gothic church by the name of Dundrennan Abbey on the south coast of Scotland. We can only assume she believed the Abbey seemed more reachable and safe. From there she could head for England and be out of harm's way.

After all the mistakes Mary had made, leaving Scotland was the worst. She would never see her homeland again.

In Mary's mind, the only choice she had was to throw herself on Elizabeth's mercy. And Elizabeth may have initially been tempted to do exactly that and take her cousin in, especially when she remembered the night she'd refused Mary permission to dock in London on her way back to Scotland from France after the death of her French husband. That night, it was as if God had unleashed a powerful, vengeful storm following her refusal and the result had been that St Paul's Cathedral had been reduced to ashes, burnt to the ground and in ruins.

But with this horrific memory came doubt. The old Mary had been dangerous enough but this new Mary was more dangerous and treacherous to Elizabeth than the one she'd sent that letter to years ago. This new Mary seemed out of control. Could she even be trusted?

If there was one thing we can be certain of is that Elizabeth would have remembered the past mangled generations of her dynasty. She would have remembered the stories of how her grandfather, Henry VII, had kissed the ground reverently as he invaded England before slaughtering Richard III and she would have remembered the stories of his tyranny. She certainly would have remembered that her father had excelled at disposing of anyone who stood in his way. Her own mother had been one of those disposable people. And I'm sure it would have been those same horrific memories that made Elizabeth hesitate and finally resist her government's advice. Beheading traitors was one thing, but beheading someone of royal blood, more to the point her own cousin, was something she could not bring herself to do. All you had to do was look at how the War of the Roses has turned out if you were in any sort of doubt. For a woman and a queen who had suffered first-hand at her family's brutality, there seemed only one option available to her. Rather than risk temporarily sheltering Mary and then returning her to Scotland at a later time with an English army, or even sending her back to France, Elizabeth imprisoned Mary in Carlisle Castle and then one month later, moved her a little further away from the Scottish border to Bolton Castle.

As it turned out, Elizabeth was wise not to trust Mary. As you would expect, Scottish supporters schemed and plotted against Elizabeth at every turn during the early months of Mary's imprisonment and in 1569, the threats became a reality.

In Elizabethan England, there was not only a religious division between the North and the South, nobles in the north felt threatened by Elizabeth's power. With the increase in threats on Elizabeth's life, the question of who would succeed to the throne of England was being asked more often. No one wanted another Catholic queen so it was becoming obvious to the government that Elizabeth needed to rid England of Mary before Catholics got to Elizabeth first. And their advice to her was she needed to do it quickly.

You can be sure Mary's supporters were thinking the exact same thing, only in their minds, Elizabeth was going to be the one disposed of.

It's not clear who first suggested the idea of a marriage between Mary and 30-year-old Thomas Howard, 4th Duke of Norfolk although his name had been floating around as a possible suitor for Mary for several years. Norfolk himself was actively discussing it by mid-October of 1568.

Norfolk was a second cousin to Elizabeth through her maternal grandmother, Elizabeth Howard, and he considered himself, as England's only duke at the time, as terribly undervalued in the English court. Self-worth had never been a problem in the Norfolk family and seems to be a familial flaw. It had led his father and great-grandfather to the executioner's block under Henry VIII and his grandfather had only been reprieved by the death of Henry himself. To add to his sense of incredible self-worth, after the deaths of his three previous wives, he had become the wealthiest landowner in the country as well as Earl Marshal of England and Elizabeth's Lieutenant in the North. As such, he had the means, the numbers, the family connection and he had the support of a Florentine banker by the name of Ridolfi behind him to make himself well and truly heard.

'The Ridolfi Plot', as it was called, was an intricate scheme in 1569 to murder Elizabeth, free Mary and marry her off to Norfolk then put Mary on the English throne. With the assistance from Catholic English peers in excess of 39,000 men, the plan was looking incredibly positive. With this impressive array of support, it seemed only logical that he could progress further and make a considerable attempt to depose Elizabeth.

It could have been a great success. Alongside the Duke of Norfolk and his family connections, they had Ridolfi's money and the support of the Bishop of Ross who was surreptitiously delivering letters to Mary of their progress while she was under house arrest in Bolton Castle. Then there were the armies of both Phillip of Spain and 10,000 loyal men standing behind the Duke of Alba from the Netherlands to back them up. They even had the go ahead and the nod of approval from Pope Pius V. But common sense tells us that the plot was doomed to fail even if it hadn't been discovered prematurely. For one thing, 10,000 roaring Spanish and Dutch soldiers waving swords and guns would have been more than a little difficult to hide. For another, they would still have been absurdly inadequate to overthrow Elizabeth's newly formed army. Thirdly, the vagueness of the invasion point was terribly confusing. What let them down at this point was administration.

The plan they'd hatched was to land at either Harwich or Portsmouth, not a bad location by any means for an invading army. But by not telling Ridolfi *exactly* where Harwich was in the first place, they made a colossal blunder because the banker had no idea where to go. Another stumbling block for Norfolk as a future king was that a lot of nobles considered him a rather dubious contender anyway. Most regarded him as a bad leader, and heaven forbid, he wasn't even a Catholic. All this, plus the fact that both he and Mary had been married three times before this new proposed marriage, seems to have made the attempt a little too farfetched for anyone to conceive.

Elizabeth's extensive spy network didn't have to work too hard to uncover this plot. Ridolfi's talkative nature was always going to be a problem and rather stupidly, he trumpeted his plan all over Europe, more particularly to Cosimo I de Medici, Grand Duke of Tuscany, who sent a private message back to Elizabeth. Ridolfi's messenger was then arrested at Dover with his pockets full of compromising letters and money and he soon spilled every bean in his possession.

From being the most powerful nobleman in England, Norfolk overnight became damaged goods. Elizabeth ordered him to be arrested and sent to the Tower of London on her 37th birthday on 7th September but he left court, evidently hurt that his cousin could believe the terrible rumours of his implication in the plot. She reissued the order later that month and he removed himself further away to his palace in Kenninghall, outside Norwich, claiming illness. His distress seemed understandable, caught between public shame at becoming a person who could eliminate the queen and the private horror waiting for him while imprisoned in the Tower.

Three days later, Elizabeth wrote again demanding his return '... *without any manner of excuse*'. By 28th, all semblance of patience was gone. Norfolk was placed under house arrest on October 3rd and he was in the Tower by the 11th. By January the next year he was tried and convicted of three counts of high treason and beheaded six months later again.

Mary watched in stunned silence as Norfolk and hundreds of rebels were executed for treason. As the death toll rose, Elizabeth's government again pushed hard for Elizabeth to sign Mary's death warrant as well. Still she refused to shed royal blood, stating that Mary would continue to remain in her prison.

That year marked the time when most recognised the fact that Elizabeth would probably never marry. Her outright refusal had finally been accepted by Parliament who had repeatedly asked her to make a decision and they'd repeatedly been refused. The House of Commons had even threatened to withhold funds from her if she did not marry and still she held her ground and refused.

Over the years, Robert Dudley tried everything in his power to persuade Elizabeth to marry him. In 1575, he decided to pull out all the stops and make on last spectacular attempt. The invitation for her to visit him at his Warwickshire estate, Kenilworth Castle, for several days of lavish entertainment was meant to be extraordinary and Elizabeth loved every minute of her visit. Still she hesitated. As genuine as her love for him, she knew that marrying him would only court disaster, sparking such intense opposition from Dudley's rivals that it might even spill out into civil war.

He waited for Elizabeth until 1578. For all his desperation to marry Elizabeth, he had been secretly courting one of her ladies-in-waiting Lettice Devereaux, formerly Knollys, now the dowager Countess of Essex for the past three years.

Lettice was one of the most beautiful women at court, bearing a striking resemblance to a younger Elizabeth and was of royal blood herself, being the great-niece of Elizabeth's mother, Anne Boleyn. The pair had enjoyed a flirtation for ten years and with his failed last-ditch attempt to persuade Elizabeth to marry him, he took Lettice as his mistress. Lettice was 29 and her husband had disappeared into an Irish fog and died of dysentery two years before, leaving her with two children.

For a time, Elizabeth was blissfully unaware that Dudley had betrayed her. But three years into the affair, Lettice fell pregnant and refused to be pushed aside any longer. Fearing the inevitable backlash from Elizabeth, Dudley agreed to a secret ceremony. Lettice wore a loose gown at the ceremony but inevitably the secret was out.

Elizabeth reacted as we would expect. She threw a Tudor wobbler. When she heard that her cousin had stolen the only man she'd truly loved, she boxed Lettice's ears and screamed abuse before banishing her from court, vowing never to set eyes on her again.

While she ranted, marriage proposals still flooded in and for a while she seemed taken with 24-year-old Hercule Francois, Duke of Anjou, brother of Mary's dead French husband.

No matter which way you look at it, it was not an ideal match. Anjou was twenty years her junior, pockmarked, tiny and a Catholic, also widely rumoured to be a transvestite. The comparison between Robert Dudley and Anjou was laughable. But Elizabeth loved to be wooed and she was still hurting from Dudley's rejection so for a time, she showed interest in Anjou, whom she affectionately called her 'frog'. Negotiations began for a while, perhaps out of peevishness towards Dudley, until she finally ended all speculation by saying, *"If I follow the inclination of my nature, it is this: beggar-woman and single, far rather than queen and married."*

But there could have been other reasons why Elizabeth backed away from the marriage, beside her love for Robert Dudley.

Hercule Francois was the youngest son of Henry II of France and Catherine de Medici and only a few years before, a terrible scandal and massacre had occurred in France. And everyone was pointing a finger at Catherine de Medici as the instigator.

It was a time when John Calvin and his writings were inspiring French Protestants and his supporters were being called Huguenots. This group was growing stronger in strength throughout the world and France, as a Catholic nation on the whole, was feeling very threatened.

It all came to a head after an important wedding on the 18th August 1572. Many leading Huguenots had remained in Paris after the wedding to discuss some grievances with the king but what happened four days later stunned Europe. Admiral Coligny, a leading Huguenot, was walking back to his rooms from The Louvre when a shot rang out from a nearby house and wounded him in the arm. A smoking gun was discovered in the window of an upstairs window, but the culprit had made his escape from the rear of the building and on to a waiting horse. In a state of shock, Coligny was carried to his lodgings at the Hôtel de Béthisy, where a surgeon removed a bullet from his elbow and amputated a damaged finger with a pair of scissors. Considering all the possibilities, the damage could have been far worse, but the bloodbath that followed was soon beyond the control of any leader.

The St Bartholomew's Day Massacre began two days later, after Catherine's son, King Charles IX, ordered, *"Kill them. Kill them all! Don't leave a single one alive."* The thinking was clear. Catherine and her advisers were expecting a Huguenot uprising to avenge the attack on Coligny but instead of waiting for it to happen, they chose to strike first and wipe out the Huguenot leaders while they were still in Paris. It was the beginning of a wave of Catholic mob violence that continued unabated for weeks.

The slaughter began in Paris but soon spread outwards to the French countryside. Estimates of the number of dead across France range from 5,000 to 30,000 but for Paris alone, the only hard figure was the payment by the crown to workmen to collect and bury 1,100 bodies washed up on the banks of the Seine downstream of the city... in the first week alone.

The horror of the massacre and the hostility it aroused still created a great deal of controversy throughout Europe and at the heart of the blame was Catherine de Medici.

With her temper tantrum at Dudley finally under control, Elizabeth was having second thoughts regarding a marriage to Francois anyway. It must have been with a great deal of relief that she felt confident and justified enough to cut all ties with the French family. But by deciding not to go ahead with negotiations with Hercule Francois, she had no idea that her decision would have a snowball effect with Spain.

For as long as Elizabeth could remember, Spain had set their sights on England. Prior to Elizabeth's reign, her sister Mary had married Philip of Spain and you'll remember that all hell had broken loose. Everyone knew that if they had children, the Hapsburgs would forever influence English politics and Catholicism would be there to stay. Neither outcome had seemed pleasant. As for Philip, he was hoping that when Mary died, with or without children, he would simply take over where Mary left off. Two years before Mary died, he'd inherited a basically bankrupt Spanish empire on his father's death and he desperately needed English money to help fill his own empty treasury.

Of course, Parliament hadn't seen it Philip's way at all. Knowing full well that part of Philip's inheritance were territories throughout Europe, in particular the Netherlands, they could see an endless supply of English cash heading across the channel to Europe to help fund the Dutch Catholics. So when Mary died, Philip was unceremoniously sent packing back to Europe, virtually bankrupt. Stinging from the insult, the threat from the Spaniards had been looming ever since.

As many other monarchs in history have done to help their dire financial situations, Philip kept increasing taxes until they'd become so high that the predominantly Protestant population in the Netherlands had reached boiling point. All at once, they'd had enough and they were rebelling.

As the riot picked up momentum, it continued expanding into Northern France until Philip knew he had to do something. And fast. Then the penny dropped. He could kill two birds with one stone if he signed a treaty with the French Guise family who also controlled Scotland. Together, the two nations could form an alliance against all Protestants, more particularly Elizabeth. After all, France and Scotland hated England as much as the Spanish did.

Elizabeth was very upset by the proposed nightmarish treaty that was obviously aimed at England. She had never officially supported the Dutch because she was afraid of aggravating the powerful Spaniards, but with the imminent treaty with the French looming, she couldn't afford to wait. She had to act immediately.

Her stand had always been not to support rebels who were rebelling against legitimate authority but with the Spaniards and the French breathing down her neck, her only hope was to perform a complete about face on that viewpoint and propose a treaty of her own... with the Dutch.

Her treaty, called the Treaty of Nonsuch, offered to finance an army of 6,400 Dutch soldiers and another 1,000 cavalrymen plus an annual subsidy of 600,000 florins to the Netherlands and in return, all they had to do was hand over four cities to England, primarily Brill and Flushing.

Elizabeth knew exactly what she was doing by asking for the two cities. Both were two commercial fishing cities in western Holland strategically situated in the most important passageway to Antwerp, not just one of the biggest ports in Belgium, but the most important one in all of Europe. For England, this meant more trade and more riches but it left Spain, still in financial crisis, out in the cold. You see Antwerp was off limits to the Spanish since they'd ransacked it nine years before.

For most wars, you can usually trace the aggravation back to one of two issues: religion or money. This current problem between Spain and England however had both ingredients. Spain, who had recently declared bankruptcy, had sent 400,000 precious florins (money they really couldn't afford) on ships intended as payment to angry troops in Holland. Spanish soldiers had been fighting without rest or pay against the Dutch Protestant rebels so the money was meant to appease them. But nature had stepped in and during a violent storm, the Spanish ships were forced to seek shelter in English ports. And of course Elizabeth had taken full advantage of the situation by confiscating the money.

With no money forthcoming, the battle-hardened Spaniards swarmed into Antwerp looting and killing everyone in their path. As you can imagine, the civilians were no match for the soldiers and over 7,000 lives were lost with a great deal of property destroyed in just three days. The shocking attack had almost destroyed Antwerp but the long-term affect was that the reputations of both Spain and the Hapsburg monarchy were forever tarnished and the attack had destroyed every accomplishment the Spanish had made in the past ten years.

So with both these ports in her possession, Elizabeth knew it was like waving a red flag in front of a bull. A Spanish bull to be exact.

To say the Dutch Protestants were astonished at her proposal is perhaps an understatement. But as the saying goes, 'Never look a gift horse in the mouth', they quickly signed the treaty and handed over the cities to England.

There was never any doubt in Philip's mind that the treaty Elizabeth devised was an act of war against Spain. To add fuel to the fire, she was offering a lot of cash to the Protestant Dutch. *His* cash, to be exact. *His* 400,000 florins. Almost before the ink had dried on the paper, Philip began putting war plans into effect. Ships were built and spies were employed with the full intention of escorting an army from Flanders to invade England. The aim was to overthrow Elizabeth and finish Protestantism in England for good. The added incentive was it would also put a stop to the English sticking their nose in where it wasn't wanted in the Netherlands.

In England, Francis Drake had just returned from a trip that had taken him around the world and he'd brought back Peruvian gold and spices as well as captured Spanish treasures. As a reward, Elizabeth had knighted him and given him his own personal coat of arms. With his experience, there was never a doubt that he would be the one to lead the expedition to attack the Spanish. In September 1585, Drake left Plymouth in command of 1800 soldiers and 21 ships freeing up Elizabeth's time so she could concentrate on Scotland.

With Drake on his way to fight the Spanish, Elizabeth needed as much support as she could get. And what she had was a rabbit in her hat, well... in her prison. Mary Queen of Scots. By then, Mary had been imprisoned for nineteen years and during the whole time, her son James had continued to petition Elizabeth for the safe release of his mother so she could return to Scotland.

Where once upon a time, Elizabeth would have scoffed at the idea of sending Mary home, considering how Mary and her supporters were continually plotting to murder her. But things had changed in that nineteen years and she began to see the value of the notion. What if she too could kill two birds with one stone? What if she gave Scotland back their precious queen, with a little quid pro quo, of course? Slowly, a plan began to formulate in her mind. What she would do would be to send James an ultimatum. On the threat of losing his 'heir apparent' status to the English throne, she would demand that James sign a treaty with England by which he pledged to protect her, and vice versa. They would both come to each other's aid in the event of any attack. Only *then* would she consider releasing his mother.

The unspoken words to James were 'Spanish attack' aimed at shutting out the Spanish and of course, with his mother's freedom hanging in the balance, James willingly signed. His mother's release was everything he had been hoping for and if her release meant pledging his support to protect England from Spain in the process, then so be it.

It was at this time when everything began to unravel. No sooner had he signed the agreement than a new plot surfaced aimed to kill Elizabeth. Letters from Mary were discovered by Elizabeth's spymaster Sir Francis Walsingham suggesting another attempted assassination and the threat from Scotland could not be denied anymore.

The chief instigator had been Anthony Babington, a young man recruited by John Ballard, a Jesuit priest who had wanted to rescue Mary and place her on the English throne. At Ballard's instruction, Babington had sent a coded letter to Mary, who added his name to the complicated plot, and Mary had responded back in code ordering the would-be rescuers to assassinate Elizabeth. When Mary had signed the letter, she had been in a dark mood thinking her son James had betrayed her since she had been dependent on the Spanish to help rescue her. She had even stated in the letter that she was in favour of a Spanish invasion of England.

Mary couldn't have picked a worse time to write the letter. John Ballard was arrested on 4th August and under torture confessed. Then he'd implicated Babington. Within days, the names of other conspirators were added to the list and all were rounded up and taken prisoner.

For Mary, the 11th August 1586 dawned like any other day except for some subtle differences and if she'd been watching closely, she would have been aware that a change was taking place. Up until that day, Mary had always been treated like a royal prisoner with every luxury at her disposal. In Bolton, she had been living very nicely in the South-West tower with a full retinue of 51 knights, servants and ladies-in-waiting. Her household included cooks, grooms, a hairdresser, an embroiderer, an apothecary, physician and a surgeon. Elizabeth had even sent tapestries, rugs and furniture from nearby Barnard Castle and she had herself loaned some pewter vessels to Mary as well as a copper kettle. But much to Mary's annoyance, she had been moved one year before to Chartley Manor owned by Robert Dudley's stepson, Robert Devereaux, 2nd Earl of Essex, because the house had a deep moat, which helped with security. She was still allowed relative freedom of her prison, along with her servants and every day she was allowed to go out riding while her servants left the house to do her laundry. On this particular day however, her servants were refused permission to leave the manor.

At the time, Mary hadn't seen this as a threat. It had surprised her, but she nevertheless continued with her plans to go out riding with her doctor and several others. But as she came to the crest of a hill, she was startled by a group of armed soldiers waiting for her in the shade of a leafy outcrop. It was only then she learnt that instead of riding back to the manor, she was to be taken to Tixall where she would wait to stand trial for treason.

If Mary thought she had a hope of defending herself, she was wrong. Even though the assassination order had not come from James, Mary's supporters had instigated it and it was the final straw for Elizabeth. Knowing she could not wait any longer, she was forced to make a fateful decision regarding Mary. Parliament was still pushing for her execution and at last, a stoic Elizabeth signed the death warrant. It was all just a formality anyway.

Within 24 hours, Elizabeth regretted it but by then, it was too late to stop the ball from rolling.

While Mary waited for word of her fate, her supporters were given no such luxury. On 20th September, seven Catholic men were bound to hurdles in the Tower of London and dragged on their final slow journey through the streets to a hastily erected scaffold in the open field at the upper end of Holborn to what is now known as Lincoln's Inn Fields. Most of the condemned were well-connected and wealthy men, wearing fine silks for their last day on earth. Just a week before they had been tried at Westminster and found guilty of treason and only six weeks before that, they had been free men enjoying the good life. Authorities had searched the homes of known conspirators who had been seen having furtive conversations and the list was a long one.

The crowd, numbered in the thousands, gathered at the scaffold and authorities had to fence off the site to stop people blocking the view. The gallows were even raised so that no one could miss seeing justice being done. Seven more executions would follow the next day.

It was customary for a traitor's death to be by hanging but this day would be different. One after another, the men were left to swing briefly by the neck until half-dead and then cut down, still alive and conscious. Then they were made to watch as an executioner hacked off their genitals with their own knives before digging out their intestines. If they were still alive after all of that, they knew their heart would be next. As their insides were cast into a burning brazier, each man's body was then dismembered and the severed head set high above the gallows.

The first man to die was Ballard, arguably the ringleader, and the second was Babington. He stood unflinchingly beside the scaffold and watched Ballard die, waiting coolly for his turn, not even removing his hat as others turned away in apprehensive horror.

The outcry from their executions was so intense that Elizabeth changed the order for the second group to be allowed simply to hang until 'quite dead' before disembowelling and quartering.

Weeks later, Mary was sent to be tried at Fotheringhay Castle in Northamptonshire by 46 lords, bishops and earls. There would be no legal counsel, no permission to review the evidence and there would be no witnesses called. Portions of the letter were simply read and Mary was convicted of treason against the country of England.

It was on the 7th February that Mary began to hear faint banging in the distance and she would have been aware that a scaffold was being erected. It wasn't until after dinner that evening that she was notified of her forthcoming execution at 8am the following morning. She was not allowed to see a priest, despite one being in the building, and she was not given permission for him to hear her confessions or to receive the Last Sacrament. She could however receive the consolation of *their* minister. She quickly distributed her belongings to her household and wrote her last will as well as a letter to the King of France, her former brother-in-law who was now King Henry III of France.

At just past eight the next morning, the Sheriff arrived for Mary and they made their way down the great oak staircase of Fotheringhay Castle. At the foot of the stairs, the Earl of Kent refused to allow Mary's servants to proceed any further but after heated words with Mary, six of her attendants were granted permission. Just not a priest.

From around the countryside, the gentry gathered to witness her death. Mary appeared in black satin and walked down the quiet hall to the cloth-covered scaffold draped in black. In the hush, she slowly disrobed revealing a blood red bodice and a petticoat of crimson velvet, the colour of martyrdom in the Catholic Church. She was then blindfolded by one of her servants and ordered to kneel in deathly silence. Throughout the hall, awed spectators watched and held their breath, expecting Elizabeth's soldiers to rush in and halt the execution at any moment. After years of refusing to kill her cousin, no one really expected Elizabeth to go ahead with it. Surely this was just a terrifying warning to the Scottish queen to stop her rebellious threats and plots. Wasn't it?

It took two strokes to kill Mary. The first blow missed her neck and struck the back of her head, at which point Mary's lips moved (her servants reported they heard her whisper "*Sweet Jesus*"). The spectators in the Great Hall gasped and screamed. The second blow severed the neck, except for a small bit of sinew that the embarrassed executioner split by using the axe as a saw. The executioner then held the head up and at that moment, the auburn tresses in his hand came apart and the head fell to the ground, revealing Mary's head of very short, grey hair. She had tried to disguise the greying of her hair by wearing the wig that had matched her auburn hair before her years of imprisonment. She was 24 years old when first imprisoned and she was 44 at the time of her execution.

As Mary died, Elizabeth sat in her room and cried.

Over the span of three years, Drake attacked cities of Vigo in Spain, Santiago, Santo Domino then San Augustina. He had learned more and more about the Armada's strengths and weaknesses and by then, he knew it was necessary to close within 100 yards to penetrate the oak hulls of the Spanish ships. By 1588, the English had spent most of their gunpowder and after leaving the Isle of Wight, they'd been forced to conserve their heavy shot and powder for one last final attack.

With the English breathing down his neck, Philip of Spain had no choice but to attack. In August 1588, he sent 130 ships from the small port of Gravelines in Flanders, close to the border with France, to meet the English in one last almighty clash.

Initially the English stayed well out of range, forcing the Spanish to fire uselessly at them in the hope that they would waste most of their dwindling ammunition before they closed in. Unfortunately, after eight hours of intense fighting, the English ships began to run out of ammunition themselves. By 4pm, they had fired their last shots and were forced to pull back and review the damage.

What they saw gave them hope. Despite running out of ammunition, many Spanish ships had been severely damaged during the early hours of the battle and five Spanish ships were lost. One galleon, *San Lorenzo*, had run aground at Calais and the galleons *San Mateo* and *San Felipe* had drifted away in a sinking condition. Drake would hear later that the ships had run aground on the island of Walcheren and the Dutch had taken them the next day. The English had managed to give themselves a little breathing space.

The next day, the remaining ships of the Armada moved northward away from the French coast in an attempt to limp home. Their plan was to keep to the west coast of Scotland and Ireland and then reach the relative safety of the open sea. But to their consternation, as they slowly sailed away, the English continued to pursue them.

By the time the Armada reached Firth of Forth off Scotland, the Spanish were suffering from thirst and exhaustion. Supplies of food and water were running out and the ships were beginning to show wear from the long voyage. In an attempt to keep the ships afloat, anchors and cavalry horses were cast overboard into the sea. Still the English followed.

The Gulf Stream is notorious for mountainous seas and unsure tides so instead of moving west, the Armada found themselves carried north and east. By the time they eventually turned south, there was nothing they could do.

In the end, it was the weather that defeated the Spanish. Off the coasts of Scotland and Ireland the fleet ran into a series of powerful westerly winds that drove many of the damaged ships further on towards the shore. Because so many anchors had been abandoned during the escape from the English ships off Calais, many of the ships were incapable of securing shelter as they reached the coast of Ireland. Most were driven onto the rocks.

The late 16th century was marked by unusually strong North Atlantic storms and the decision for the surviving ships to make for the western shore of Ireland to replenish their supplies of water was a disastrous decision. It's believed that 5,000 men died by drowning, starvation and slaughter at the hands of English forces after they were driven ashore.

In the end, only 67 of the 130 Spanish galleons survived manned by fewer than 10,000 men. Many of the men were near death from disease as the conditions were very cramped and most of the ships had run out of food and water. Many more died in Spain, or on hospital ships in Spanish harbours, from diseases contracted during the voyage. As a result, more ships and sailors were lost to cold and stormy weather than in direct combat. It was reported that when Philip learned of the result of the expedition, he declared, *"I sent the Armada against men, not God's winds and waves".*

As for the English, they had not lost a single ship and their losses stood at between 50 and 100 dead with only 400 wounded. It was hailed as a great success despite typhus, dysentery and hunger killing a number of sailors and troops.

Like many past British monarchs, after dazzling accomplishments came terrible disasters.

One of the last recorded sightings of Elizabeth and Dudley together was at a palace window watching a celebratory parade staged by his stepson, Robert Devereaux, Earl of Essex. Over the years, she forgave Dudley for his betrayal but their relationship lost the intimacy that had defined it for so many years. One week after the sailors had paraded down the streets of

London to the cheers of the crowds, Robert Dudley had dinner with Elizabeth.

He had been showing troubling signs of bad health for quite some time and malaria was suspected although that didn't explain the continual pain in his abdomen. He took his leave of her and one week later, he was dead.

Distraught, Elizabeth locked herself in her apartment for days until the door was eventually broken down. In her hand was a letter he had sent her six days before his death and one day after their final meal together. At the end of the letter, he wrote, "*I humbly kiss your foot... by Your Majesty's most faithful and obedient servant.*" He would have known that it would be his last words to her.

On her deathbed fifteen years later, the letter was found in a bedside treasure box labelled "*his last letter*".

It cannot be disputed that Elizabeth loved Robert Dudley deeply and it may explain why she began to indulge his stepson, Robert Devereaux, towards the end of her life.

It's true Devereaux was handsome and charming and many described him as *'the darling of Elizabeth's old age'*. In fact, he was probably her greatest headache. He was spoilt, ambitious, moody and headstrong and in his arrogance, he saw her as a tiresome old lady who, if she could not be cajoled, would have to be bullied. This led to stormy rows between them and often he would sulk like a spoiled child afterwards. He had a dark side and when his temper was roused, he would become rashly impulsive.

Despite increasing irresponsibility on his part and against the advice of her adviser William Cecil, Elizabeth continued to appoint the young and somewhat petulant young man to highly sought-after military posts. That is, until he deserted his command in Ireland in September 1599 and returned to London. He had been obsessed with fears of what William Cecil was saying about him back home to undermine his influence and this obsession led him to making a truce with the Irish rebel leader (against Elizabeth's wishes) and returning to London without her permission. This rash act amounted to nothing short of desertion and disobedience, something Elizabeth could not and would not tolerate. The situation was made worse when he strode into her bedchamber unannounced and saw her without her makeup and wig.

The next day, he was brought to the council session to explain himself and Elizabeth reportedly cuffed him round the ear. To the amazement of everyone present, he half drew his sword in anger and as a result, he was committed to the custody in his own York House and deprived of his public office. As a further punishment, the source of his income – the sweet wines monopoly – was not renewed.

By underestimating Elizabeth Devereaux made the worst mistake of his life and ultimately it was his pride and need for recognition and power that led to his undoing. Everyone knows '*Pride comes before a fall*' and he was about to fall hard.

He may have wormed his way back into her favour if he had only swallowed his pride and appealed for mercy and apologised. After all, Elizabeth had a soft spot for him and she was very used to his impulsive behaviour. Instead, he made the fatal error of trying to enlist the support of the Scottish king, James VI, to attempt a coup to overthrow her the following March. Why not, he must have thought. He was Elizabeth's great-nephew and she had no children of her own. Why not appoint him as her heir?

His plan was to demand that Elizabeth summon a Parliament in which he would have William Cecil and Walter Raleigh impeached and himself named as Lord Protector. It backfired spectacularly.

It was on 7th February 1601 that he received an ominous letter from Elizabeth that he was to present himself before the Council. With the letter clutched in his hand, he decided to bring the coup forward. He summoned 300 followers, telling them that both Cecil and Raleigh were planning to assassinate him and that he was demanding their attendance the next day.

The 200 soldiers that marched with him on 8th February thundered their way through the city and Londoners were smart enough to remain indoors instead of joining him on his march. His group were intent on entering the city of London to force an audience with Elizabeth.

With his connection to Robert Dudley, Essex had believed that he was untouchable but this time, he'd gone way too far. He took no heed of the warnings along the way and in retrospect, he should have. William Cecil was quick to proclaim him a traitor and a barrier was placed across the street at Ludgate Hill. When Essex's men tried to force their way through, a scuffle broke out and close friend was badly wounded in the cheek, forcing the group to withdraw back to Essex House.

Elizabeth knew she had no choice. He'd broken every rule in the book and had pushed every boundary to the limit. On 19th February, she had him formally arrested and tried for treason and the next day she signed his death warrant. He had committed two unforgiveable sins. He had set out to turn Londoners against her and he had attempted to touch her sceptre.

Six days later, at just before 8am, Devereaux was brought to the scaffold on Tower Green. He beseeched God to forgive him before removing his gown and ruff and kneeling at the block. He said the Lord's Prayer then rose to take off his doublet, revealing a scarlet waistcoat, signifying martyrdom, before once again placing his head on the block.

As a bit of trivia, the executioner was Thomas Derrick, a man previously convicted of rape but pardoned by Essex himself on the condition that he became an executioner at Tyburn. It took three strokes for Derrick to complete the beheading.

During her last years, conflicts with Spain and Ireland continued, the tax burden grew heavier and the economy was hit by poor harvests as well as the cost of the war against Spain. Prices rose and the standard of living fell. And Catholicism strengthened. But during it all, Elizabeth never forgot her people. She gave her country everything she was never able to give to a man and England responded with a loyalty that amounted to love, despite knowing she could be vain, arrogant, spiteful and frequently unjust. But England never seemed to mind. They knew she was also brave and fierce during war and amazingly clever.

During Elizabeth's reign, her whole court was packed up on more than two dozen separate occasions and hit the road as she visited many of her nobles and selected gentry. Elizabeth didn't travel too far as she only visited the parts where she was popular and she never went near the Pro-Catholic north.

During these visits, she would be absent from London for many months at a time. Tapestries and paintings were removed from the walls and put in storage along with the silverware and other valuables, ready for her return. Even though this was supposed to be an exercise to show herself to her people, I can see how this would have been financially beneficial for her as well. The outings were a huge undertaking requiring around 2,000 men and women in her entourage. Also needed were 300–400 carts driven by 2,400 horses, all carrying what was needed, including 200 of Elizabeth's dresses.

To the nobles she visited, it must have been an enormously costly two-day visit. The grocery list for her entourage would have included 11½ cows, 17½ calves, eight stags, 1200 chickens, 2500 pigeons, a cart load of oysters and so the list goes on and on. Take into account an average cow in those days cost people around £2 each and was a labourer's wage for six months. And then there was something needed to wash all this down with. Water was far too risky and anyway, Elizabeth's court liked something a little bit stronger. In two days, they would go through 2,500 gallons of beer alone. But that was not for the gentlemen. They preferred to drink wine, which was imported at great expense and regarded as a status symbol. For these gentlemen and ladies, they drank an average of 63 gallons of white wine and 378 gallons of claret. In just two days.

Elizabeth's health remained good until the autumn of 1602 when a series of deaths among her friends plunged her into a severe depression. Six months later, the death of another close friend seemed to finish her completely.

In her last sickness, knowing her end was near, Elizabeth had the ring she had worn since her coronation filed off her finger. It was a risky business as the skin had grown over the gold. But then, it was meant to be a tight fit. It was her wedding ring to England for when she had been coroneted 45 years before. In March, she fell sick and shortly afterwards, she died.

By the time of her death, Elizabeth had become a legend and over the centuries, instead of that legend decreasing, her legend has grown. She has become one of the most talked-about monarchs of England and I like to think her father would have been very proud of her.

But with her legend came some astounding stories and theories.

Are you sitting comfortably? This could take some time because there are a few theories from varying sources. One rather spectacular theory in particular.

The question has always been *'Why didn't she marry?'* and many people have speculated. Being Henry VIII's daughter, there would have been no greater thought on her mind. A few historians believe they know the answer but it was the 19th century fiction author, Bram Stoker, who first published his astounding theory.

Bram Stoker wasn't just an author. He was also the personal assistant of the actor Henry Irving who had been looking for a house in the Cotswolds in

Gloucestershire. It was in the village of Bisley that Irving came across the legend of 'The Bisley Boy' and he passed the story on to Stoker who was keen to investigate. Stoker was intrigued by the fact that the village's May Day celebrations involved a boy, The May Queen, dressed in Elizabethan costume. Such traditions are generally based on historical events or legends and Stoker wanted to find out more about this one. Why a male Queen, he thought? His meticulous digging resulted in uncovering an astounding and fascinating legend. He was so fascinated with it, he made it the final chapter of his book 'Famous Imposters' called 'The Bisley Boy'. Stoker seemed to be convinced of its truth.

Okay, here we go. According to the legend, a lie began on an autumn morning 470 years ago when panic swept through a manor house in a Cotswold village in Gloucestershire. The 55-year-old king, Henry VIII, was due at any hour, travelling from London to visit his daughter Elizabeth who had been sent there the previous summer to avoid an outbreak of the plague. Unbeknownst to Henry and within days, she had fallen sick with a fever and after weeks of bleeding and vomiting, she was too weak to keep fighting. The night before the king's arrival, his only child to Anne Boleyn, lay dangerously ill. By morning, she was dead.

Elizabeth's governess, Lady Kat Ashley and her guardian, Thomas Parry, had good reason to fear telling Henry this awful news. Four of Henry's children had died in infancy and of the survivors, Edward was a sickly boy of seven and the other was Mary, an embittered, unmarried woman in her late 20s. This 12-year-old child was England's most valuable child in many ways. She could be married to a French prince, or even a Spanish one, to seal a much-needed alliance and when she gave birth, Tudor blood would continue to flow throughout the coming centuries. It was what Henry had so desperately craved.

It was Kat Ashley and Thomas Parry's sole duty to keep Elizabeth safe and they knew that when the king discovered that they had failed, there would be a penalty worse than beheading. They would be bound and dragged for miles to a scaffold. They would be hanged, cut down and then disembowelled. Their entrails would be ripped from their bodies and held in front of them until they died. Their limbs would then be hacked off and displayed on spikes to be picked bare by the birds. Henry was quite capable of ordering this sort of punishment and they knew it.

Their only chance was to conceal the truth from Henry in some way if they could, giving themselves a few days to flee the country.

Kat Ashley's first thought was to find a village girl and dress her up to look like the princess and try to fool the king. Henry rarely saw his quiet daughter and when he did, he was used to seeing her with her chin resting on her chest and saying nothing. The last time she had seen him was when she'd visited his new Queen, Kateryn Parr, and she had been trembling with terror. Elizabeth was known as a gentle, studious child, and painfully shy. Certainly not the sort to speak up to someone who had beheaded her mother. And his arrival would be late in the afternoon at dusk.

By this time in his life, Henry was grossly overweight, ill most of the time and crippled by festering sores. Once his duty was done and he had seen his daughter, they felt confident that he would eat and then quickly adjourn to his bedroom for the night.

It was an elaborate plan but it was the only one they had.

After searching high and low, they could not find a girl of Elizabeth's age. And I'm sure they looked very hard. The closest they could find was a boy from a local village of Bisley with the family name of Neville. He was a gawky, angular youth a year or so younger than Elizabeth who had been her companion and fellow pupil for the past few weeks. The best thing was, he knew her mannerisms.

Stoker's suggestion is that this boy was the son of Henry's illegitimate son, Henry Fitzroy who had died at almost 17 of tuberculosis. Henry VIII had allowed the marriage of 15-year-old Fitzroy to 14-year-old Lady Mary Howard, a Neville, but had declared that the marriage was not to be consummated until both of them were older, believing that too much sexual activity at such a young age would hasten their death. Of course, unbeknownst to Henry, and against his precise orders, they did.

Lady Mary Howard was the second daughter of Thomas Howard, 3rd Duke of Norfolk, a very powerful and ambitious man. His driving force was to make his family more powerful and the possibility of bringing his family closer to the crown after the execution of his niece, Anne Boleyn, was uppermost in his mind. You can see why this match was such a triumph for the family. From birth, Mary was just a pawn for her family, much the same as any woman of noble birth in those days. Through her father, she was first cousin to both Anne Boleyn and Catherine Howard as well as second cousin to Jane Seymour. Her marriage to the acknowledged son of the king, although illegitimate, was quite an achievement for her family.

But sixteen seems to be a dangerous age if you were a Tudor and Henry Fitzroy was no different. He had been suffering from tuberculosis for the past year before his death at 17 years of age, leaving Lady Mary Howard a 16-year-old widow. By then Catherine Howard, Henry VIII's fifth wife, had fallen from grace and Mary's entire family were arrested and briefly imprisoned with the prospect of being hanged overshadowing them.

After Fitzroy died, Mary went to live with her family near Bisley and Stoker believes it was there she secretly delivered a baby boy. At the time of Elizabeth's supposed death, Henry VIII's grandson had worn his red hair long, his bones were slim and he had a feminine look about him.

In any case, there was no time to look further so Parry and Ashley took the desperate measure of donning the boy with his dead friend's clothes.

Remarkably, the deception worked. In the dimness of a dark oak-beamed hall lit only by candles in latticed windows, it was not so surprising that the king, tired and irritable, failed to realise the quiet child at the end of the table was not Elizabeth. He had no reason to suspect his daughter had been ill, and he was exhausted and in pain. It was as short a visit as expected.

But after he left the next morning, the deception began in earnest. Both Parry and Ashley knew without a doubt that they couldn't admit what they'd done. The king's fury would be infinite. They may get out the country but their families would surely suffer. On the other hand, few people knew the princess well enough to recognise her (they could simply dismiss anyone who seemed doubtful) and there was no female look-alike to replace the replacement.

The Neville boy's family didn't argue. They hated Henry VIII for the terrible things he'd put their family through in the past. He had after all beheaded his wives, Anne Boleyn and her cousin Catherine Howard, both cousins and both from the Neville family. It was a twist of fate that after those brutalities, they would have the last laugh and a Neville would sit on the throne after all. As they buried Elizabeth in a stone coffin in the manor grounds, they decided to teach the boy how to be a princess.

Of course, this entire story sounds absolutely and completely absurd and yet many corroborating details around this extraordinary tale about the Neville boy were enough to convince Bram Stoker. Stoker had heard persistent stories that a clergyman from the village of Bisley had discovered a coffin during the 1800s with the skeleton of a girl dressed in Tudor finery with precious gems sewn onto the cloth (enter Twilight Zone music). It seemed to blend with legends that persisted for centuries that an English monarch had in reality been a child from the village.

Above all, Stoker believed that it was the most plausible, although not only, explanation why Elizabeth had changed so dramatically at Thomas Seymour's trial when she was 14 and why at age 25, she had still not married. As we know, it was her most urgent duty as the last of the Tudor line to produce an heir. Yet she described herself as a 'Virgin Queen' and vowed she would never take a husband. And she stayed true to that oath, almost provoking a war between England and Spain when she refused the offer of marriage to the son of the Emperor of Spain. But she did not waver and never took an acknowledged lover although she declared herself 'fond' of Robert Dudley.

She often proclaimed that she was more a king than a queen and '*I have the heart of a man, not a woman, and I am not afraid of anything*'. And then, in a famous speech to her troops at Tilbury as the Spanish Armada approached, she roared '*I have the heart and stomach of a king, and a king of England, too*'. Could she have been telling the literal truth?

Again, you're probably muttering 'rubbish', but just stop and think about it for a minute because here's something else to consider. When the princess reached her early teens, she was assigned a new tutor, Roger Ascham, who was puzzled by her behaviour. He had been led to believe that she was exceptionally bright, poring over her books and learning as quickly as her tutors could teach her. He found she was actually slow at her lessons, and though far from stupid, more an academic plodder than prodigy. He began to make her lessons shorter. He commented that the girl who had been said to soak up facts like a sponge was more a shallow cup: if liquid poured in too quickly, it would simply splash out.

And then we should look at her appearance. An early picture of Elizabeth exists as a pretty child painted by a court painter depicting her with slender shoulders, a delicate neck and a heart-shaped face with ginger hair and eyebrows. In the next portrait, shortly after she was crowned queen, her broad shoulders and neck are disguised with heavy furs, her jaw was heavy and pointed and her lips were pursed. She took to wearing wigs and heavy makeup, had her eyebrows plucked bare and she always wore unflattering clothing that concealed her body. She also refused doctors to examine her and she commanded that there would be no autopsy performed after her death.

Kat Ashley and Thomas Parry, two of the select few who were allowed to come close to her, remained loyal to Elizabeth throughout their lives as the political pendulum swung wildly after the death of Henry VIII. They were her closest friends during Edward VI's reign and they stood by her during her years of imprisonment in the Tower when Bloody Mary decided that the best place for Elizabeth was under lock and key where she could not threaten the throne.

When Mary died, one of Elizabeth's first acts as queen was to make Kat Ashley her First Lady of the Bedchamber and for the next seven years, until Kat's death, she controlled all access to the monarch. Elizabeth began wearing thick white make-up and heavy wigs at all times, and no one was permitted to see her without them.

Elizabeth's chief minister, William Cecil, may have discovered the truth, as he seemed to have a supernatural ability to read people. He was certainly surprisingly tolerant about the queen's determination never to wed. If indeed he knew, he could not afford to have the secret get out. If it did, the country could be plunged into civil war, as there was no obvious heir. There was only Mary I's former husband, Philip II of Spain, Britain's greatest enemy, or the Catholic, Mary Queen of Scots, in Scotland.

Of course, with every pro there is a con. Firstly, Henry VIII was not thick. Surely he would have noticed a change in his daughter's appearance no matter how long between visits and no matter how dark the room or late the night. And then we know for certain Elizabeth was vain and delighted in wearing low cut necklines, even in her old age. If that is true, that is certainly not the way to conceal a lack of breasts. Also Elizabeth was not bald. She chose to wear wigs to hide her greying hair. And how could a teenage boy disguise the changes during puberty? Wasn't it Philip II's own emissary who bribed the queen's laundress for details of her health, and bodily functions, i.e. menstruation? And then there's Robert Dudley. If you can believe they had an intimate relationship, surely Dudley would have known that she was a man. You can argue that it meant they were gay lovers but it would be such a long stretch of the imagination if you were to believe such a thing merely to justify Bram Stoker's theory.

In any case, it's certainly an interesting fun story, which will never be proved. Or disproved for that fact

And now, let me tell you another very story of a young Elizabeth that *is* widely believed.

Many Tudor courtiers, who had been around her for years, suspected that Elizabeth had a 'secret' as many of them had seen the young woman growing into womanhood. You will remember that during her two-year stay with Kateryn Parr and Thomas Seymour, Elizabeth and Thomas engaged in 'playful romps', which ended abruptly when the heavily pregnant Kateryn caught the two of them in an embrace. Elizabeth was sent off to Waltham Abbey and later transferred to Hatfield House.

Months later, Kateryn died days after delivering a daughter and Thomas 'renewed his interest' in Elizabeth, even petitioning his brother, who was the Protector of young King Edward, for permission to marry Elizabeth 'immediately'. Of course, this request was vehemently refused. Any whiff of a scandal would bring the world's anger down around them. But... are you ready for this... what if Elizabeth had actually been pregnant at the time? It's actually not too hard to believe.

She was sent to Waltham Abbey for a period of time around May 1548 and remained in seclusion until September 1548 with her governess, Lady Kat Ashley and her guardian, Thomas Parry. Even though historians state that Elizabeth was there because of illness, there are no reports of a doctor having visited her until October of that year.

What is recorded, however, is that a midwife reported that she was taken to a household blindfolded and there she attended a young fair-haired woman, who gave birth by candlelight. The midwife was woken in the middle of the night by a loud rapping on her door. When she opened the door a crack to see who was knocking, a well-dressed man pushed the door wide open and demanded that her services were needed urgently. She was told she would be paid well but she was not to ask questions and do exactly as she was told. She gathered her tools of trade together and she was bustled into a waiting coach where she was blindfolded.

The coach clattered through the streets of London then out to the countryside down narrow tracks. The journey was furious and lengthy and she had no idea of where she was. Eventually they came to a stop and she was helped down from the coach and led through a door and up a set of stairs. Her blindfold was removed when she came to a bedchamber where a young lady lay in labour. The midwife was told most certainly that she must save the young mother, no matter what happened to the child. She was also told to remember that she should not tell anyone what she had seen that night.

The healthy child was delivered but before she could hand the baby over to the mother, she was ushered out the door into a small room. With a bag of gold pressed into her trembling hands, the midwife was shown out of the room and driven home. The child had been born July 21st, 1548.

There is no doubt that when she turned up at court 18 months after being sent to Waltham Abbey, Elizabeth was a totally different person. She was silent and subdued, dressed in a simple, drab dress with plain and unadorned hair, contrasting sharply with the other ladies who dressed in bright showy splendour. It was almost as if she was trying to live down her reputation with Thomas. It was an amazing transformation.

Hampstead Park has strong connections with Elizabeth. It was given to her by her brother Edward VI in 1550 and had belonged to her stepmother, Kateryn Parr, before her death in 1548. If both rumour and legend is true, Elizabeth must have travelled to Hampstead Park before it came into her possession. Shortly after her accession to the throne in 1558, Elizabeth gave Hampstead Park to her faithful friend, Thomas Parry, one of her two friends in Elizabeth's exclusive circle of friends. He had also been questioned extensively about Elizabeth's relationship with Thomas Seymour but had not disclosed anything. Was Hampstead his reward for silence of Elizabeth's pregnancy?

But that story is just the tip of the iceberg.

The Tudor era has seen many people making claims that they were heirs to the throne. There was Perkin Warbeck who claimed to be Richard Duke of York, one of the princes who died in the Tower during Richard III's reign. There was also Lambert Simnel who pretended to be Edward Plantagenet, son of George Duke of Clarence (Edward IV's brother).

So if we can't quite bring ourselves to believe Stoker's theory, and can't quite believe the midwife's story (although that *would* substantiate the fact that Elizabeth was indeed a female) then the question still remains '*why didn't she marry?'* What I discovered during research has been called 'The Great Tudor Cover-up'.

We all know of the rumours of an affair with Robert Dudley. William Cecil, her most trusted adviser wrote at the time that he feared the pair would be the *"ruin of the realm"*. So what if Cecil actually *did* know a secret and that secret was that she had become pregnant to Robert Dudley prior to the death of his wife and she delivered an illegitimate child to him? It has already been noted that during 1560–1561 there is very little documented information regarding Elizabeth. However, there are reports that during the summer of 1561, the Spanish ambassador commented that she was *"swelling extraordinarily"* and was *"dropsical"* and she had a swelling of her abdomen. According to witnesses, she was supposedly suffering from dropsy, now called oedema, the same ailment that Mary of Guise had suffered which was a build-up of fluid in the body. It is not too much of a jump to imagine this might also have been due to a pregnancy. Put that with the fact that Elizabeth was 'fond' of Robert Dudley, whose bedchamber adjoined hers. She could have given birth during the winter of 1560/61 when marriage to Robert would have been impossible due to the scandal surrounding his wife's death.

And then we have Arthur Dudley.

In the summer of 1587, a Spanish ship intercepted a boat off the coast of San Sebastian that had been heading to France. One of the passengers was a young man who claimed to be a Catholic undertaking a pilgrimage. The Spanish arrested him suspecting he was a spy. The man asked to see Francis Englefield, a Catholic who had been the adviser to Mary I and who was now in exile at the Spanish court. He told Englefield his name was Arthur Dudley and this was his story.

He had been raised by Robert Southern, a man who had once been a servant of Kat Ashley, Elizabeth's governess and friend, in a village around 60 miles outside of London. On Southern's deathbed, he had admitted to the young man that he was not his father. The young man was the son of Robert Dudley and the queen.

He told Englefield that Southern had been handed a baby after being summoned to Hampton Court and that he had been instructed to name him Arthur and raise him as his own. He had assumed initially that it was the child of one of the queen's ladies. He later found out from Kat Ashley's husband that he was 'someone important' and he was to be given the education of a gentleman.

Arthur told Englefield that he had taken flight abroad in fear of his life when he found the secret of his birth. After officers named Blount and Fludd (yes... those names did actually exist) took him before Robert Dudley, Dudley showed him "*affection by tears and words*". It was a long and complicated story, with plausible events and real names, telling of his fear that he would be tracked down and murdered to keep him quiet. If he was indeed the son of Elizabeth, he had every reason to be afraid. If publicised, the story would have sparked an international crisis and possibly a civil war.

Arthur wrote a letter to King Philip of Spain asking for his protection by spreading a rumour that he had escaped and that nobody knew where he was. Englefield believed the reason for this was because Elizabeth was planning to acknowledge Arthur as her son and nominate him as heir to the throne to obstruct the claims of James VI of Scotland and King Philip. That, however, was supposition on his behalf.

Whoever we believe Arthur was, historical evidence shows that he definitely existed and we even know from a letter sent to William Cecil in May 1588 that a young man, who states he was 27 (that would make him born in 1561), and that he was the son of Robert Dudley. He stated that Arthur was costing him six crowns a day to keep imprisoned. But Arthur is never mentioned again and it was assumed he remained in Philip's prison until his death.

Ultimately, only Dudley and Elizabeth knew the truth and neither of them were telling. Dudley died in September 1588, one year after Arthur visited him, and Elizabeth followed him 25 years later.

But if we are to believe that Arthur was indeed the child of Elizabeth and Robert, why didn't she admit to having a child? At her age, having a child was out of the question, which would mean there would be no heir to the Tudor dynasty. It was everything her father believed in and based his life around and she would have been totally aware of that fact.

For me, if the child was indeed theirs, I find it hard to believe the pair didn't discuss the issue of their son over their last meal together. Having acknowledged his son one year before, wouldn't Robert have brought the subject up? Was the child even hers? Was Arthur just one of Walsingham's 'secret agents' sent undercover to gather information on foreign enemies? Or was it the fact that after a lifetime of professing herself as a Virgin Queen, Elizabeth would have to admit to her subjects that she was perhaps *not* that person she had portrayed? Was it the shame? Or was it the fact that she didn't want to repeat another episode of fighting that had occurred during the War of the Roses? Let's not forget Richard III had usurped the throne from his nephews when his brother Edward had died due to the question of their legitimacy. The war had almost destroyed Britain and she would have been well aware of that fact and would have avoided a repetition at all cost.

A wise woman recently said, 'The truth is both a beautiful and terrible thing and must therefore be treated with caution.' Whatever the truth was, it died with her. And with her, the Tudor dynasty died as well.

Elizabeth's death marked the end of one of the most controversial reigns in English royal history. Throughout her life she dazzled everyone with her charm and clever wit. Even her enemies were enthralled. But through it all, she managed to keep her very private life a mystery.

On March 24th, 1603 Elizabeth died and England would soon know what it was like to have a Scottish king as their ruler. Their new king was nothing like Elizabeth and he would certainly take a little getting used to.

SOCIETY IN 17TH CENTURY ENGLAND

*E*ngland was changing dramatically. The population was growing steadily and had reached 5½ million at the time of Elizabeth's death. With that population growth came a growth in wealth as England became steadily richer. Trade and commerce was growing and industries such as the manufacture of glass, brick making, iron and coal mining were an increasingly important part of English economy that was expanding every day. With the importance of trade, awareness of merchants increased and with that awareness, their status grew as well.

As England grew more commercial, the lending of money became more important. London merchants had been depositing their gold at the mint for safety but in the future, Charles I would confiscate that gold and from then on, people began to deposit their gold with goldsmiths instead for surety. By the early 17th century, it was usually the goldsmiths who lent and changed money. The goldsmiths gave receipts for the gold in the form of notes promising to pay on demand and in time, merchants and tradesmen began to exchange these notes as a form of money. The goldsmiths presumed that not all of their customers would withdraw their gold at the same time so it was a pretty safe bet for them to issue notes for more gold than they actually had.

Let's take a quick walk around London in this era. Imagine it's been a rainy day and you're out for a walk. Water puddles had formed in dark alleys and the drains have overflowed down the middle of the cobbled streets as people huddle in their bedraggled hats and cloaks under dripping eaves. A horse-drawn carriage with clattering wheels speeds past on the uneven stones and carelessly splashes water on anyone who has braved the inclement weather. Normally the streets are packed with people and carriages and most days a blanket of smoke hangs over the city. The pollution gets in your eyes and the stonework of every building is blackened with it. Many of the houses are hundreds of years old and their timbers are deeply scarred with rat holes teaming with life. The houses are so close in the narrow alleys that occupants can reach out and touch hands with their neighbours if they chose to.

But there is a reason you're out and about on this day.

After a downpour, you get the clearest view of the city with the sky washed clean of smog although the city air still smells of coal smoke. But it's not just the burning coal that affects your nostrils. There are noxious fumes coming from the parts of the city where tanning is taking place and aromatic horse dung still lies in piles in the streets. As the day wears on, the smells are intensified by the stench from cesspits in cellars and from the carts filled with dung-pots left in the streets by rakers, whose business it is to empty private cesspits. Pigeons fly out from under the eaves of the old houses and their dropping leave white streaks on everything below. Rats scavenge behind crates avoiding the rubbish collectors in their horse-drawn carts collecting rotting matter from kitchens. You will be able to smell the flocks of sheep and herds of cattle driven by hoof to the abattoirs where their dung and blood add to the aroma on the streets.

Very soon, the streets will fill again, not just by permanent residents who contribute to the overcrowded feeling, but hundreds of thousands of people who come to town daily to go to markets, fairs and to do business in the city. Very soon there will be crowds of people and animals everywhere so you know not to linger.

And then you listen to the sounds of London. Oxen are led into the city and slaughtered every day and the squeals and bellows they make in their pens is considerable and disturbing. There is the sound of iron wheels of coaches grinding over the cobbles and the hammering of blacksmiths and candlestick makers. There are the bells of rakers driving their dung-carts, the yelling of those gathering around a cockfight, the shouting of vendors pushing their carts, householders leaning out their windows and shouting to neighbours and you would hear the hourly chimes of more than a hundred churches. This London is so crowded, smelly and noisy you will barely be able to hear yourself think.

As always, at the top of the ladder of English society was the nobility. Below them were the gentry: a group of men not quite rich but certainly well off. Below them again were the comfortably well-off yeomen who worked side by side with their farmers. Not on the ladder of success at all were the vast mass of the population: craftsmen, labourers and the poor who were coming in their droves from the countryside looking for work in town. And then there were the prostitutes.

Both Henry VII and Henry VIII had made attempts to close down the brothels after continued outbreaks of syphilis. It was a largely unsuccessful attempt to douse the spread of the disease because red light districts flourished again after Henry VIII's death, and this time they did not restrict themselves to the south bank. There was the lucrative Southwark, a den of vice in Central London, to consider. Not only did they rub shoulders with thieves and sleazy characters on their way to bearbaiting or cockfighting pits, they mingled with the middle and upper class clientele on their way back from theatres and inns.

For these two classes, life had grown pretty comfortable. They were eating meat every day and living the high life, conveniently unaware that others less fortunate than themselves were only eating meat three times a week while some only ate it once, if they were lucky. This last group had to rely on charity to help them survive. For the poor, life had changed very little since early Tudor England.

With the increase in population, diseases lurked around every corner and in every shadow. Everyday life meant being aware of the flu, dysentery, typhoid and smallpox and then there were always outbreaks of plague to be aware of. If you had a swelling in your armpits, if you were exceedingly thirsty, had a headache and if you were vomiting, you knew you were in serious trouble. You also knew to air your bedding in case there were fleas.

You were certainly aware that fleas caused the disease but if you found any or you had been bitten, it was already too late because nobody had any idea how to treat it.

Plague broke out in London in 1603, 1636 and in 1665. Each time it killed a significant part of the population but each time London recovered. Of course, other towns as well as London were also periodically devastated by the plague. However, the plague of 1665, which affected London and other towns, was the last recorded outbreak and no one is very sure why because rats still scurried through the dark streets and people were still throwing dirty water and other rubbish from their windows into those same streets.

17th century London was a dangerous place to live if you were poor but if you were rich, you were lucky enough to build grand houses west of London or along the Thames. Transportation was no problem for you. You could easily walk from one street to another or you could travel by boat along the Thames. You could even hire a horse-drawn carriage called a 'hackney carriage' to take you around London if you desired. The streets were lit for the first time and an oil lamp was hung outside every tenth house. Not that the oil lamps gave you much light but they were certainly better than nothing at all, which was a fact of life on the other side of town.

In your grand house you had grand furniture that was more comfortable and much more finely decorated than the plain, heavy oak furniture of Tudor times. This century, furniture for the rich was often made of walnut or mahogany and was decorated in new ways. A new concept was veneering, the layering of thin pieces of expensive wood over cheaper wood, although you could also opt for inlaid pieces where wood was carved out and the hollow was filled with mother of pearl. Lacquering had also arrived in England and pieces of furniture could be coated with lacquer in bright colours to match the drapes.

If you wanted something completely different by Stuart England times, chests of drawers were becoming commonplace as were grandfather clocks. Later in the century the bookcase would be introduced. Chairs had also become far more comfortable and were upholstered (padded and covered) and very soon, the first real armchairs would appear.

In the Middle Ages, ordinary people's homes were usually made of wood. However in the late 16th and early 17th centuries, many were built or rebuilt in stone or brick and by the late 17th century, even poor people lived in houses made of brick or stone. It made life a little more comfortable since they were warmer and drier than the old wooden ones, although they still remained very small and crowded. Most of the poor lived in huts of two or three rooms while some families managed to survive in just one room. Your furniture, such as it was, remained very plain and basic because enhancements in furniture were not a part of your life.

But there were some more improvements on the horizon. In the 16th century, chimneys had been a luxury only the well-off could afford. But during the 17th century they became more common and by the late 17th century the vast majority had them. Windows however took a little longer to become commonplace. Glass was definitely a luxury so those who could not afford it made do with linen soaked in linseed oil. However during the 17th century glass became cheaper and by the late 17th century everyone had glass windows, sometimes casement windows (ones that opened on hinges). Later on, sash windows that slid up and down vertically to open and shut, were being introduced.

The poor lived in houses east of the city where the streets were narrow and dark, well away from the wealthy people. Unfortunately, in these overcrowded, heavily populated areas, crime and danger was ever present and in a place where so many had so little, it's not so surprising. Tempers and alcohol produced volatile situations and you made sure you kept a dagger close by to protect yourself. You learnt to keep your wits about you on the way home from the local pub especially as ale was the only available liquid to drink due to the unsanitary condition of the water. Looking at the rivers running with excrement, they had a good point.

However, more improvements were on the way and a piped water supply was being created. Water from a reservoir travelled along elm pipes through the streets then along lead pipes to individual houses. Unfortunately, you had to pay to be connected to the supply and it was not cheap.

In the early 17th century people began eating with forks for the first time. New foods were being introduced into England such as bananas and pineapples and new drinks such as chocolate, tea and coffee had arrived. By late 17th century, coffee houses had popped up all around town and merchants and professional men alike could meet to read newspapers and talk shop.

But not everyone was so lucky. Ordinary people existed on food like bread, cheese and onions and they ate pottage each and every day. This kind of strew was made by boiling grain in water to make a kind of porridge to which you added vegetables and pieces of meat or fish, if you could afford it.

Everyday life was a challenge and a hazard so it's not surprising that the average life span in the 17th century was considerably shorter than today. Average life expectancy at birth was only 35 and many people died while they were still children. Out of all the people born, between one third and one half died before the age of about 16. However if you could survive to your mid-teens you would probably live to your 50s or early 60s. Even in Stuart times some people lived to their 70s or 80s.

If you were a wealthy man at the beginning of the 17th century, you were probably wearing a starched collar called a ruff on your linen shirt, a knee length trouser-like garment called breeches with stockings and boots. You also wore a kind of jacket called a doublet with a cape on top to keep out the cold. At times, your doublet became a waistcoat and you wore a frock coat over the top instead of your cape. Together with the breeches, it was rather like a three-piece suit. To finish your ensemble, your hair was long, you probably wore a beard and a wig, and your beautifully dressed wife walked beside you wearing a small black patch on her face, much like a little star or a crescent moon, to enhance her beauty. Under her long dress, she wore a linen nightie-like garment called a shift, followed by a frame made of wood or whalebone, called a farthingale. Her dress came in two parts: the bodice and the skirt and sometimes she would wear two skirts. The upper skirt was gathered up to reveal an underskirt but not too far... because she never wore knickers.

Because of the state of the water, keeping yourself clean wasn't an easy task. You did that, not by washing, but by rubbing linen cloths over your body and through your hair to soak up the sweat. To take care of your body odour, you used perfume to improve the smell of your clothes. After taking care of your body odours, you had to take care of your breath. Thankfully, the Chinese had invented the toothbrush in 17th century and it had been introduced to England so there wasn't as much need to chew cumin seeds or aniseed anymore. However, after brushing, you still rinsed out your mouth with white wine.

To pass the time, you played games such as cards and bowls with the occasional tennis and shuttlecock as well as board games like chess, drafts and backgammon. Among the cruel 'sports', you liked cockfighting and bull and bearbaiting where a bear or bull was chained to a post and dogs were trained to attack it.

And of course, the theatre remained popular with the stage jutting out into the audience where boys played women's parts. That would soon stop after 1660 when actresses came into their own. Too soon though, the Puritans would arrive and they certainly disapproved of any such frivolity. They would ban it completely in 1642 although it would be revived again when Charles II returned home in 1660.

Stagecoaches were running regularly between the major English towns from the middle of the 17th century although the wealthy were still being carried around in sedan chairs while out and about in town. You paid dearly for the luxury of a stagecoach, and to top it off, they were very uncomfortable on the rough roads because none of them had springs. And of course, there was still the danger of highwaymen.

The word 'highwaymen' conjures up characters like Dirk Turpin but these men were not so polite. In 1560 in Essex, there were 60 court cases alone relating to the theft of money and jewellery stolen on the highways and unlike the 18th century, these robbers were just common thieves. If you were unlucky enough to come across these ruffians, there would also be another group cutting off your retreat. They would not only take your money and jewels, they took your clothes as well. Some killed their victims but most were left tied up in the forest in such a way that you could work yourself lose in an hour or two and make your way to the nearest inn or town in your underwear. If you survived the trip, you would be grateful to arrive unharmed but even these establishments housed thieves and unsavoury characters.

Heaven help you if you needed to see a doctor because barber-surgeons were still performing operations. Their knowledge of anatomy was improving but still left a lot to be desired. In 1628 William Harvey published his discovery of how blood circulates around the body and doctors had discovered how to treat malaria with bark from the cinchona tree.

But even with these improvements, medicine was still handicapped by wrong ideas about the human body. Most doctors still thought that there were four fluids or 'humours' in the body – blood, phlegm, yellow bile and black bile. Illness resulted when you had too much of one humour. When that happened, you needed to be bled. Nevertheless, during the 17th century, a more scientific approach to medicine emerged and some doctors thankfully began to question traditional ideas.

At the heart of everything was your awareness that war could begin at any time. Up until 1700s, firearms were either a matchlock, (a slow burning match touched to the powder when the trigger was pulled) or a wheel lock, (a metal wheel spun against iron pyrites making sparks). During the 17th century both of these were gradually replaced by the flintlock, which worked by hitting a piece of flint and steel making sparks. That is until the cartridge was invented and changed everything. The musket ball was placed in a container, which held the right amount of gunpowder to fire it. Killing became easier and quicker because a soldier no longer had to take so much time to measure powder from a powder horn into his gun.

Apart from artillery there were two branches of an army: cavalry and infantry. The cavalry was usually armed with wheel lock pistols and sabres, back plates, and breastplates. Helmets protected their heads and torsos. But life wasn't as easy if you were an infantryman. The infantry consisted of two groups of men: some armed with pikes and others with muskets. Because it took a long time to reload muskets making soldiers very vulnerable while they did so, there was a need to be protected by men with pikes. In theory there were two musketeers to each pike man but when the bayonet was invented, a nasty looking blade fixed to the musket to jab at your enemy, pike men were out of a job.

But if the need for pike men had disappeared, the need for an army hadn't. War was always just around the corner.

This is the beginning of 'Early Modern Britain'. It was a time of Renaissance, English and Scottish Reformation and a debilitating English Civil War. And as always, to the victor goes the spoils. It was a time of rulers who were vain, greedy and downright corrupt. It was a time of adulterers, swindlers and cowards. And it was a time in British history when war would tear the country apart. It would become the most religious decade Britain had ever seen since the Middle Ages and society would be dominated by Christian beliefs and a willingness to severely punish people for ungodly behaviour. They themselves became victims of Puritanism.

But I don't want to get too far ahead here. James VI of Scotland had just arrived and became James I of England and a new dynasty was beginning – the Stuarts. This new king lacked the charisma and charm of Elizabeth and always seemed to be in conflict with someone or other.

JAMES VI OF SCOTLAND / JAMES 1 OF ENGLAND

Born 1566
Reign 1603 – 1625

Being the only son of Mary Queen of Scots and the ruler of Scotland since he was 13 months old seems incredible enough on its own, but James' early childhood years were lonely ones, full of murder and intrigue, and they undoubtedly had a profound effect on him.

He had heard the story of his father's death presumably planned by his mother and executed by her lover who then fled when his complicity was discovered. He knew of his mother's desperate attempt to escape only to be arrested and imprisoned in Loch Leven Castle after abdicating in his favour and he knew she'd been forced to leave him in the care of her half-brother, James Stewart, Earl of Moray, while she had fled to England in the dead of night to escape the consequences. Instead of sanctuary, his mother had found herself spending the last nineteen years of her life in Elizabeth's prison, plotting endlessly for her cousin's murder. Eventually, Elizabeth had had enough. His mother's position as Queen of Scotland had made no difference at all to England when the crime was the attempted assassination of their queen. The expected punishment for treason had been beheading and Elizabeth had not wavered at the end.

To him, these stories were wild, romantic tales told by men sitting around a fireplace with a tankard of ale in their hands while the bitter cold winds blew snow in from the north. He was unaware that those same men were determined that the wild stories they told held just the right amount of danger to ensure James would remain submissive and pliant. They were meant to show James what would happen if he didn't comply. What they actually did was fill James heart with a desperate longing for the shadowy figure of his mother. She was a figure he had no hope of ever remembering since she left Scotland when he was only thirteen months old, never to be seen again. Despite this, or possibly because of this, those old men failed. James desperately wanted her to come back to him at any cost. He *longed* for it. It was a yearning however that was never fulfilled.

Scotland was ripe for a change when his mother had fled to England and there seemed no end to the ruthlessness that men were prepared to go to. As a consequence, James had seen four of his regents die horribly one after the other. When he was four years old, the Earl of Moray had been assassinated and James' care had been transferred to his paternal grandfather Matthew Stewart, 4th Earl of Lennox. Two years after that, his grandfather was shot dead in a skirmish with Mary's supporters and replaced by the Earl of Mar who in turn was poisoned at a banquet given by James Douglas, Earl of Morton two years later again. Morton lasted for ten years until James' second cousin, the then current Earl of Lennox, established himself as James' dominant male 'favourite' and convinced James to have Douglas executed for the overdue complicity in his father's murder 15 years before. For a sensitive young man not even out of his teens, James had been surrounded by death and intrigue for most of his life.

By then, the juicy carrot of the English throne had been dangled in front of him and James wanted it more than anything else, even as much as his mother's return. After all, it was his due as the great-great-grandson of Henry VII. But that same carrot was also being dangled in front of another member of the Stuart clan: his cousin Lady Arbella Stuart.

For some time, from around 1592, Arbella was being considered as one of the serious candidates to succeed Elizabeth I. Arbella's father Charles Stuart, 1st Earl of Lennox, and James father, Henry Stuart Lord Darnley, had been brothers and both brothers were great-grandchildren of Margaret Tudor – James through Margaret's first marriage to James IV and Arbella through Margaret's second marriage to Archibald Douglas. This made them both great-great-grandchildren of Henry VII and both with equal rights to the English throne. Everything depended, of course, on Elizabeth's choice of heir and it could have gone either way.

At 17 years of age, Arbella had many childbearing years ahead of her while at 26 years of age, James was displaying little interest in women and the government was beginning to show signs of uneasiness as male favourites came and went at a steady pace. Things weren't looking very rosy for James at this stage.

Then Arbella made a big mistake. Word had reached Elizabeth that Arbella was making plans to marry Edward Seymour, the son of Edward Seymour, Duke of Somerset, eldest brother of Jane Seymour and Elizabeth was far from pleased with her choice.

It wasn't the fact that the Seymours were a powerful family who had rightful claims to the English throne. And it wasn't the fact that while Edward's father had been regent for her young brother, Edward VI, people were suspicious at the speed with which he accumulated his wealth and power. Both were bad enough, but it was more Edward Seymour's predisposition for clandestine marriages that made Elizabeth hesitate.

Edward's first marriage had taken place in December 1560, without Elizabeth's permission, to a potential claimant to Elizabeth's throne, Lady Catherine Grey (the sister of Lady Jane Grey, the Nine Day's Queen). It had been kept hidden until Catherine was so visibly pregnant in August the next year that the secret could no longer be kept quiet. She had confided in Lord Robert Dudley of her predicament and there had been no doubt that Robert was going to tell Elizabeth. When the truth came out, both were sent to the Tower, where their first son was born. It was only after Catherine died of consumption eight years later that Edward had been released from the Tower.

His stay in the Tower apparently hadn't taught Edward a single thing. In 1582, he married a gentlewoman of the Privy Chamber by the name of Frances Howard and that marriage had been kept a secret as well for almost a decade. The truth only came out when he had tried to have it set aside so he could establish a relationship with Arbella.

Of course, Arbella denied any intention of marrying Edward without Elizabeth's consent but the damage had already been done. Elizabeth's opinion of Arbella hit a disastrous low and Edward was once more sent to the Tower, only to be released when Frances died in 1598.

During all of this, James was feeling pretty buoyant. Only months before his mother's death in 1587, under the threat of losing his 'heir apparent' status, he had been 'requested' to sign a treaty with England assuring them of his allegiance and support and he had willingly signed. Having done everything Elizabeth had asked of him, he was quietly confident that Elizabeth would keep her word. By signing the treaty, he had cleared the way for his succession to the English throne after Elizabeth's death no matter whom his cousin Arbella married. Even still, it was touch and go for a while.

But James' big problem was that he needed an heir just as urgently as Elizabeth did. To achieve this, James needed a wife and the search was on to find him one. Denmark became the prime choice since it was a growing and affluent country and James had very little money in his Scottish bank. Scottish ambassadors initially focussed on King Frederick's elder daughter, but they were informed she was out of the race because she was already betrothed. Their attention then shifted to King Frederick's younger daughter, Anne, at James' suggestion, although she had only just turned 14. Despite her youth and within months of the initial negotiations, everything was quickly finalised and James married Anne by proxy at Kronborg Castle in Demark. Within weeks, she set sail for Scotland to meet her new husband for the first time. Who said romance was dead?

Despite being spellbound with Anne at first, James' enchantment quickly evaporated and whispers resumed of his fondness for male company. As for Anne, she had been very underwhelmed by her new husband and her eyes had been caught wandering on many occasions.

As with most queens, Anne had been very aware of her role and producing heirs to the throne was her main duty in life. Finally, and to everyone's relief, she gave birth to her first child four years later, a boy they named Henry and over the coming years, two further children would arrive.

In 1603, James' prayers were answered when Queen Elizabeth died in the early hours of 24th March and he was informed that he would indeed be the next King of England as James I. A month later, eager to start their new life in England, full of wealth and promise, James, Anne, and their three children left Edinburgh for London. With a fervent promise to parliament that he would return every three years, James set off with his family on their high adventure.

His promise to return was one he had no intention of keeping after hearing the endless stories of English wealth, told around his inadequate fireplace on cold wintery nights. Compared to Scotland, England offered incredible prosperity and he was going to take every advantage of it. That fortune was now his and he had no intention of being parted from it, or the benefits of having it, for any length of time whatsoever.

As he travelled south to London, his new position as King of England began to truly sink in as he was received everywhere with lavish hospitality. He was even heard to say it was like *"swapping a stony couch for a deep feather bed"*.

Despite a sudden outbreak of the plague when people naturally locked themselves away from the rest of the population, the streets of London were overflowing with onlookers when James entered on 7th May. People hung out of windows and onlookers craned their necks to catch the first glimpse of their new king. You see no one had any idea of what he looked like.

What they saw was a rather plain-looking, dishevelled man in bulky clothing that exaggerated his notably spindly legs. They watched in silent shock as he dismounted awkwardly and walked gracelessly towards Westminster Abbey. As he looked around open-mouthed at his new kingdom, his protruding tongue lolled to the side of his mouth. Some bystanders went so far as to pull an expression of revulsion.

By the time James inherited the throne, England had changed dramatically from when the Tudors had first laid claim to the realm. Spain was no longer a threat and the nobility were beginning to feel their own strength. England felt secure enough to take a hand in their own management without relying on the opinion and wishes of a sole monarch, much less a Scottish one.

From the very beginning, parliament was determined to make it perfectly clear to James that he would be crowned the King of England with the usual pomp and ceremony, but the practice of total obedience to their monarchs had died with Elizabeth. What they didn't know, but were going to find out very soon, was that James firmly believed in his Divine Right to rule and he was going to enforce that belief. There had never been a time in his life when he hadn't been regarded as the rightful King of Scotland, always to be obeyed, and he wasn't about to let that submission cease now. With his cloistered upbringing sprang arrogance and he fully expected England to conform to his way of ruling. Even before the coronation, this sensitive issue had already reached a crisis. It wasn't a good start for James.

It was definitely the wrong attitude to bring to his first parliament and it was a total disaster from the beginning. The House of Commons had already drawn up a document in firm but definite language reminding James that their liberties included free speech, free elections and freedom from arrest at Parliamentary discussions should their opinion differ from his. Everyone was very aware of Henry VIII's fondness for lopping off the heads of anyone who disagreed with him and that particular clause was a safeguard that everyone eagerly agreed upon, especially with this relatively unknown ruler from the barbaric north.

It's pretty safe to say that all James was interested in was how much money was in the treasury. So when he read through the documents handed to him, he brushed them aside with contempt as if they were personal insults. Then, to add insult to their injury, when James, a devout Presbyterian, proceeded to say he hoped to secure peace by 'profession of his true religion' and his divine right to rule, brown stuff instantly hit the fan. If first impressions are vital, then James had failed miserably.

The understanding in Scotland was that England was a wealthy country. Fanciful stories had morphed into something more like fairy tales as they drifted around the Scottish court. Reports of Elizabeth's fabulous jewels, of her plentiful visits to her nobles with over 2,000 men and women in attendance, of her bounteous feasts, her incredible navy and as the stories grew in splendour from person to person, James waited eagerly for his turn. He was in for a bit of a shock. All too soon, he found himself hard pressed for money with the country in debt for the massive sum of £400,000. Elizabeth had certainly been a penny pincher, taking her extensive court on routine visits to wealthy landowners on a regular basis to lessen her expenses, but the war with Spain and Ireland had been costly and every year, the country's revenue was worth less and less due to inflation in Europe.

As a result, the expenses of James' court increased at an alarming rate. His lack of money meant summoning more parliaments, which again cost him more money, creating a vicious circle he had no way of controlling. When he asked for more money, Parliament came back with the comment that a monarch should 'live off his own' and any revenues from crown lands should be used for the upkeep of the public services not his personal use.

Again, James disagreed. After all, he had *no* money of his own.

It had only taken one year but England already had had enough of him. And it's not so surprising that by May of that same year, a man by the name of Robert Catesby was hatching a plan. This burly man with burly friends had two things in common: they were all Catholics and they all disliked James intensely. By then, James had denounced the Catholic Church and ordered all Jesuits and Catholic priests to leave the country and had reimposed the collection of fines for those who refused to attend Anglican services. The anger had only deepened when he allowed his Scottish nobles to collect the 'recusancy' fines. This one fine alone gave James a total of £5,000 a year (equivalent to over £10 million by today's standards).

What happened next, and the incredible reasoning behind it, is like something out of a tacky novel. The conspiracy, famously called 'The Gunpowder Plot', was actually hatched over a few pints in the back room of a pub called the Duck and Drake between Robert Catesby, Thomas Wintour, John Wright, Thomas Percy and Guy Fawkes.

Their plan was to assassinate James and his Protestant supporters by digging a tunnel under Parliament house and hiding thirty-odd barrels of gunpowder (two and a half tonnes by the way) in order to blow it up during the next sitting of parliament. At the same time, they would organise a riot in the Midlands to act as a decoy.

Thomas Percy, a member of the King's Bodyguard was able to lease lodgings that were situated adjacent to the House of Lords and Guy Fawkes, a man who had been fighting for the Spanish in the Low Countries, was the man chosen to put the plan into operation. His role was to light the match to a slow fuse and then escape across the Thames before high-tailing it to the continent for safety. He could then leave the others to complete the said plan. When James was dead and Elizabeth was on the throne, he would return triumphantly to celebrate and reap the spoils. After James was killed, they would then kidnap his nine-year-old daughter Princess Elizabeth and place her on the throne as the new Catholic monarch.

Elizabeth was chosen after considering all their options. Prince Henry, they believed, would die alongside his father, Charles was too weak and feeble and Mary was too young. Elizabeth was just right. She was young enough to be a puppet queen, brought up as a Catholic and later married to a Catholic bridegroom and having little Catholic princes and princesses.

An oath was taken and they all went home, ready to make more plans at other meetings and organise just how they were going to surreptitiously transport all this gunpowder and have it in place before the next parliament opened in February 1605.

Was this rather amazing and intricate plot *ever* going to work? Imagine them. Four of the five men were tall and powerfully built with thick reddish-brown hair, flowing moustaches and bushy reddish-brown beards and they more than likely had big voices fuelled on by alcohol to complete the package. Is it just me or is this just a group of rather large obvious-looking men speaking in drunken whispers at the local pub most Friday nights over several rounds of drinks, plotting to kill the king and rule the world? With the way they looked, it's not likely they could hide anywhere.

Not surprisingly, things began to go awry very early on in the planning stages. Firstly the re-opening of Parliament was delayed due to concerns over an outbreak of the plague, which meant that rather than sitting in February, Parliament would not sit again until 3rd October. The delay however meant they had more time to dig the tunnel beneath Parliament.

The Palace of Westminster in the early 17th century was a warren of buildings clustered around the medieval chambers and halls of the former royal palace that then housed both Parliament and royal law courts. It was easily accessible by merchants, lawyers and others who lived and worked in shops and taverns within its precincts.

On 25th March the plotters had purchased the lease of a ground floor brick-lined storage room, which may have been part of the palace's medieval kitchen, beneath the first-floor House of Lords. The room was ideal since it was alongside a passageway called Parliament Place, which itself led to Parliament Stairs. Unused and filthy, its location was ideal for what the group planned to do.

Twenty barrels of gunpowder were brought in first, followed by sixteen more on 20th July and the plan was ready to be put into action. It was then they heard of yet another delay. The ever-present threat of the plague had risen again and the opening of Parliament was delayed once more until 5th November. While the plague raged, James had decided he would spend much of the summer away from the city, hunting and staying wherever convenient, which meant the plan had to be delayed until he returned.

When the men regrouped in August, it was to discover that the stored gunpowder had decayed. More gunpowder was brought into the room, along with firewood to conceal it, and the remaining details of the plot were finalised in October in a series of taverns across London.

Not so strangely, it was at this time that an anonymous letter found its way to Lord Monteagle just one week before parliament opened and the letter was then passed on to James. He in turn authorised a quiet search and shortly before midnight on 5th November, Fawkes was caught red-handed leaving the cellar after placing the last of the gunpowder in place.

The outcome of their trials was never in doubt and the jury found the defendants guilty of high treason Their punishment was read aloud in the court as the men listened in shock to their fate. They were to be drawn backwards to their death by a horse to the very building they had tried to destroy. Before dying, their genitals were to be cut off and burnt before their eyes and their bowels and hearts removed. They would then be decapitated and dismembered. The dismembered parts of their bodies were to be displayed so that they might become 'prey for the fowls of the air'. In January 1606, the sentence was carried out.

By then, it was obvious that it wasn't just Parliament who hated James. His wife Anne despised him intensely as well. And the feeling was entirely mutual. They fought openly in public with James sending her messages saying, "*His Majesty took her continued perversity very heinously,*" to which she replied "*the king drinks so much, and conducts himself so ill in every respect, that I expect an early and evil result*".

No one had ever called James handsome. He wasn't even close. James had not been able to walk properly until the age of five. Invariably, he leaned on men's shoulders for assistance and for some reason, his fingers were always embarrassingly fiddling with his codpiece. He was of medium height and weight, but he appeared much larger because he continued to wear bulky clothing, padded to protect him from the daggers of possible assassins. His conversations were usually longwinded and full of lengthy theories mingled with coarse jokes, although few could understand him as his speech was quite garbled with his strong Scottish accent. His protruding tongue seemed too large for his mouth and gave the impression that he ate liquids rather than drank them, slobbering his wine down his chin and onto his clothing.

And James liked wine. He liked it an awful lot. He rarely drank water, but then, who did? Looking at the rivers running with excrement, the key to staying on the healthy side was to *not* drink the water. As a result of so much wine, his urine and faeces were usually quite concentrated and... umm... odorous and he had occasional bouts of abdominal pain when passing this dark and bloody urine. He even complained of a constant fever. To add to his problems, he had melancholic episodes, particularly at times of stress, accompanied by bouts of diarrhoea.

Like some of his descendants, James most likely suffered from the hereditary disease porphyria, which primarily affects the nervous system resulting in abdominal pain, vomiting, depression, paranoia and mental disturbances. This disease can also affect the skin with itching and swelling and increased hair growth on areas such as the forehead. James' urine would have had a purple or red hue although he may also have had a series of chronic kidney infections, which would have given it the distinctive colour.

As James' general appearance, disposition and health deteriorated, it was no surprise that Anne made the decision to have no more children to him. She moved herself into Greenwich Palace, then later Somerset House, naming it Denmark House. To show Anne how little he cared, at the vulnerable age of 40, James began a fling with a tall Scotsman by the name of Robert Carr.

The two first met when a friend of James by the name of Thomas Overbury introduced the handsome young man to James while out riding. It seems to have been love at first sight for James so when Carr was thrown off his horse, breaking his leg, James insisted that his own physicians take care of him.

After Carr's recovery, James appeared everywhere with his arm around the young man's neck, constantly kissing and fondling him. James would lovingly feel the texture of the expensive suits he chose and bought for him, pinching his cheeks and smoothing his hair and kissing lasciviously in public. They couldn't keep their hands off each other. As a sign of his affection, James made Carr his Gentleman of the Bedchamber and was given the title of Viscount Rochester and later Earl of Somerset. Soon, it was openly joked that *"Elizabeth was the king: now James is the queen!"* One year later, James knighted Thomas Overbury and the threesome became inseparable.

With a wife and family to support, plus a lively new addition to his court, James was always on the lookout for money. Apart from the endless gossip that grated on him, he hated the fact that he had to beg parliament for financial help. He was the Divine Ruler after all, so why should he have to stoop to such desperate measures? As the king, the money was his anyway, wasn't it?

For a man who had lived most of his life on a shoestring budget, James had become so extravagant with his spending that it seemed there was no solution to his dwindling finances. Not only was James tired of having to ask for money, Parliament was tired of listening to him. As a way of compromising, they came up with a financial solution that involved a little *quid pro quo*. The suggestion was that Parliament would grant him an enormous lump sum of £600,000 (a sum roughly in excess of £600 million by today's standard) to pay off his debts plus an annual grant of £200,000 for his personal use if he would pass ten articles, up to now refused, at the next parliamentary sitting.

It was more than James had hoped for. He wholeheartedly agreed and the suggestion was passed on to the House of Commons. But that's where it all came to a screeching halt. The House of Commons agreed on the annual sum part of the proposal but absolutely refused to give James the money to pay off his personal debts. That, they stipulated, he would have to find for himself.

James was livid. After eight weeks of raging arguments, James had finally had enough of the lot of them. On 31st December 1610, he dismissed Parliament and all of its members. Then he promoted Robert Carr as the new Treasurer.

We can all see where this was going. Of course, his financial problems were solved and James now had the money he needed to pay off his debts with a never-ending supply available on tap from his close friend. But it would be seven long years before another Parliament was called and by then, England's finances would be in ruins.

The year 1612 was monumental for James. In October, his 14-year-old daughter Elizabeth met her future husband, Frederick V, Count Palatine of the Rhine, and both seemed happy from the very beginning. Even her elder brother Prince Henry was delighted with the match. The only person not happy was her mother, Queen Anne. As the daughter of a king, the sister of a king, and the wife of a king, Anne expected to be the mother of a queen as well and although Frederick had a mild manner and generous nature, she simply felt that he was not quite good enough for her only daughter.

As always, James completely disregarded anything his wife said, and with Elizabeth standing firmly by her choice as well, there was nothing Anne could do. The betrothal, then the marriage, went ahead regardless of what she thought.

Everything was going extremely well for James. He had money in his pocket. He had a new friend by his side and his daughter had made a rather significant marriage. There wasn't much else a man could ask for.

Then one month later, Prince Henry caught typhoid and all of England held their breath while the heir to the throne struggled to survive.

Although somewhat priggish, Henry was a popular prince with the people. His younger brother Charles however, could not stand him. As older brothers tend to do, Henry played pranks on his younger brother and Charles had never forgotten an incident that had occurred when Henry was nine years old and he was four. Henry had snatched the hat off a bishop and put it on Charles' head saying that when he was the king, he would make Charles the Archbishop of Canterbury and Charles would thankfully have to wear a long robe to hide his ugly rickety legs.

It was just a prank and poor Charles *did* have ugly rickety legs like his father, but he didn't need to be reminded of the fact by his stronger, more handsome, elder brother. Screaming and crying, Charles had repeatedly stomped on the cap and had to be dragged away in tears. And he never forgot the humiliation.

Henry's quick death was certainly not what anyone had foreseen. The strong young man, full of vigour and always brimming with good health, had gone downhill rather rapidly and all of a sudden, Charles was thrown onto centre stage as the heir apparent. Despite his past grievances, Charles became the chief mourner at the funeral when his father and mother were too physically ill to attend.

His son's death almost destroyed James. He grieved in private and believed above all else that he only had his true friend Robert Carr to lean on. But there was another blow looming that James hadn't foreseen. Carr declared that he had fallen in love with the Earl of Suffolk's daughter, Frances Howard (not to be confused with a previous Frances Howard married to Edward Seymour).

While Robert Carr was the man with James' ear, and… ah… other parts, Sir Thomas Overbury was actually the brains of the outfit and more than a little smitten with Carr himself. Sir Thomas Overbury disliked and distrusted the Howards immensely and he believed he knew exactly what they were up to. In his opinion, the Howards were a conniving bunch who were scheming to take control of the government. They had been watching Carr climb, not so slowly, up the ladder of success and as such, were more than happy to welcome Carr into their family.

The only fly in the ointment was that Frances was already married to Robert Devereaux, 3rd Earl of Essex, and she needed an annulment before marrying Carr. Frances had been married at the age of 14 to the 13-year-old Devereux and she stated that her marriage had been a sham from the beginning, ordered by her family in the first place, and more of a political relationship than a love match. They were separated after the wedding to prevent them from having intercourse due to their youth and Devereaux had been sent away to Europe for two years. When he returned, seriously ill with smallpox, Frances had made every effort to avoid him. She claimed later that after his return to health, she had made every attempt to be sexually compliant to her husband and through no fault of her own, she was still a virgin. In turn, Devereaux claimed that he was capable with other women, but not able to consummate his marriage to Frances. It backed up everything she was saying and left the way open for her to proceed with plans for an annulment.

From the start, Overbury was violently opposed to the affair and told Carr so in no uncertain terms, even going so far as to point the finger of immodesty at Frances. But Carr was infatuated and he wanted to marry her no matter what his friends thought.

Carr wasn't the first man to divulge secrets to his lover after a romp in bed and he told Frances everything: what Overbury had said, how he planned to stop the marriage and how he was going to tell James about Frances' past indiscretions. He spilt every bean there was to spill and when the Howard faction in turn heard what Overbury was planning, they put a deadly plot into action in order to remove him from court permanently.

The timing seemed perfect when a position become available as the English ambassador in the court of Michael of Russia. The plan was for the Howards to convince James to offer the lucrative job to Overbury as a reward for his loyalty, fully aware that it had twofold benefits for them. Firstly, if he accepted, it would remove Overbury from court leaving the Howards free reign, and secondly, and this is what they were really hoping for, a refusal would be seen as tantamount to treason to James who liked everybody doing just as they were told. Either way, they would come out winners.

Just as they had hoped, Overbury declined the offer, stating that he wished to remain in England, close by his friend, Robert Carr's side.

If Overbury thought Carr would stand by him and persuade James to see it his way, he was wrong. As for James, his world had suddenly turned upside down. His eldest son and heir had died, his close friend Carr had left him and then, to top it off, his dearest friend Overbury had defied him. He had no choice. On 22 April 1613, Overbury was placed in the Tower of London at the king's 'request'. Two months later, James finally agreed to annul Frances' marriage to Robert Devereaux on the grounds of impotence and the happy couple were free to marry.

Unfortunately, it was not to be such a happy ending for Overbury. He died in prison three months later of 'natural causes'. And of course, as we know, natural causes can range anywhere from poisoning, strangulation, drowning in a barrel of wine or a red-hot poker finding its way up the victim's bottom. Overbury's 'natural' death was by poisoning.

James had not seen Carr's marriage to Frances as too much of a hindrance. It was more of an annoyance since Carr had already withdrawn himself from James' bedchamber anyway. He continued to shower Carr with gifts despite reproaching his friend many times on his absence, until 1615 that is, when things came to a nasty head and the two had a serious falling out. The truth had finally come out regarding Overbury's death and a seriously miffed James demanded a trial be held to uncover the truth of the matter.

There was never any doubt of Frances' guilt and she simply owned up and confessed. Carr's part in the plan is far more difficult to uncover. The evidence against him rested on mere presumption and he consistently declared himself to be innocent. The probability is, on the whole, that he had no part in the actual murder and was no more than an accessory after the fact.

James repeatedly sent messages to the Tower pleading with Carr to admit his guilt in return for a pardon. But rather stupidly, Carr remained firm and never replied. James was left with no alternative but to let matters take their own course. By then, James had moved on and he'd met his last and greatest love, dashing George Villiers.

In the throes of a new love, James was happy to let the court pass judgment on both Carr and Frances and of course, they were both found guilty, along with four more of her family members. Those four were convicted and subsequently hanged, but Frances and Carr remained locked in the Tower for another seven years until Frances was eventually pardoned. Carr unfortunately had to sit and wait a further two years for forgiveness.

By then, he was a broken man

By all accounts, George Villiers was a charming man with stunning good looks and James fell hopelessly in love with him. But let's have a closer look at George.

George Villiers was the son of Sir George Villiers and his second wife, Mary Beaumont. Mary seems to have recognised George's potential to become a figure of political importance and played a crucial role in making sure her son was fit for high society. Although she is said to be penniless when she married his father, she somehow found the money to send him to the French court, where he learned the courtly skills of fencing and dancing. Having then found the necessary funds to outfit him with a suitable wardrobe, she sent him to the English Court and deliberately placed him in James' path where he rapidly became the new favourite. As George rose, his mother, brothers and half-brothers rose with him. James even said that *"he lived to no other end but to advance the Villiers family."* It's pretty obvious that Mary, and all the members of her family, were ambitious.

Having said that, Mary was simply making the most of the very limited opportunities she had as a woman in early modern England. She was from a gentry family, not a working-class one, but had never been able to access money on her own other than what she was able to gain firstly as a widow and secondly through her son George. She had no power in life except through the men she married or her male children. She was driven to survive and thrive any way she could.

The pair were quite open about the whole affair, *even hinting* coquettishly at activity in bed. Rather amazingly, James had officially only recently condemned sodomy as one of the sins that cannot be forgiven, but no one was about to remind him of that minor little detail.

As the romance flourished, James began calling Villiers his 'wife' and Villiers responded by calling him 'husband.' Before England knew it, George had taken Carr's job and was appointed the new Gentleman of the Bedchamber. The very next year, he became Viscount Villiers and between 1617 and 1623, he was created Earl, then Marquis, and later on, Duke of Buckingham and Lord High Admiral of the Navy. *"Christ had his John,"* James once wrote, *"and I have my George."*

Perhaps it was James and his behaviour or perhaps it was his religious beliefs that tipped a small group of people, calling themselves Separatists, over the edge. It was September 1620 when 102 passengers and about 30 crew members boarded a ship called the Mayflower bound on an iconic voyage to the harsh New England winter in the Americas. This ageing English merchant ship, with his high, castle-like structures, was nearing the end of its working life when it set sail against the prevailing Westerlies of the North Atlantic making it a dangerous place for sailing. She was about 100 feet in length, 25 feet at her widest point and the bottom of her keel was about 12 feet below the waterline. It was fortunate that she could carry a cargo of about 180 tons because as well as many stores the pilgrims needed, the ship was laden with tools and weapons, cannons, shot, gunpowder as well as some live animals, including dogs, sheep, goats and poultry. Horses and cattle would come later on the next ship.

The passage was a miserable one, with huge waves constantly crashing against the ship's topside deck and an eventual shortage of food. Despite this, there were only two deaths, although this was only a precursor to what happened after their arrival in Cape Cod on 9th November. After two months, the passengers of the Mayflower arrived at the beginning of a bitter winter in below-freezing temperatures and set foot on land wearing wet shoes and stockings that soon became frozen. By spring, only 53 passengers remained and half the crew although most were still happy to be in a new land they could make their own. Anything was better than King James it seemed.

James had never been a robust man but as he aged, his health deteriorated at an alarming rate. His weak legs started aching more and more and the pain seemed to be settling in his joints. Swelling of both feet had been occurring and finally, arthritis took over in his knees, hands, and shoulders. Hunting and riding became impossible and he was often unable to even walk more than a few short paces.

And then, people began noticing other disturbing issues. Never known for his clean habits, James was rarely washing and was developing a somewhat dishevelled appearance. He lost weight and became thin and cadaverous. He began hiccupping, sneezing and belching, and if it was possible to be even more repellent, painful looking sores began to appear on his lips and his bad breath was astonishing. He lost interest in his parliament and was unable to concentrate for long on anything, often behaving childish and irritable. Business was becoming more burdensome to him and decisions were more difficult, fears more acute and emotions more overpowering. He was agitated by constant mistrust of everyone and he had a perpetual paranoiac fear for his life. He'd be swearing one minute and then a transformation would appear and he'd be instantly and openly weeping.

James was just as confused as the nobles, which left him even more unsure and mistrustful. As James withdrew more and more, George began 'acquainting' himself with James' son Charles, just as a serious conflict in Europe became evident. The Catholic Holy Roman Empire and the Protestant Bohemians were banging heads and at the centre of it was James' son-in-law, his daughter Elizabeth's husband, Frederick.

Bohemian nobles, wanting to rid themselves of the Catholic Hapsburgs, had offered Frederick the throne of Bohemia just one year before. Somewhat doubtfully and after lengthy consideration since it meant moving his wife and four children to Prague, Frederick eventually accepted. The problem was Ferdinand II King of Spain, being the Hapsburg they were ridding themselves of, did not agree with the decision. He believed the throne of Bohemia was rightfully his and he declared war on Frederick.

Frederick went into full panic mode and sent an urgent letter to James begging for troops to help him, unaware that James was in no physical condition to help anyone. While he fretfully waited for James to reply, he raised taxes and conscripted soldiers in a desperate attempt at preparation for war. By August, he still hadn't heard from James but he couldn't afford to wait any longer. His army was ready with the help of Prince Christian of

Anhalt and by November, one year and four days after assuming the throne, both armies had assembled at White Mountain, ready to fight.

If Frederick could have changed anything, I'm sure he would have chosen not to fight in the middle of winter. At dawn on Sunday 8th November, the hills were covered in a dense fog as both armies stood anxiously watching ghostly shadows shift and move. Thankfully for both sides, by nine o'clock, the fog was beginning to clear, but it left Frederick's apprehensive army of 25,000 conscripts facing Ferdinand's seasoned army of 30,000 over a low plateau in the light snow. Now that it had come to the final showdown, neither side seemed particularly willing to actually start the battle since the weather had turned so cold and wet.

What had started out as the full intention of a full-scale war between two unrelenting armies, suddenly dwindled into just a nasty skirmish that was over in an hour. With morale extremely low due to the fact that no one had been paid for months, most of Frederick's men had simply downed their weapons when they saw the size of the other army on the other side of the plateau. Before the battle even started, a lot of them had already gone and by midday, Frederick found that his army had been reduced to about 15,000 disgruntled men who had already decided that there was little chance of victory anyway.

And so as a relatively small part of the Spanish force approached the Bohemian flank, they began to crumble. When the Spanish cavalry charged, most turned tail and ran in the opposite direction and by the end of an hour, the Bohemian army was in tatters with 4,000 men either killed or captured, while Ferdinand of Spain had only lost 700 men.

In the aftermath, there was no other choice for Frederick but to flee the country to his uncle Maurice, Stadtholder of the Dutch Republic in The Hague, with his heavily pregnant wife and his children. And as it turned out, it was a good decision because Elizabeth only just made it. Within days, she delivered her fifth child.

When James heard of their lucky escape into the Netherlands, he was desperate to help his daughter but as usual, he was out of ready cash. George Villiers was proving to be very expensive by then, since the accumulating titles James was loading on him came with healthy incomes and handsome benefits. Seeing no other way to find the money, James tucked his tail between his legs and reluctantly summoned parliament.

As it turned out, they were more than happy to help. With of course, a couple of stipulations. They wanted war with Spain and they also wanted his son Charles to marry immediately to reinforce anti-Catholic laws instead of the Catholic doctrine that Spain was encouraging.

You would think that after seven long years, James would have learnt that you catch more flies with honey than with vinegar. But in the end, he did what he always did. He told them in no uncertain terms not to interfere in royal matters or else they risked severe punishment. Of course, they reacted by indignantly by reminding him that *he* was the one who'd come to *them* not the other way around and they had their rights as well, including freedom of speech. Remember? They even showed him the very document that he had signed at his first sitting of Parliament.

A couple of times in his reign James had shown composure, but on the whole, serenity was not one of his best qualities. Furious at their impertinence, he literally ripped the documentation out of the record book and promptly and unceremoniously dissolved Parliament. Again.

In his heart, James knew Parliament had a valid point regarding war against the Spanish but he also knew that the Spanish had almost 30,000 men, flush with victory, waiting to see who else wanted a thrashing. And James was still wise enough to know he didn't want to be on the receiving end of it. The only real hope he saw of restoring his daughter and son-in-law to their position in the Palatinate was for Charles to marry the Spanish Infanta Maria, the *Catholic* Infanta Maria by the way, and settle the volatile situation down once and for all. The offer of marriage would be done with or without Parliament's nod of approval, although he knew he would absolutely never get it any way. In fact, he knew they'd be downright apoplectic.

For a while, things were looking good with the negotiations. There was communication between the two countries and for a while everything seemed almost civil. But for some reason, there was less and less communication from Spain and negotiations began to drag on and on with no foreseeable result in sight. Finally, feeling absolutely frustrated at the lengthy delays while his sister waited in the Hague in limbo, Charles decided that he and his friend, George Villiers, would seize the day and the initiative and travel to Spain to talk to the Infanta directly.

It was a desperate move and it left King Phillip IV of Spain flabbergasted and dumbstruck at their impudence. They had no idea that it was Maria herself who was strongly opposed to marrying a non-Catholic and that the Spanish, who had only been delaying the negotiations to keep England out of the war, would never agree to the match. The only way they would even consider it was if Charles converted to Catholicism and spent the first year in Spain to ensure he kept his side of the bargain.

Leaving England for a year while his father's health was declining rapidly was something Charles would never do. Angry words were flung backwards and forwards until finally, Charles and George stormed out of the Spanish court and returned to England empty-handed. When they arrived back home, Charles demanded that his father declare war on Spain for the insult.

Since this was what Parliament had wanted in the first place, they were absolutely delighted. But not so James. Declaring war on Spain was still out of the question for him and once again he steadfastly refused. The only other option left for Charles was to find another love match. And then suddenly, he remembered Henrietta Maria, the youngest sister of King Louis XIII of France.

Charles had met the 15-year-old at a French gathering while he was on his way to Spain with George. At the time, his impression was that she was an undereducated, frivolous young woman who could not even speak English. He also remembered that she had long arms, uneven shoulders and some of her teeth were sticking out of her mouth like tusks. Her only redeeming quality was she had pretty eyes and a good complexion.

But for Charles, she had one other redeeming quality. She bought with her a huge quantity of expensive possessions, including diamonds, pearls, silks, gold plate, chandeliers, pictures, books, ladies in waiting and twelve priests as her pages. It was an impressive haul and Charles immediately sent an agent to Paris to start marriage negotiations. Very soon all was agreed upon, and preparations for the wedding began.

But not everyone was as happy as Charles with the outcome. When Spain heard the news, it was like a slap in the face. Just a short time ago Charles had been declaring his intention of marrying their beloved princess and here he was, doing an about face. Worst still, he was intending to marry a *French* princess. It was like waving a red flag in front of their faces and they were livid. James' worst fears suddenly became a reality and before he knew it, war was on. And you guessed it, to raise the funds for both the wedding and the war, James reluctantly had to call another Parliament.

It had all been a terrible strain on James and as it turned out, before any decisions could be finalised, all war and marriage negotiations froze in September 1624 due to his ill health. His hands had become so crippled with arthritis that he could not even sign his name. By Christmas, he was seriously ill.

Ironically, James had been crowned during an infestation of bubonic plague and it looked like he was to die during one as well. In early 1625, when London was suffering at its worst from the disease, 50-year-old James made an attempt to outrun it by escaping to Hertfordshire. But even there, he suffered recurrent attacks of fever, diarrhoea and fainting spells. By then, his teeth had fallen out and soon he had difficulty swallowing and speaking.

On occasions, he had convulsions.

For two months, James steadily grew worse, until finally on March 27th, he died from a violent attack of dysentery, which led to a stroke. George sat by his side to the very end.

For all James' flaws, in his 22-year reign, he had retained a certain level of affection from his people although not too many people could say that they actually liked him. He had his unpopular male favourites, he lacked financial responsibility and he also believed in absolutism when it came to his belief in the Divine Right of Kings. This, he believed, set him apart from the rest of us mere mortals.

Over the years, his son Charles had taken on board everything his father taught him. Add that to it the fact that he despised Parliament more than his father had and you have a recipe for disaster.

It would ultimately be Charles' downfall.

CHARLES I

Born 1600
Reign 1625–1649

As much as Charles wanted the throne, the timing of his father's death could not have been worse. There was widespread starvation throughout England at the end of a devastating harvest, inflation was high and parliament was seriously annoyed at seeing the Stuart's use of precious money spent lavishly on themselves and their friends. To top it all off, it was right in the middle of a devastating bout of the bubonic plague.

The character of the epidemic was appalling. The disease itself, with its frightful symptoms, was swift. First, blotches appeared. Then came the hardening of the glands under the armpit and the groin, followed by the horde of virulent pustules. After that the victim developed a hacking cough that would produce blood, then vomiting. Breath, sweat and excrement stank and delirium, followed by insanity, completed the suffering before you thankfully died.

As the second son of James I, Charles was never expected to become king. He had been a sickly and frail child and it was not until he was three and a half years old that he was able to walk along the halls of Dunfermline Palace in Scotland while the rest of the family had moved south to England.

Because of his fragile health, he was left behind with a guardian. It was only after he was put in boots made of leather and brass to help strengthen his weak ankles that he was sent to join the rest of his family. Eight years later, his elder brother Henry was dead from typhoid and his sister had married a Catholic, Prince Frederick V of Palatine.

Despite his shaky youth, by the time Charles was 25 years old he had few physical faults. Although he could never have challenged his brother in athleticism, he had become a good horseman and a good shot with a crossbow and a gun. And he was intelligent. Make that *very* intelligent. His only physical failing was his stammer, which was as a result of infantile paralysis.

His personality however was something else entirely. He was self-righteous and arrogant and he had an uncanny knack of making wrong decisions. Some went so far as to say he was his own worst enemy.

By the time his father died, Parliament had strengthened and they'd begun to take the lead again. For them, the unsettling events unfolding in Bohemia rated just as high as domestic issues. As always, religion was uppermost on everyone's minds. England's very survival depended on a victory against Spain and everyone watched intensely, ever vigilant, at every event, good or bad. When Elizabeth and Frederick were finally ousted to The Hague and the Catholic Ferdinand of Spain took over, Parliament knew action needed to be taken.

Where once Tudor authority had been welcomed with open arms after the disaster of the War of the Roses, that same authority did not fit anymore in England's society. When Parliament looked back, they saw their strength beginning to emerge with the Lancastrians, even as far back as King John and the Magna Carta. But a society more complex than the one of Tudor England was coming into existence. Trade was expanding and coal mining was developing. Thousands of large companies had formed in London and in the countryside and the gentry (who formed the House of Commons) were steadily growing richer.

As with Charles, this Parliament was all for war against Spain and they knew that this would force him to come to them for financial assistance. This assistance, once given, meant more power for them. His father had avoided the trap but Charles and George Villiers, now the Duke of Buckingham, were high-spirited young men who had been slighted by the Spanish rejection of Charles' offer of marriage to Infanta Maria. This rejection meant Charles' vanity and pride had taken a serious beating and he wanted war just as much as Parliament did. Maybe even more so.

As for Charles, he couldn't wait to begin both his reign and his marriage to the Catholic French princess. The marriage gave him the added bonus of French assistance and that put him in a strong position to help his sister and brother-in-law who were living in exile.

Declaring war was one thing but to marry a Catholic princess, a French one at that, was abhorrent to Parliament. No one was happy. By now, Parliament contained quite a number of Puritans who disliked Charles as much as they had disliked his father and all of them voiced their anger loudly. Most were sure that if Charles went ahead and married a Catholic, he would lift restrictions on English Catholics, which in turn would undermine the Church of England.

Charles feigned shock that Parliament would conceive such a terrible thing of him and adamantly consoled them that he had no plan to do any such thing. Butter wouldn't melt in his mouth. In actual fact, that was exactly what he had already promised in a secret marriage treaty with Louis XIII. Not just that, he had promised the support of his Navy to Louis as well if the Protestant Huguenots in France rebelled any further.

It took two months of intense bargaining and promises for everything to be finally agreed upon but eventually Charles married 15-year-old Henrietta Maria by proxy in May. It was a further month again before she was able to join Charles in England where they were then married in a Catholic ceremony at St Augustine's Church in Canterbury.

To say that Henrietta had definite ideas of how to be treated is perhaps an understatement. She was the youngest sister of King Louis XIII, trained along with her sisters to ride, dance, sing and partake in French court plays. She could read and write, although not in English, but she fully expected to be treated with the same dignity and respect as she had been in France. Add strong Catholic beliefs and a huge expensive entourage and you have a Parliament who was ready to send her back on the next boat. They pointed out to Charles that her accustomed extravagance was something England simply could not afford if they were intending to head off to war.

While Parliament huffed and puffed that Charles' new wife was flagrant and unapologetic when it came to her religion (she had even been seen praying for the Catholics that had been hung on the Tyburn Tree) Charles was experiencing some problems of his own.

Apart from Parliament's opinions on her religion, things had not been going so well for Charles and Henrietta anyway. Instead of the meek wife he had expected, he found her belligerent, argumentative and frigid. If that wasn't bad enough, she took an immediate dislike to Buckingham. And then, when he ultimately became aware of how much she was actually spending, he finally blew a gasket and put his foot down, demanding that she dismiss all of her servants. It was only after Charles had his armed guards physically eject them that she begged to keep just seven of her original staff. Somewhat mollified, Charles agreed.

With everyone watching intently, Charles was crowned on 2nd February 1626 at Westminster Abbey – without his wife by his side. There had been the inevitable row over her attendance at the Protestant ceremony but in the end, she had stood her ground, reluctantly agreeing to only watch Charles being crowned from a discreet distance. Already unpopular with the English, her decision not to be included in the important ceremony was further seen as an insult to their tradition and only made matters worse for her.

With the coronation out of the way, Charles did not waste any time with his war plans. He had money in his pocket from Parliament and the support from France and he immediately declared war on Spain.

Parliament was ecstatic. It was everything they had hoped for. However, elation soon turned to dismay when Charles stated that his friend Buckingham would lead the expedition and match the successes of Sir Frances Drake who had defeated the Spanish Armada during Elizabeth's reign. Parliament had no doubt at all in their minds that Buckingham would fall flat on his face and fail dismally.

As they expected, instead of victories, the war went rather badly for Buckingham. The initial idea of seizing the main Spanish port at Cádiz and burning the fleet in the harbour was strategically sound as was the plan to land further up the coast and march his army south on to the city before anyone knew what was happening. What let him down were his troops. They were undisciplined and badly trained and they loved a tipple or two. When a warehouse filled with wine was discovered along the way, everyone dropped their weapons and indulged themselves. With none of his soldiers sober enough, the attack had to be called off.

From there, Buckingham decided to head out to sea to intercept a much anticipated Spanish silver fleet from the New World. What he didn't know was that someone had already forewarned the Spanish of the plan and they were ready and waiting for him, protecting their treasured cargo well before his proposed ambush. It was yet another failure to add to the others and with supplies running short and men sick and dying from starvation and disease, the fleet were forced to limp home in embarrassment.

As we know, Parliament had a longstanding dislike for Buckingham since James' reign, and perhaps someone was actually brave enough to say, '*I told you so*' to Charles. Feeling confident and seeing this fresh failure as an opportunity to rid themselves of Buckingham's meddling once and for all, they demanded that they prosecute Buckingham, sure in the fact that Charles would agree with them. After all, Buckingham had disgraced both himself and his country, not to mention the amount of money he'd wasted.

Instead of listening to his Parliament, Charles did what his father would have done. He dissolved it.

Things were going from bad to worse for Charles. It wasn't too long before he realised that his rather hasty decision to dissolve Parliament, based on saving his friend, had in fact created more problems than he could handle. He also knew that they'd been right about his marriage to Henrietta as well. That too was in ruins.

War with Spain had originally started with his sister's exile from Bohemia, and marrying the French princess had seemed like the only way to fix the situation, especially after the Spanish had been rude enough to turn him down. But as time passed, it turned out the marriage to Henrietta had been a colossal mistake from the beginning and France had never any intention of helping him out in the first place. Instead of creating an alliance against the Hapsburgs of Spain, France showed no interest at all in fighting to recover his sister's position in the Palatinate on England's behalf. King Louis and his Chief Minister Cardinal Richelieu declared that their main priority in the kingdom was to suppress the Huguenots not to help Charles with his personal family problems. Charles angrily pointed out to Louis that he had signed an agreement at the wedding. Charles would supply English ships if France needed them and they would supply support if he needed it. Remember? Well, now he needed that support.

Louis still refused.

As things deteriorated with France, domestic quarrels between Henrietta and Charles worsened as well. At a time when every bit of spare money was meant for war, she had resumed spending vast amounts on clothes and new staff to her household. The straw that broke the camel's back was when she openly began practicing Catholicism in the palace. In a fury, Charles once again expelled the vast majority of her French entourage and then turned his anger on France. He simply got lost in his anger.

The decision to launch an attack on the French coast at a town called La Rochelle and help the Huguenots came at a time when Buckingham really needed to redeem himself. While Charles jailed anybody who objected and imposed taxes on property owners to raise money, Buckingham set off in high spirits for France.

On 12 July 1627, an English force of 100 ships and 6,000 soldiers invaded the small island west of France called Île de Ré with the plan to control La Rochelle and encourage a Huguenot rebellion in the city. As a starting point, Buckingham hoped to capture the fortified city of Saint Martin-de-Ré by landing at the beach of Sablanceau. What he hadn't counted on was the island's governor, Marquis de Toiras resisting so strongly. With his own force of 1,200 infantry and 200 horsemen, Toiras hid behind the dunes before finally attacking. On the first day alone, English losses were 12 officers and well over 100 men.

For three days, Buckingham held his position while Toiras took all available provisions from the island and fortified himself in the citadel of Saint Martin. But as Buckingham attempted a siege around the citadel, he was plagued with overwhelming problems and a string of unforeseen misfortunes. Firstly, the English siege engineer had drowned during the landing. Then they found that there were not enough cannons and even the ones they had were too small. As well as that, disease had started to take its toll on the English troops. Urgent messages were sent back to Charles for reinforcements and supplies and all Buckingham could do was to try and hold on for as long as he could while the siege continued. When supplies eventually arrived, they were totally insufficient.

Finally, in September, two thousand Irish troops arrived, along with a small supply fleet of 400 raw troops, with the promise of more help on the way from Scotland. Buckingham, who was more than a little panicked by then, welcomed the news with relief but that breather soon disappeared when he heard that the Scottish fleet of 30 ships and 5,000 men had been lost as a result of a storm off the coast of Norfolk.

The French, despite their own difficulties, were holding their own. They had managed to get a supply fleet through the English blockade, only losing six of their 35 ships. Of the 29 ships that had survived, 4,000 additional troops had landed on the southern end of the island from the mainland.

Buckingham just wasn't having any luck. Guessing that the French garrison was just as exhausted as the English army, there seemed no other choice than to attempt a last desperate attack on Saint Martin. Once again, fate stepped in. It turned out that his ladders were far too short to scale the high fortress walls, making it impenetrable.

Altogether, Buckingham lost more than 5,000 men in the campaign out of a force of 7,000. With such heavy losses and the French troops pursuing him hotly, he finally retreated towards the northern part of the island with the plan to return shamefully to England once again.

Buckingham's war had been costly for England with nothing to show for it and while Charles tried frantically to salvage the situation, Parliament watched and waited patiently. They knew before too long, Charles would need money desperately.

Charles could see the writing on the wall but there was nothing he could do about it. Buckingham had used every bit of spare cash in the treasury and Henrietta kept spending what was left. His only recourse was to summon Parliament again and ask for their help.

But this time, Parliament came well prepared.

As the members walked silently into the room, they handed Charles a 'Petition of Right'. He looked from man to man solemnly before looking down at the piece of parchment in his hand. There were four main conditions. He was to promise not to attempt to tax without the consent of the House of Commons. He was to refrain from arbitrary imprisonment. He was to refrain from quartering troops in people's homes and he was not to impose martial law in a time of peace. It was a big ask for Charles but he had no other choice left to him. Reluctantly, he agreed.

Heaven knows Charles was far from perfect and most would agree that he'd made some terrible blunders in the past. But his next move seemed one of deliberate dishonesty. By 7th June, he'd signed the petition and he had the money he needed. By the end of the month, he changed his mind and had suspended Parliament again. Of course, he kept the money they'd given him.

As Charles turned more and more people against him, Buckingham couldn't forget his shocking defeat at La Rochelle. Instead of putting it behind him, he tried to organise a second campaign knowing full well that the public feeling towards him was that he'd been the one responsible for the disaster in the first place. It all came to a head on 23rd August 1628.

Buckingham was dining at the Greyhound Pub in Portsmouth where he was trying to organise the next campaign. Standing and watching from the shadows at the back of the room was an army officer, who it turned out had been wounded in the earlier military campaign and been passed over for promotion because of it. The soldier made his way slowly from the back of the crowded pub and came up behind Buckingham. Before anyone knew what was happening, the soldier stabbed Buckingham in the back. He lived long enough to attempt a chase, but inevitably and before too long, Buckingham fell down dead.

Distraught is too light a word to describe the feelings Charles felt when he heard the news. According to the Earl of Clarendon, he *"threw himself upon his bed, lamenting with much passion and with abundance of tears"*. Charles remained grieving in his room for two days, refusing to see anyone. In contrast, the public rejoiced.

Buckingham's death brought a couple of colossal changes to Charles life. Even though the disagreements between Charles and Parliament continued relentlessly, the war with Spain came to a sudden end. Buckingham's death also coincided with an unexpected improvement in Charles' relationship with Henrietta and by November 1628, their old quarrels were at an end. She became pregnant for the first time and nine months later, delivered their first child, a baby boy they named Charles.

With the arrival of an heir, Henrietta's position at court improved greatly. Where Charles had never consulted her regarding state matters in the past, he suddenly began discussing his concerns with her more and more, despite the fact that she was still unpopular with Parliament. This newfound camaraderie with Charles only helped to increase their intolerance level towards her and pretty soon, that intolerance gradually shifted towards hatred. It almost reached explosion point when a Scottish doctor was flogged, branded and mutilated before being imprisoned for life after criticising Henrietta in a pamphlet. Her newfound confidence and power was a serious thorn in Parliament's side.

In January the next year, Charles opened Parliament again with a small speech on new taxing issues and as expected, Parliament exploded. It seemed that a Parliamentary member's property had already been confiscated for failing to pay the very same tax that Charles had promised *not* to impose taxes on months ago in the Petition of Rights. Showing a surprising level of serenity, all but temporarily, Charles quietly ordered another adjournment of the issue and Parliament exploded again. Tempers erupted and some members had to physically hold the Speaker down in his chair so that other issues could be covered before the session ended.

Charles' calmness was just a ruse. The way he saw it, he had two options. Option One was he could ignore the whole episode and pretend it never happened. A pointless exercise really, but that was Option One. Option B was he could dissolve Parliament again and imprison the main instigators. He much preferred Option B because the Speaker's resentment towards him was just too much. With his face flushed with anger, his eyes burning feverishly and his voice as sharp as glass, he dissolved Parliament. To show he meant it this time, he had nine parliamentary leaders imprisoned as well, many of whom would die during their incarceration.

But once the dust settled, Charles realised yet again that he had to find money from somewhere. But this time, he had several ideas where he could do exactly that.

Charles knew that during financially pressing times in 13th century, King John had been short of cash as well. As a means of fundraising, he had resorted to finding money anyway he could. One of those ways was with a tax called the 'Distraint of Knighthood'. This tax required that any man who owned land that brought in more than £40 per year be required by law to have been present at the King's coronation. Relying on this antiquated law, Charles fined individuals who had failed to attend his coronation three years ago. With a mere flick of the quill, he had earned himself £173,000.

Another tax that was a good earner was called 'ship money'. Regardless of profession or how often the seas were used, anyone who lived within fifteen miles of the coast in any county, was to be taxed. Charles argued that this tax, which was originally only to be applied *to coastal towns during a time of war*, was his prerogative to collect throughout the kingdom, even if it was during peacetime. He was, after all, the king, and he owned the sea. This little enterprise earned Charles between £150,000 and £200,000 annually.

His third tax was directed at Scotland. Charles decreed that all gifts of church land made to the Scottish nobility since 1540 were to be revoked, and anybody using that land in the future was subject to an annual rent to be paid to the King of England. Namely him. In addition, the boundaries of the royal forests were extended to their ancient limits, which meant more revenue as well through rent, and another £100,000 per year in his pocket. To add fuel to the fire, he also ordered the use of a prayer book in Scotland that was almost identical to the 'English Book of Common Prayer' without consulting either the Scottish Parliament or the Church.

Hindsight is a wondrous thing and I'm sure Charles would have regretted his decision to aggravate the Scots every day of his life. Everyone knew that you didn't poke the Scots. They had a reputation for being fierce and once they started a fight, it was vicious to the end. This final tax was the spark that started a war with Scotland and it quickly spun out of control. By July 1637, riots were erupting all over Edinburgh while Charles fumed in London, itching to fight back.

If nothing else, Charles was a smart man. He knew that if you were going to show someone who was the boss, you needed the help of an army. But without a Parliament and without any sort of financial backing, raising one was almost impossible. Knowing all of this, he still refused to summon Parliament.

Against all odds, and using the money he'd raised through the taxes, he managed to gather an army. It was a raggedy bunch I'll give you, but an army of a few thousand men is always better than none at all and together they marched resolutely on to Berwick, on the English side of the Scottish border. Camped on the Scottish side were 12,000 angry Scotsmen.

By 16th century, Berwick had become a prosperous town and the Scottish people held it dear in their hearts. In 1291, John Balliol had betrayed them when Edward I had tried to take the Scottish throne from them in the Great Hall of Berwick Castle. An arm of their hero William Wallace had been displayed at Berwick after his execution and quartering in 1305. In 1314, Edward II had mustered 25,000 men at Berwick, who later fought (and lost) the Battle of Bannockburn. In 1461, Margaret of Anjou surrendered Berwick back to Scotland on behalf of her husband Henry VI, during the Wars of the Roses. Berwick meant a lot to the Scots. An *awful* lot. Berwick was their line in the sand. And they were about to show Charles that he should never have crossed over it.

Some of the Scotsmen were old and gnarled with bald scalps scarred and pitted from past battles. Others were young enough to have been their grandsons. All were covered with dirt and sweat and their matted beards stank of smoke and rancid grease from countless campfires. Most of them could trace their ancestors back to the Vikings who had thieved and slaughtered their way across Europe to finally settle in the cold storm-racked Scottish islands. Not all the clans saw eye to eye. The Campbells and the MacDonalds hated the sight of each other. But now they put past family differences aside and stood steadfastly together, united unwaveringly to keep the English king out of Scotland.

Berwick was a terrible failure for Charles. After several minor skirmishes that were basically push and shoves, Charles knew he really *did* need money to raise a decent army if he wanted to defeat the Scots. And unfortunately, there was only one way for him to raise that desperately needed money. He summoned every Parliament in his kingdom. Again.

An Irish Parliament was summoned first, headed by Lord Strafford, the Lord Deputy of Ireland, who pledged £180,00 by the end of May. The English Parliament was not so easy. Once again, they refused to agree to help unless Charles promised to forfeit the ship tax he had imposed. Take it or leave it, they said. Furious, Charles dissolved them again.

Encouraged by the turn of events in England, the Scots surged into Northumberland.

Try to picture a late summers evening in August on the Banks of the River Tyne. On the north side was the historic village of Newburn, the river wound lazily through flat meadows lying between steep banks covered in scrub and gorse bushes. The village had Roman connections with Hadrian's Wall cutting across its northern half before running toward Throckley. From the 8th century, it had been a royal town but it didn't become an important settlement until Plantagenet times when Hugh Percy was the last to inherit Newburn Manor House. It had always been considered among the greenest areas of Newcastle. But on this evening, before the Battle of

Newburn Ford in Northumberland, tensions were high and no one was admiring the view.

Under the command of Alexander Leslie, the Scottish army had increased to 20,000 men, sitting high and dry around coal fires intending to cross the river the next morning and attack Newcastle. Leslie knew well that the people of Newcastle would be expecting the attack to come from the north, which is why he had planned to come from the south.

The English were led by Lord Conway and consisted of around 3,500 men with a promise of another 2,000 re-enforcements to come the following morning, led by Sir Jacob Astley. But when Conway saw the massive number of Scots on the hill, he was sorely tempted to order a retreat. Only one night ago, his army had passed through the streets of Newcastle eager to start the battle. With many drinks under their belts, his men had been in high spirits, brandishing their swords and guns, drinking at every other door to the health of the king and swearing they would fight to the last gasp. Every one of them had pledged to exterminate at least a dozen Scots. But that was last night and they had been very drunk. This morning, they were sober and a sea of angry Scotsmen could be seen across the plains.

Conway looked across the grasslands at his enemy. Smoke wafted above the fields where the Scots camped and save for the warbling of skylarks hovering high above and the soft snuffling of horses, there was very little sound. A thin drizzle was falling but the wind had died to nothing and the silence made it all the more unnerving. He knew he was out-numbered, out-gunned and in a strategically disadvantageous position, camped in the flood plains and meadows below the medieval town of Ryton. They were hunched in hastily built trenches and they were in full view of the Scots. He also knew that his men were basically untrained, ill-paid and were largely reluctant to fight a battle for which they had little commitment.

But he had received an order from Lord Strafford and he had no choice. The order was very explicit. He was told that if the Scots tried to cross the Tyne, he was to fight them with every means at his disposal. To the very end if necessary. With these direct orders, retreating was not an option.

Meanwhile, the bonfires in the Scottish camp burned brightly as the Scots watched and waited for dawn.

The next morning, the two wary armies eyed each other silently for several hours across the river as they watered their horses. Somewhere about one o'clock in the afternoon, a Scottish officer came out from one of the thatched cottages nearby and rode his horse to the river. While his horse was drinking, an English sentry, thinking that he was taking far too long about it and thinking he was actually taking stock of English positions, shot him. It was the first shot fired in the battle.

The whole riverbank seemed to erupt and come ablaze at once. The sound of cannons roared from both sides of the river and the sound of screaming men and horses filled the air as well as smoke and blood. For three hours, guns were fired from both sides of the river and Lord Conway struggled to control his men and keep them at their posts. Most of his men were raw troops who had not been under fire before and they were complaining bitterly that they had been on duty all night and that none of the promised troops had been sent to relieve them. When a canon shot dropped into their midst, it completely demoralised them. They threw down their guns and ran.

From across the river, Commander Leslie watched in delighted disbelief as the English scattered. It was low tide, about four in the afternoon and dusk was fast approaching – usually a time to regroup his weary men and wait through the dark hours of night until the next day to continue the battle. But Leslie wasn't about to let this once in a lifetime opportunity pass him by. He'd been summoned to kill the English troops and that's what he fully intended to do. He ordered 1,500 men to wade across the Tyne and attack and soon after, he sent another 10,000 Scottish infantry to follow them. By ten o'clock that night, most of the English foot soldiers had fled to Newcastle and by midnight, Lord Conway had followed them. Two days after the battle, the city of Newcastle had surrendered to the Scots.

When the news reached Charles, he desperately reconvened Parliament.

One by one, each member stood up, silently standing before him. Just as silently, he returned their gaze. Even then, there must have been a growing feeling of uneasiness gripping his heart. He would have noticed that most were carrying a bible and wearing their hair closely cropped around their heads. He would also have noticed someone new in the assembly, standing quietly alert to one side with passion and determination burning brightly in his eyes. This newcomer was the member for Cambridge and his name was Oliver Cromwell. At this stage there was no need to respect him, still less to fear him.

As Charles stared at the group, he would have realised that this new parliament would be much more difficult than his last 'Short' parliament.

These men were ready for him this time.

If Charles thought they had learnt a lesson the last time they opposed him, he was wrong. Parliament knew that Charles was desperate for money and by now, they'd had enough of his antics of dissolving them every time they crossed him. This time they had a good organiser and a military commander with them who fit into Parliament perfectly. This time they had Oliver Cromwell on their side and he had come up with a couple of conditions of his own to put forward.

As soon as Parliament was seated, John Pym, Parliament's nominated leader, stepped forward and handed Charles a document for his signature. As Charles read it through, he knew exactly what they were doing. This new Parliament was demanding that they be summoned at least once every three years and it was meant to stop him from dissolving them at will. Grudgingly, Charles agreed and signed. When they informed him they intended to begin proceedings to impeach Charles' leading counsellors for high treason, he knew he was in serious trouble. One of his advisors had already seen the writing on the wall and had escaped to The Hague. Three others were not so lucky. They were taken into custody to await their trial. One of the slow ones was Lord Strafford.

Strafford was Parliament's prime target and unfortunately for him, he was to find there would be no such thing as a trial. They simply declared him guilty of treason and pronounced the death sentence on him.

However tyrannical Strafford may have been, his offence was definitely not treason and angry complaints poured in from all over Ireland. *How could carrying out the king's wishes be classed as treason?* they demanded to know. Pym listened silently to the complaints but nothing was going to persuade him to change the sentence. Strafford's sentence was death and nothing less would be considered. All that was needed was Charles' signature on the document to seal the deal.

Charles knew there was nothing he could do. They wanted Strafford's head and he needed money. Reluctantly and sadly, he signed the order and two days later, Strafford was beheaded.

Unfortunately for Charles, nothing seemed to help his money situation. He was still having arguments with Parliament over taxation, military expenditure and the role of Parliament in government. While his father had held the same opinion as Charles regarding his Divine Right to rule, James had enough charisma to persuade the Parliament to accept his policies. That gene was not in Charles' DNA. What he did have was bargaining tools. He had his children.

As with every monarch to date, sons were the heirs to the throne while daughters were used to make allies and mend grievances through marriage. For his eldest daughter, Mary Henrietta, he began to consider that a marriage to either a son of the Spanish king or a marriage to her first cousin, The Elector of Palatine, would do the trick. When both proposals fell through, he approached Frederick Henry, Prince of Orange, with the suggestion of his son William as a prospective suitor. To his surprise, all was agreed upon almost immediately. The marriage took place in Whitehall Palace in London despite Mary's age of nine and William's age of 15. As an afterthought, he forbade the marriage to be consummated for several years due to their youth.

As Scots surged into England and Parliament argued with Charles, another crisis erupted, this time in Ireland. Ireland was split into three groups: the Gaelic Irish who were Catholic, the Old English who were descended from the medieval Normans and mostly Catholic and the New English who were Protestant settlers from England and Scotland. It was only this last group that supported the English Parliament.

During Elizabeth I's reign, England had simply taken over Ireland and the Irish certainly hadn't forgotten or forgiven that slight. Many Scottish and Welsh settlers had arrived by the droves in the country and government was being enforced according to English law. Many lords had lost their lands and their authority and for the first time throughout the whole island, Irish culture, law and language were being replaced. During James' reign, Catholics were even barred from all public offices.

By early October 1641, the Irish had had enough. Their resentment against the Protestant settlers had intensified with another poor harvest followed by a recession until finally, Catholics banded together and surged into key towns to address their grievances. With resentment came anger and by the end of October, they had taken over Dublin Castle.

It was intended to be a swift, bloodless coup but the anger grew so quickly, that it was soon out of control and had worsened into full-scale war.

Protestants were robbed and evicted from their lands. Farms and houses were burnt to the ground and cattle were stolen. As the violence escalated, the mob began killing settlers as well. And then, one day in November, in County Armagh, 100 men, women and children were thrown off a bridge to drown in the River Bann. Within days, Tyrone and Leinster had risen and Drogheda was besieged.

Out of a population of around 40,000 Protestants, it was reported that 12,000 had been murdered with thousands more fleeing back to England with shocking stories. Eventually, those stories would make their way back to Scotland. It would be yet another issue that increased Scottish hatred for Charles.

When the stories reached Charles, he must have felt surrounded by enemies on all sides. If it wasn't France, it was Scotland. When it wasn't Scotland, it was his own Parliament. With everything happening at the same time, the last thing he needed was for Ireland to revolt as well.

At that point in time, if Charles had stopped to take a count of his allies, he would have found none. And if all of that wasn't bad enough, he still didn't have enough money to raise an army. Another plea to Parliament met with the same negative reply. In actual fact, they had already voted against collecting the money necessary for Charles's army to move against Ireland's Catholics because they were afraid that with such an army at his disposal, Charles could, and would, try to re-establish his power over them too. No one trusted Charles anymore.

As bad as the trouble was in Ireland, something else had been bothering Charles regarding the Scots. It seemed no matter what he did, they were always one step ahead of him and his suspicious mind was working hard to understand the reason. And then, a rumour reached him. Just as he had suspected, some members of his Parliament were conspiring with the invading Scots and passing on vital information. One of the names given to him was John Pym. It was the final straw for Charles. He'd had enough.

Trying to keep his overwhelming anger under control, Charles stormed into Parliament with 400 soldiers and made an announcement. Parliament was to give up five of their members, including John Pym, from the House of Commons, on the grounds of treason. If they didn't hand the traitors over immediately, he would take matters into his own hands and have them all physically arrested and charged on the spot.

Shocked and affronted, Parliament adamantly refused to comply.

Charles' plan had very nearly worked except for the fact that all five had been forewarned and they'd already fled to Europe. As he stared around the room, his expression was so intense; members shuffled their feet in nervousness. It took all of his strength to contain his anger. In his anger, his jaw clenched and his eyes blazed.

In the aftermath, Parliament began taking sides. Those who staunchly supported Charles tended to be aristocrats, comprising mainly of the House of Lords, calling themselves Cavaliers. On the other side, whoever remained of Parliament, were called Roundheads, because of their short hair and as their leader, the Roundheads chose Oliver Cromwell. The king and his Cavaliers had their army, and Parliamentarians had theirs and a civil war was about to begin.

It was January 1642, only a few short days later and Charles feared for the safety of his family. With tension growing, Charles bundled them up and dispatched them off to Europe, while he hurriedly travelled northwards to set himself up in Oxford. Later he would be told that during the flight, two of his children, one-year-old Henry and five-year-old Elizabeth, had been captured and were imprisoned in the Tower. His wife and remaining children had thankfully escaped unharmed.

Like past monarchs, Oxford had a meaning for Charles. King Harold died there. Richard the Lionheart was born there. Henry V was educated there and Elizabeth had partied there. It was a place of theology and learning where poets had lived as well as politicians, clergy and scientists.

For Charles, it was his sanctuary.

As Charles' power gradually weakened, Cromwell's grew. War raged for six years indecisively and sporadically with wins and losses on both sides. Too few places were left undisturbed by the violence. Through the horror, peace talks were mentioned a few times but neither of them wanted to be the first one to start proceedings. No one wanted to be the first to give in.

While Charles struggled to hang on to his power, Scotland was having problems of its own. The army, sent to Ulster in Ireland in 1642 to protect the Scottish settlers from the Irish Catholic rebels, had suffered huge losses. To top it off, a religious group called the Covenanters were prospering and making their presence felt. In the growing unrest, Charles and his nephew Prince Rupert of the Rhine had had an early win in a battle against the

Parliamentarians and were eager to keep up the pressure. But then Cromwell's army moved on to capture York and everything turned belly up for Charles.

The battle of Marston Moor was probably the turning point for Charles. Rupert had been sent with a small force to hold out until reinforcements arrived from Cumberland and for a short while, he had managed to do just that. By 1st July, his troops numbered 14,000 with more to come. His biggest mistake was delaying his attack by just one day.

As he gathered his troops, the sky had darkened threateningly. Within an hour, the clouds had opened and they found themselves in the middle of a sudden torrential thunderstorm. As they scurried for shelter from the downpour, a distant, almost monotonous, hum drifted across the moors to them. At first they struggled to comprehend what the sound could be. And then, it finally dawned on them. It was the singing of psalms through the rain they could hear and there was no doubt at all in their minds that the enemy was waiting close by.

What they didn't know was that standing beside the Parliamentarians were thousands of Scotsmen. And then, in the shifting wind, the stench of thousands of men and horses slowly drifted towards them. The realisation must have sent shock waves through every last man as they stood with their heads tilted slightly upwards to catch the breeze. They would have heard horrendous stories of the barbarians from the north and they would have known that those same barbarians were close by, waiting for the right moment to attack. As the horses stamped nervously in the mud, the humming suddenly ceased and silence hung heavily over the waterlogged moors.

Stories have been told of Prince Rupert's deep affection for his dog, named Boy. This rare white hunting poodle was Rupert's constant companion, always by his side throughout the campaigns. Boy had a reputation throughout Europe. Numerous accounts of his abilities suggested he was the Devil in disguise. Stories abounded of the poodle's ability to find hidden treasure and it was rumoured that he could even catch bullets in his mouth that had been fired at him. Some even said he was a witch transformed into a white dog.

Then through the hush, a sound, feint at first, began to build until it sounded like thunder. Out of the darkness, like ghosts through the rain, came Cromwell's army. They were fully deployed and they were attacking.

In the chaos, heads and limbs were hacked off with swords, cannonballs destroyed bodies, and soldiers on both sides were impaled on the end of the long pikes. In the space of two hours, Rupert lost 4,000 men and a further 1,500 were captured. Along with all their guns, hundreds of weapons had fallen into the hands of the Roundheads.

Rupert was devastated. It was the first time that he had been decisively beaten in war but he had also suffered a personal loss. During the battle, Boy was killed after escaping from the camp and chasing after Rupert as he ran from the battle.

Understandably, in his grief, Rupert's enthusiasm for the campaign dwindled with the loss of his companion and things slowly began to fall apart for Charles. Still he refused to concede defeat and he pressed on. By May of the next year, he was ready to continue the fight with a somewhat subdued Rupert by his side.

News that Cromwell's army were on the march again and were about to attack Oxford reached Charles, and he was eager to show his new strength. Moral was high and Charles knew that if he was quick, the Parliamentarian leader, Commander Thomas 'Black Tom' Fairfax, would need a lot more support if he expected to win with only 2,000 men. This time, Charles had 9,000 at his disposal and the result would be a very different one than the result the year before. Naseby, he decided, was the ideal spot and it would send a clear message to the Parliamentarians that he would not be giving up his fight in a hurry.

What Charles didn't know was that Cromwell was once again one step ahead of him and had already joined up with Fairfax. Their troops had swollen to 13,000 and Cromwell was eager to press his point.

The early morning fog on 14th June 1645 rose from the valley and drifted through the trees like cold grey smoke. The overnight frost had not quite melted so the leaves were still white-dusted and crisp beneath boots and horseshoes. Mist blanketed Charles' horsemen as they shuffled nervously. The only sound was the gentle fall of hooves on the soft earth, puffing horses and the metallic chink of bridles. His men were nobles, armoured up and bearing heraldic shields as their horses stomped the ground, and most were trying to calm their nervous horses. Their steamy breath floated above their heads along with banners and pennants fluttering in the gentle breeze and around them stood an army of raggedy soldiers. To the side of them sat Charles.

At 10am, the armies clashed and the beautiful green hills overlooking Naseby turned red with blood.

Ironically, the battle started well for Charles. Prince Rupert smashed the Parliamentarian left wing and his pikemen and musketeers pushed Cromwell's back almost to breaking point. But his charge meant his left wing were scattered and Cromwell took full advantage of it. There was very little Charles could do but to order a retreat. He barely escaped with his life.

After the battle Cromwell's men rampaged through the baggage train where armies usually kept their supplies. While snaring great amount of gunpowder, arms and food, the real treasure was seizing private papers left behind in the retreat. These papers showed that Charles had been trying to raise an army of Roman Catholic soldiers from Ireland as well as negotiating for help from the French and Spanish, also Catholic. Parliament wasted no time in publishing copies of this damning correspondence for the whole nation to see. It put Charles in a terrible light showing him to be duplicitous and seemingly only caring about being in power no matter the means.

It was a discovery that Charles would never recover from. By May the next year, in his desperation, Charles made a fateful decision without thinking too far ahead of the consequences.

Charles believed the only way to rid his country of Cromwell was to join forces with the Scots. In his anxiety, he had forgotten Drogheda, Newburn and Berwick. He'd also forgotten the tax he'd imposed on Scotland's church as well as his insistence that they discard their own bible and use the English book of Prayers. In his mind, all he could think was that he was a Scotsman by decent and they would support their own.

It is hard to imagine how one mistake in judgement would catapult Charles headlong into disaster. He was so sure that he would be welcomed with open arms and you can understand his reasoning. He *was* Scottish after all. Born in Scotland of a Scottish king, James VI. His blood was their blood and he was so sure they would support him. What could possibly go wrong?

It was all very dramatic when Charles confidently appeared in the camp of the Scots army, his smile wide and his teeth gleaming white against his olive skin. Instead, the Scots stared back at him in chilly silence. As he looked around at the grim faces staring back at him, hope must have drained from his heart. I would have been the first inkling that he'd committed a colossal blunder. When he was forbidden to leave the camp, he knew for certain.

By November, Charles knew he needed to escape but by then, it was way too late. By August the following year, it was all over. There had been some sort of effort made at negotiations but it had all failed miserably. Before Christmas, the Scots had handed Charles over to Oliver Cromwell in exchange for £100,000 and by January 1649 Charles was standing in Westminster Hall listening to charges being brought against him.

By rights, there should have been 135 judges to decide if Charles was guilty or not. In fact, only 68 turned up at all on the first day. The others were less than happy about being associated with the trial and there were plenty who did not want a trial at all. The number of judges allowed into Parliament was reduced even further when Cromwell would only allow those he thought supported him to enter through the front door. That left only 46 men. Of these, only 26 voted to try the king. Regicide, they argued, was a huge risk and they risked alienating England from the rest of Europe if they went ahead with it.

As Cromwell and the judges walked into the packed hall, soldiers stood shoulder to shoulder trying to hold back the jostling crowd. Voices rose to a deafening crescendo as the Chief Justice Bradshaw, who even had the foresight to make himself a special hat lined with metal to protect his head against an attack, walked to his seat and turned to face them.

When everyone was seated, Judge Bradshaw read out the charges. The king was charged with *'accomplishment of designs and protecting himself and his adherents in his and their wicked practices...'* Charles was told he had traitorously and maliciously levied war against the present Parliament and invented entitlement for himself and his family against *'public interest, common right, liberty, justice and the peace of the people of the nation'*. He was also being held accountable for the 300,000 people who had lost their lives during the wars.

After the announcement, a lot of talk about God erupted. Charles claimed that he had a trust committed to him by God and that God would call those trying him to be accountable for their actions. In turn, those trying Charles proclaimed themselves the instruments of God's justice.

They called on God for guidance, and they spoke of God's will being done.

After their speech, Charles eyed the judges with scorn and an uneasy murmur rippled through the assembly. Perhaps they expected him to beg for mercy or at least show a little contriteness. What they received was a heated response that did little to help his situation. He told them that it was *they* who were committing treason and that no court had jurisdiction over a monarch.

On the third day, they refused to listen to him anymore. To the low whisper of 'God save the king', he was removed from court after being refused permission to speak any further. As he walked out, surrounded by soldiers, he straightened his back and held his head high as he caught the eye of Cromwell. He noticed that Cromwell did not have the look of a man who wanted his enemy beaten. He had the look of a man who wanted his enemy dead. As for Charles, if there was one quality he had shared with his father, it was his family's absolute refusal to concede defeat, no matter what the consequences. He defiantly turned his eyes forward and shrugged off the soldier's hands that were holding him as he defiantly walked out the door.

Over the coming days, 30 witnesses were called and on January 26th, 1649, Cromwell simply declared Charles guilty as charged without waiting for the final vote. Together, he and his commissioners signed Charles' death warrant and the beheading was scheduled for four days' time.

As the scaffold was being built, England held their breath, sure that this was just a terrible threat and Cromwell would suspend the execution to life in prison.

At the same time, the Scots looked on in horror. When they'd handed Charles over to Cromwell, they had never imagined what he'd had in mind. This was, after all, regicide and it was something that had never been done to a King of England before in all of history.

From France, in an attempt to save his father's life, Charles Prince of Wales had signed a carte blanche in a desperate attempt to spare his father's life. Alongside Charles stood his distraught mother as well as his younger brother James and his even younger sister Minette. They were the only ones who remained in France after Cromwell's men had captured their baby brother Henry and sister Elizabeth eight years ago, both still imprisoned in the Tower. But nothing was going to stop Cromwell from performing what he saw as his duty.

On the day before the execution, Parliament allowed Charles to see his two children. In their final moments together, Henry aged nine and Elizabeth aged 13 sobbed ashen-faced on their father's knees. They had seen the boiled heads driven on spikes on London Bridge and the thought that their father's head would join them frightened the children until they were both trembling with grief.

Charles kissed them both then took Henry onto his lap and held his face as he stared into his son's eyes.

From Elizabeth's diary, a wrenching account of his words was found among her possessions.

He bid us tell my mother that his thoughts had never strayed from her, and that his love would be the same to the last. Withal, he commanded me and my brother to be obedient to her; and bid me send his blessing to the rest of my brothers and sisters, with communications to all his friends. Then, taking my brother Gloucester on his knee, he said, 'Sweetheart, now they will cut off thy father's head.' And Gloucester looking very intently upon him, he said again, "Heed, my child, what I say: they will cut off my head and perhaps make thee a king. But mark what I say. Thou must not be a king as long as thy brothers Charles and James do live; for they will cut off your brothers' heads when they can catch them, and cut off thy head too at the last, and therefore I charge you, do not be made a king by them.' At which my brother sighed deeply, and made answer: 'I will be torn in pieces first!'

With one final kiss to each of them, he allowed the guards to take them away, shrieking for their father with their arms outstretched. It would be Charles' last sleepless night.

People say that when you know your life is ending, you reflect on your past. I'm sure as he sat in the golden light of a candle staring out of his icy windowpane, he would have been going over everything in his mind. Had he wished he'd had a glimpse of the future when he accepted the throne 24 years ago? Did he wish he'd had a quick flash of what lay ahead? If he'd known what was coming, could he have avoided certain choices and selected a different fork in the road? Could he have changed his future? If he only knew, he could perhaps have exercised discretion and restructured his life accordingly. No one will ever know what Charles was thinking in those last few hours.

A light shower of snow fell icy and wet from a grey, winter sky on 30th January as the morning dawned bitterly cold. By mid-afternoon, when the weather had still not improved, Charles called for two shirts to prevent the chill from causing shivers that could be mistaken for fear. He walked briskly through the snow under guard from St James' Palace to the scaffold that had been erected in front of the Banquet Hall in Whitehall.

With his head held high, he merely proclaimed his innocence and wished that God would forgive his executioners. There was a shadow in his eyes and his breath was heavy as if a huge weight was bearing down on him. He took a long deep breath, summoning up his courage, then he knelt down, ready to lay his head on the executioner's block. He said a silent prayer then signalled to the executioner with his hand. In the utter silence, his head was severed with one blow. As his head was held up, the huge crowd let out a terrible groan.

This was not just the killing of a king. It was the killing of a king who, at the time, had the support of almost the whole of Britain by his side, even though, through his arrogance, self-righteousness and unscrupulous behaviour, some said he had brought it all on himself. He had a tendency to make bad decisions and those dubious decisions began the moment he ascended the throne after the death of his father. They had led the country into civil war, the abolition of the monarchy and ultimately it had cost him his life.

But they knew his mistakes hadn't come from a personal need for power. He had truly believed it was his divine right, given to him by God, to rule as he saw fit. And many had agreed with him.

To most of Europe, at the moment the axe severed the head of Charles from his body, his eldest son became King Charles II and within six days, the Scots proclaimed Prince Charles the King of England, France, Scotland and Ireland.

In exile across the sea, young Charles did not hear the news immediately. When he did, he was addressed as *Your Majesty*. When those two words sank into his brain, it proved too much for the young man. Grief tightened his throat and his eyes suddenly blurred before he ran from the room in tears.

Henrietta Maria, now a widow, was almost catatonic with shock. But there were none more shocked by the execution than his sister Mary, who had married Prince William of Orange. In his room, Prince Charles slowly went from shock to anger. He had neither army to back him nor money of his own at the moment, but that could wait.

Eventually, he would win his throne and when he did, the wait would be worth it. Revenge would be all the sweeter for the wait.

OLIVER CROMWELL

Born 1599
1649 – 1658

Cromwell didn't waste any time taking over. He saw the opportunity and he took it. He had no wish to let England discover that his victory had been with a meagre army of barely 20,000 opportunistic, military and religious fanatics. To keep them in their place, he wanted the people to believe it had been with a ruthless army that would not hesitate to deal with any other rebels and he was prepared to use that army anyway he saw fit.

But from the very beginning, Cromwell found it difficult holding his own supporters together because many were openly outraged by his order to execute the king. No matter what Charles' faults, you simply did not kill a monarch.

While Cromwell concentrated on establishing himself as Lord Protector of the Commonwealth, Parliament made sure to look after Henry and Elizabeth. They were still young enough to be influenced and the two children could be useful and easily persuaded to the Protestant way of thinking. And that could mean that Charles, living in Holland with his mother, could eventually be persuaded as well. With this plan in motion, the children's home became Carisbrooke Castle on the Isle of Wight.

Carisbrooke Castle was impressive, there's no doubt about it. A cousin of King Cynric of Wessex had died and was buried there in 544 AD and the Jutes took it as their fort in the late 7th century. Around 1000 AD, they built a wall around the hill as a defence against Viking raids and for the next two centuries, the ramparts were maintained and a keep was even added. Elizabeth I then added to the fortifications when the Spanish Armada had been expected. It was the strongest castle on the island and it was visible from a great distance away.

But the stone castle on the Isle of Wight was a cold, lonely place for two little children to live, especially when both of them were heartbroken and grief-stricken after their father's death. To make things even worse, if that was at all possible, the winter of 1649 was particularly cold so it wasn't too long before things started to unravel.

In the frigid conditions, Elizabeth was particularly inconsolable. She was a fragile 14-year-old who had always been delicate so the cold she caught on 3rd September took a firm grip of her in her weakened state. One week later, she was dead of pneumonia; found with her head resting on the very Bible that her father had given her. When told of the young girl's death, Cromwell seemed totally unconcerned with the tragedy.

For a man who professed himself to be a pious, religious man, the hypocrisy of Cromwell's actions was not lost on his supporters although by then, he couldn't have cared less what anyone thought. He had more important things on his mind. Before England knew it, Cromwell showed what he was capable of and declared that the House of Lords was useless before he abolished it.

Perhaps Cromwell had forgotten why Charles had been executed but Parliament hadn't. Outrage turned to shock when Cromwell then declared he would be sending his army to fight against the *'idolatrous and bloodstained Papists in Ireland'* who had murdered Protestants in 1641. People began looking at each other in open-eyed fear when he began to discharge anyone, with no arrears in pay, who would not volunteer to tame the Irish in this war.

What they'd expected was for him to do something about the Dutch, not the Irish. With the weakening of Spanish power, many colonial possessions were up for grabs and former allies were now openly fighting each other. The Dutch had made their peace with Spain, which in turn replaced the English as dominant traders in the Iberian Peninsula, but the English and Dutch were still butting heads. English resentment was growing as the Dutch steadily grew richer because the Dutch system was classed as 'free trade' while the English goods still had heavy duties and taxes laid on them. As a result, Dutch products were less expensive in the world market while England was struggling to cope.

Cromwell knew he would have to do something about the Dutch eventually. It wasn't just about the trade restrictions. Charles' daughter Mary had married Prince William of Orange and at his father's death, William had become the ruler of Holland as the Stadtholder of five of the seven provinces. Together, the pair were incensed at the atrocity of Charles' execution. As enraged as they were, Cromwell did not want to do anything about the situation right then. His focus was totally on Ireland.

His Irish campaign that began on 3rd September 1649 was coldblooded, brutal and full of Old Testament sentiments. Drogheda was chock-full of Catholic Irish Royalists, 3,000 people to be exact, and the massacre that followed startled everyone. Everyone was put to the sword despite Cromwell's promise to treat everyone who surrendered to him with respect. In the mayhem, no one escaped. Even priests and friars were butchered and churches ransacked. Then he moved on to Wexford.

In the end, over 40% of the Irishmen who clung to Catholicism were butchered over the next two years. The remainder of the population almost wished they had been given such a quick death. In the aftermath of the fighting, they suffered through a crippling famine as well as another outbreak of plague. When they were thinking that things could not get any worse, Cromwell went one step further. He ordered that all Irish children were to be rounded up and sent to the Americas and West Indies to work as slaves in sugar plantations. He knew full well that they would more than likely die out there but that didn't concern him in the least. Dead Catholic children could not grow into Catholic adults and have more Catholic children.

As he rampaged through Ireland, Scotland watched in horror, scarcely believing that they were the ones who had helped Cromwell in the first place. Their part in Charles' murder had been unintentional and with every day that passed, they regretted handing him over to Cromwell in the first place. They had been naïve enough to think that Cromwell would be fair in his dealings but in the end, all he had shown was contempt. They'd known he meant business but nothing had prepared them for *this*.

Finally, they decided to act. They couldn't bring Charles back from the dead and fix their terrible mistake but they could do the next best thing. They could bring his son back from exile to take his place. While they weren't too sure of what they *did* want, they certainly knew what they *didn't* want and they didn't want a Republic led by Cromwell. Prepared to go to war with England again, the Scottish government sent word to young Charles in The Hague.

What they proposed startled Charles beyond belief. What they were offering was to join with him and re-establish him back on the throne of England. But on one condition. To regain the throne, he had to go against everything he believed in, not to mention what his father and his grandfather had believed in. He would have to embrace their strict religious 'Covenant' beliefs and agree to enforce a religion that was odious to everyone who had fought with his father. It was pretty obvious that if he wanted to go back to Scotland as king, it had to be on their terms, not his.

It was a big ask, and give him his due; he did hesitate for a while. But in the end, he knew that if he wanted his family to return to England with him as king, his only choice was to agree to their demands, despite his mother arguing hotly against it. He wanted his throne back and if that's what it took, then so be it.

Plans were made for his trip to Scotland, leaving behind every member of his family in the care of his sister Mary and her husband, King William II of Orange. Once he was fully established, he promised to bring them all back home to Scotland as well. At the moment, it was still too dangerous and uncertain.

As Charles held tightly to the railing on board his ship bound for home in the driving rain, he must have wondered what was waiting for him. Scotland had never been kind to him or his family and he knew full well what they'd done to his father when he'd walked confidently into their camp. Troubled thoughts bubbled slowly to the surface as he stood resolutely in the deluge. He knew the potential risk he was taking in returning to Scotland but he also realised that everything depended on this new agreement:

his life, his throne and his future. Like his father, Charles had many faults but cowardice wasn't one of them.

The short trip did not give him a lot of time to ponder on his decision. In the cold, grey half-light before dawn as white-topped waves crashed over the shore, Charles' ship landed in Scotland and he stood before a silent crowd. It was certainly not the reception he had expected. As he looked around at the sombre faces, he must have been wondering if this was the same reception his father had received when he'd walked innocently into the Scottish camp many years ago. Immediately, Charles found himself whisked off to his house in Aberdeen.

Inside the stonewalls of the castle, the scent of the sea would have permeated the whole castle as the faint roar of the waves pounded the rocks below. Although protected to a certain degree from the harshness of a Scottish winter, the cruel wind would have found its way through every available crack. And then, he would have looked out of his window through the heavy rain, and the brutal reality would have chilled him further. Nailed to one of the walls was the hand of his friend and supporter, James Graham, Lord Montrose.

Montrose had been a loyal supporter of both Charles and his father. After his father's murder, Charles had heard how Montrose was captured and brought to Edinburgh on 20th May 1649 and hung the next day. His head had been removed and placed on a spike outside St Giles Cathedral and his body was dismembered into numerous pieces and sent to the places where Montrose had won battles.

Charles' room, overlooking one of the dismembered parts, was just the finishing touch. The meaning was clear to him. He was a virtual prisoner and he would have to do exactly what he was told.

With news that Charles was back in Scotland, Cromwell hurried back from Ireland with his army, fresh from the killing spree, ready to move his attack to Scotland. There was no chance anyone was going to yank his prize away from him, especially not some wet-behind-the-ears son of a traitor.

By now, it was fast becoming obvious that not all of Cromwell's commanders agreed with his actions. Commander 'Black Tom' Fairfax had flatly refused to invade Scotland stating that the expense and danger in keeping armies in the field would be incredible. When it became obvious that Cromwell wasn't about to listen to anyone, Fairfax resigned his commission at the same time as Scottish troops invaded the Lowlands. It looked like everything was changing for the worse.

It was 3rd September again, just one year after Drogheda. It was four o'clock in the morning and the Scottish army, sitting high on Doon Hill at Dunbar, had made the decision the day before to advance down to attack the English army on level ground. During the night, dark clouds had gathered and the skies had opened up with heavy downfalls of bitter cold rain. With the weather worsening even more, the Scottish army found themselves with no shelter from the driving wind and rain on their exposed hilltop. They were positioned badly and their left flank had no room whatsoever to manoeuvre.

In the English camp, Cromwell was a little more optimistic. He had decided to launch an all-out attack on the exposed right flank in the morning and while he waited, he would use the darkness and heavy rain to cover his army's position.

During the night, the Scots had found no rest or warmth in the rain-soaked fields. As they huddled together shivering before dawn, the alarm was raised in the Scottish army that the English had begun to move forward. To their relief, the heavy rain had eased a little and the clouds were breaking up but it was still dark when the fierce artillery fire began. After an hour, both sides stopped simultaneously and hesitated, waiting for the oncoming dawn. Then it was on again.

The air was filled with the frenzied neighing of horses and the screams of agony as men were crippled and gutted. Two hours later, it was all over. In that short time, 3,000 Scotsmen had died and another 10,000 were taken prisoner. All Scottish artillery and baggage was captured.

For Charles, it was a monumental disaster with heavy losses that could not be replaced. For Cromwell, it was more like a nosebleed. Only 30 of his men were killed and with every movement he made, his absolute confidence was evident.

The march to Newcastle was gruesome and many Scottish prisoners, who were already exhausted and drained, did not survive the long trek. Some were shot because they refused to march, the remainder were given very little to eat or drink. Disease was rampant. Others were so fatigued, they simply sat down in the mud and waited for the bullet to end their misery.

It was then the English realised they had a serious problem on their hands. Holding such a large number of prisoners was a costly business but letting them go was even more dangerous. Then Cromwell had a brilliant idea. He would send most of them to the coal mines, salt works and iron works. The rest could have sailing orders and be sent to New England in America. One week later, it was a done deal and Cromwell moved his army on to Edinburgh.

There has never been a time in history when Scotland has simply given up and they weren't about to do it then. Putting the disaster of Doon Hill behind them, Scotland dug their heels in with a fresh sign of resistance. As a sign to Cromwell that they were a force to be reckoned with, they crowned Charles as the King of England in Scone and made serious plans. Their strategy was to gather as many English Royalists together that they could find and march them south into England, leaving Cromwell behind in Edinburgh. It would mean stressing the Royalist cause rather than the Presbyterian one, but a win was a win, right?

It was a good plan but there was one major flaw. Of the soldiers who had been executed at Dunbar, most of them had been officers. This new group had the true Scottish fighting spirit flowing through their veins but they had no leadership qualities that could be utilised. As Charles looked around at his passionate men, all eagerly waiting to prove their loyalty to him, he would have realised that an attack of this size was incredibly risky and the move was a dangerous one. But there was little choice left for him. It was his final chance to remove Cromwell from the equation and he was going to give it his all.

In chilling silence, Charles resolutely marched into England at the head of his troops. Once they were in the city, he allowed his men to rest and gather supplies. And then he waited until 3rd September. It was one year to the day after the Battle at Doon Hill but this time, the result would not be a defeat. This time Cromwell would be the one running for his life.

If Charles thought that Cromwell would be taken back by this daring move, he was wrong. It fuelled Cromwell on further and made him even more determined to put Charles in his place.

This time, Charles barely escaped with his life. Leaving his bodyguard to hold off pursuit, he hid in the hollow of an old leafy oak tree for 24 hours while Cromwell's soldiers looked desperately for him everywhere. The weather had turned blisteringly cold and wet and he had no food or drink but if the alternative was being discovered and taken to Cromwell, then staying put in the tree sounded like a pretty good option.

After six weeks of narrow escapes, and with a price of £1000 on his head, Charles finally made it to Normandy and then further on to his family in The Hague. The confident young man who had left with a dream of avenging his father's death had gone. In his place was a crushed and defeated man. But he was alive.

Meanwhile Cromwell settled himself in and got down to the business of ruling, just like any other king would do.

Despite being a Puritan, Cromwell was a passionate man and his main passion was a deep hatred for the Catholic Church. While everyone had hoped that savage times had gone with Henry VIII and his daughter Mary, Cromwell began showing a new disturbing side to his character. Maypoles were cut down and village dances were considered an immorality. He shut down the inns and theatres, sports were banned and any boys caught playing football on a Sunday could expect a whipping.

Sunday was set aside as a Holy day and with it came many other restrictions. The only walk allowed on Sundays was the walk to church and back home again. Most forms of work were banned on Sundays and any women caught doing 'unnecessary' work could look forward to being sent to the stocks. Anyone who swore could also anticipate some time in prison. He demanded that one day a month was to be set aside as a fast day, during which time no one ate or drank at all for the entire day. And of course, Christmas celebrations were banned as most people saw it as a time to eat, drink, and be merry. *That* little exercise was certainly off limits. On that day, decorations were especially banned and soldiers were ordered to walk the streets and enter every house, taking any food that was being cooked for the celebration. Cromwell was making very sure that the English knew who was the boss.

By 1651, England was in a terrible economic slump and they needed money badly. For two years Parliament had been carefully grooming young Henry on the Isle of Wight but Cromwell was tired of having to feed and house a former king's son with nothing to show for it. After witnessing his father's murder and hearing about his sister's sudden death, they had expected a meek 11-year-old who would not hesitate to do as he was told. Instead, what they actually had was a stubborn child who indignantly resisted everything they suggested. It was almost like having Charles back again, only in a smaller package.

As for Henry, his father's words were imbedded in his memory.

'Thou must not be a king as long as thy brothers Charles and James do live; for they will cut off your brothers' heads when they can catch them, and cut off thy head too at the last, and therefore I charge you, do not be made a king by them.'

He was simply doing what his father had told him to do. Day and night, he prayed for his freedom and the thought of being reunited with his family one day kept him going.

Then the very day arrived that Henry had yearned for. Out of the blue, two members of Parliament walked in and told him that he was to leave on the next ship for France.

As Henry stood on the deck of the ship, his coat buffeted by the gale force winds, he watched the white cliffs of Dover slowly disappear into the thick fog blanketing the shore. He was eager to leave the place that had been so unkind to him for most of his young life but he was also filled with trepidation. He'd been so young when he'd last seen his family, only a baby, and he actually had no memory of them at all. From stories told to him by his sister Elizabeth, he knew his brother Charles was dark and his brother James was fair, but that was it. As for his sister Henrietta, he had no idea what she looked like at all. He had spent so long exiled from them that they were total strangers to him and the very thought of meeting them filled him with fear. What if they distrusted him? What if they didn't like him? What if they didn't want him back at all?

He needn't have worried. As the ship landed, he saw his brothers and sister standing on the dock eagerly waiting for him and he bolted down the gangway to embrace them. At 22, Charles was tall and strong, resembling his Medici ancestors, and already the father of a three-year-old son to his mistress Lucy Walter. His eyes were as dark as night, his glossy black hair fell in waves down his back and he had a swarthy, striking handsomeness that would turn the head of any woman he passed. 19-year-old James was fair and even more handsome than Charles, just more angular like the Stuarts, and his sister Henrietta was a young girl who would certainly grow up to be a beauty. It was then he learned that they were heading off to Paris to join their mother and his uncle King Louis XIV of France.

It was during the joyous celebrations, after Louis had greeted him with open arms, that news arrived informing them that William of Orange, their sister Mary's husband, had contracted smallpox and died.

Smallpox started out just like a cold. There was a fever and a headache and severe tiredness. When you started vomiting, you knew something was terribly wrong but you still had no idea what was coming. A few days later, when the red spots appeared on your face, hands and forearms and later on your body, you knew you were in serious trouble. These spots would turn into blisters filled with clear fluid that later turned into pus. Sometimes, lesions developed in the mucous membranes of the nose and mouth and they quickly turned into open sores. If you were lucky, scabs would form eight to nine days later and if they did, you knew you had survived. These scabs would then eventually fall off, but you would be left with deep, pitted scars to mark your survival.

Mary was heavily pregnant when her husband had contracted the disease and the fear that she could contract the disease as well at the late stage of her pregnancy must have been horrendous. Every precaution was taken and thankfully she was spared, unlike her husband who was not so lucky. Even though she had watched the progression, his death had been a blow to her. She desperately needed someone to support her, considering that his parents disliked her immensely due to her steadfast sympathies for her family, the Stuarts. At her husband's death, she immediately sent for her family.

As soon as they heard, the three brothers left their mother and sister in the French court and headed for The Hague. Just a few days after they arrived, Mary delivered a frail baby boy she named William, in honour of his father.

Back in England, when Cromwell heard the news that the Dutch ruler was dead and Mary had delivered a feeble son, he had a brainwave. Johann de Witt, the leader of the Dutch Republic, had already taken advantage of the situation and had immediately snatched control of the country in the absence of a ruler. In the past, and over a short period of time, his party had grown in strength at a phenomenal rate. As Cromwell thought more about it, he knew it was an opportunity he couldn't resist. He wanted a piece of the action.

The order went out that any trade coming into British colonies from anywhere in the world could only be brought in by British ships. No one else would be granted permission to dock. More importantly, anyone who kept in contact, or sympathised with Charles and the Stuart clan, were forbidden to enter British waters at all. Effective immediately. To make the point clearer, 140 Dutch merchantmen were instantly seized on the open seas.

Parliament couldn't have been happier. After all, that was what they had expected Cromwell to do in the first place instead of terrorising Ireland, and although it was a little late in coming, they were relieved that he had finally left Ireland alone and turned his attention to the Dutch. War was on.

In the first few months of the declaration, convoy after convoy fell to England and by January the next year, thirty Dutch ships were captured at sea and taken to English ports. Of course, the Dutch protested vehemently to England and they demanded their booty back, but their protests fell on deaf ears. The loot was too much for Cromwell to resist and the English Parliament showed no inclination whatsoever toward controlling the seizure of Dutch ships. The revenue coming in was far too good to pass up.

The last thing the Dutch wanted to do was to admit defeat, especially to the English, but by October 1653, after Britain had frozen all trade to the Dutch coast, their economy was beginning to collapse. Eventually, they knew if they didn't do something, the situation would escalate and it would lead to starvation.

Cromwell was well aware what the outcome would be. He had it all mapped out. The Dutch would be unable to feed their dense population without a regular supply of wheat and rye and the prices of these commodities would soar leaving the poor unable to buy any food at all. He knew he was in a win-win situation.

As he had predicted, by April 1654, the Dutch folded and a treaty was proposed.

As with most treaties, there are concessions on both sides. One party will concede some points and the other side does the same thing. Ultimately, a solution is established and both parties come to some kind of mutual agreement. That wasn't what Cromwell had in mind at all. He was the victor and he wanted Johann de Witt to know that little fact from the very beginning.

There were thirty-six humiliating stipulations in the treaty for the

Dutch to agree upon, two of which targeted the Stuarts. One stipulation was Charles had to leave his refuge in the court of his sister Mary in The Hague and find lodgings elsewhere. The Lowlands of France near Belgium, owned by the Spanish, were strongly suggested and very soon, Charles was informed that he was to start packing immediately. Another condition was that any descendants of the House of Orange, once again meaning the family of Charles I and his daughter Mary and new-born baby boy, were not allowed to rule. Ever.

And of course, De Witt signed willingly.

Cromwell was in his glory. In his nine years as Protector, his passion had never wavered and he had convinced himself that God had chosen *him* as the Supreme Ruler of Britain. He was, however, ready to share his power with Parliament as long as they agreed with him on absolutely everything and passed the laws and taxes he required.

But while Cromwell crowed, anger and hatred welled up in Britain towards him. For nine years, they'd forgone everything they had held dear. Their children would never know what it had been like to dance around a maypole on midsummer's eve and they would never know the joy of watching actors dancing and singing on a stage. They would never know the happiness that came from decorating a Christmas tree or to smell a fresh fruit mince pie that had just come out of an oven. The more they reminisced, the more they remembered how Cromwell had intentionally ordered the murder of their king and they began to remember what it had been like when there was a king, not just a Protector, on the throne. Sure, kings had harassed the nobles and taxed the poor but that was their divine right and everything that Charles had done was based on his certainty of that belief. Cromwell was just someone who had climbed to his status with violence and bloodshed. He had removed everyone in his path, including their king, to get there and in the process, they'd forfeited everything: their rights, their traditions and ultimately their freedom.

It seemed somehow befitting that his death should come in the middle of a howling storm on 3rd September. It was the anniversary of the Battles of Dunbar, Worcester and of the siege of Drogheda. It was when Elizabeth had first contracted the cold that had turned into pneumonia and it was one month after the death of his own daughter.

Cromwell had been suffering from a bout of malaria and a kidney infection and over a period of a few days, his condition had worsened. Eventually, it had turned into septicaemia. At the age of 59, as thunder roared and lighting flashed, the skies had opened up and Cromwell died.

To depose, well actually *murder*, a monarch whose family believed in familial transfer and then embrace that exact same concept yourself is incredible, even hypocritical. But that's exactly what Cromwell succeeded in doing. Under the Protectorate's constitution devised in the first few months of his rule, Oliver Cromwell was required to nominate a successor and although his eldest son Richard had only a minor role as member of the Council of State, it was Richard he chose to succeed him.

But it wasn't the lucrative job that Richard thought he was inheriting. He was going to find out that filling his father's shoes would be very difficult, especially since he had also inherited an economy in debt of £2 million.

CHARLES II

Born 1630
Reign 1660 – 1685

For a short while after the death of Oliver Cromwell, Charles considered his chances of regaining the throne as very slim. Cromwell was dead but his son had stepped up to the mark, despite the delicious rumours he was hearing of his unsuitability. But then to Charles' amazement, the tides slowly turned.

To say that Richard Cromwell was not the man his father was is probably a gross understatement. From his first day, he was faced with two problems. Firstly, the fact that he had no military experience, or more to the point, had never even participated in any of his father's wars, had grated on most members of Parliament. Most of them had fought on the battlefields of many of the English Civil Wars and his apparent lack of respect for the army was alarming, not to mention insulting. And secondly, the rate which money slipped through his fingers astonished everyone. If he couldn't even control his own finances, how could he be expected to control a country with a debt of over £2 million? From their point of view, he had been handed the job on a silver platter without actually earning it and he was certainly not the man for the job. In their disappointment at the turn of events, the phrase 'Good Old Cause' began to be bantered around by Parliamentarians and every second or third pamphlet in bookshops had the phrase as its title.

The phrase was open to interpretation but to its supporters, it meant that their Commonwealth had been based on Regicide and Cromwell's dictatorship had been an interruption of the natural course of things. They left off cleverly at the question of whether it had been necessary or justified along with any effectiveness Cromwell had, but the insinuation was clearly evident.

Within barely six months, the debt had doubled to £4 million and when Richard's Parliament refused to pass a vote for increased taxation for crucial revenue, there were fears that, out of desperation, he had begun formulating plans to make cuts to the military to reduce costs. To the army's way of thinking, cutting back on their army was like shooting yourself in the foot. You had to support and pay for your army somehow, and if higher taxation was the only way to fund the government's costs, then so be it.

Watching closely from Scotland was Cromwell's lieutenant, General Monck. For the past eight years, he had practically been the ruler of Scotland, commanding an army of 10,000 men and acting as the linchpin. Richard Cromwell's popularity had reached an all time low by then, (he was even being called 'Tumbledown Dick') when Monck realised that it was time for someone to step in and deal with the deteriorating state of affairs. Things were going from bad to worse and he'd finally had enough.

He had only meant to go to London to help set up a more stable government. But in the short time it took for him to make the trip, Parliamentary members were resigning at an alarming rate and there were less than forty members sitting in the 'Rump' Parliament. London was in a mess. He held an emergency council meeting and with the approval of his officers, he sent a writ to Richard demanding that he pack his things and leave. And of course, Richard refused.

When Monck began massing his troops threateningly in Westminster, Richard realised he had no other choice but to listen. He was duly summoned and given an ultimatum. They would treat him honourably and pay off all of his debts as well as give him a pension, but on one condition. All he had to do was resign.

To a man in Richard's sorry position, the idea must have been very tempting indeed. He had virtually no supporters, no money and contempt was evident on everyone's face. He didn't need to be a genius to know his time was up. He signed the document and by April, he had the money in his pocket and he was on his way to France. In his rush to leave, he forgot to take his wife and family with him.

The whole messy business of getting rid of the Cromwells had gone far easier than England could ever have hoped for. Richard was gone without too much of a fuss and it had seemed like a godsend as they watched him sail away through the growing thunderstorm on his way to France. But with their relief came a new question. *Who was there to take over?*

The question must have been lurking in the back of Monck's mind even as he travelled down from Scotland. The solution would have started to formulate and he would have voiced his thoughts at the general meeting. These were men who were planners and strategists and they never left anything to chance. They would have known exactly what they were doing. They were tired of constitutional experiments and the resultant upheaval the dictatorship had produced. What they wanted was the return of a monarchy and a return to their previous way of life. What they wanted were the Stuarts to return home.

Luckily, that was exactly what the Stuarts wanted as well.

As Richard Cromwell floundered and Monck was making his presence felt, Charles was keeping a vigilant eye on what was happening in England. He and his brothers had been seeking refuge wherever they could, ever since Johann De Witt had signed the treaty with Cromwell, ordering the Stuarts to leave The Hague immediately and find lodgings elsewhere. Destitute, they had asked France for sanctuary but Louis XIV had already sided with Cromwell due to trade agreements so that option was out as well. It meant Charles had to turn to his old enemy Spain for help.

The diplomatic choice of Spain over France caused Charles and James to quarrel endlessly. But exiled and poor, there was little that either of them could do. Ultimately, James and Henry joined the Spanish army while Charles raised a ragtag army of his own from his exiled subjects and the poorly-equipped and ill-disciplined bunch became the nucleus of his military campaign. Since then, he'd been waiting four long years to make his move. And then Oliver Cromwell died and things took a decided turn for the better.

Within a month of Richard Cromwell's flight, Charles could hardly believe his luck when he was handed a letter from Monck requesting that he return to England to reclaim his throne.

From the very start, Charles knew it wasn't going to be easy. In negotiations, there are always conditions and both parties need to know where they stand. On the positive side, he had never expected to be asked to return at all so with the letter clutched in his hand, he was already in front. But when he'd finished reading the letter and the stipulations, he sat back and took a deep breath and thought about it for a while.

If he accepted, the conditions were specific. He had to settle the back pay to all English soldiers and with that, he had no problem. He also had to promise religious tolerance and he knew he could live with that as well. But what irked him was the fact that he had to promise a general pardon to any of his and his father's old enemies. That was the clause that made him hesitate. They had however, allowed one compensation. They would allow Charles to administer punishment to the men who had signed his father's death warrant. If he agreed to all of the conditions, they promised to send him money to help him return home and they would give him an annual income for life of £1.2 million to run the government. To Charles, who was totally impoverished, it was almost too good to be true.

By 23rd May 1660, Charles and his two brothers, James and Henry, were on their way from The Hague bound for London. The 29th May was Charles' 30th birthday and he was about to have the best birthday he could ever have imagined. Alongside them was their sister Mary, who had happily pawned her jewellery and left her young son William in the care of her in-laws so she could return home with her brothers. The youngest sister, Henrietta, was left behind with their mother, who was busy making preparations for her to marry her cousin Philippe of France, the younger brother of King Louis XIV of France.

General Monck greeted the three men with something like reverence when they landed. Behind him were rows of soldiers, standing silent and respectful. A throng of people had crowded to see them: some cheered while others openly wept uncontrollably as if Charles had been the one who had woken them from a nightmare. The Lord Mayor and members of the Presbyterian clergy presented him with a Bible amid enthusiastic greetings while both Houses of Parliament acknowledged and welcomed him.

All around him, the rich and the poor stood side by side, rejoicing at his return. Church bells were peeling and the smell of pies, pastries and roasted chickens wafted on the morning breeze. The city was ablaze with colour.

Charles' brothers and their handful of supporters gazed about in astonishment and Charles himself must have wondered if he was asleep and dreaming. It had been eleven years since Cromwell had first deposed him. It was ten years since the Battle of Dunbar and it was eight years since he had hidden in the oak tree to escape capture. Throughout his exile, he had always hoped to return to England as the king but he had never imagined it would be with such overwhelming acceptance. Grinning widely and showing gleaming teeth beneath his dark moustache, Charles must have sent many hearts racing as he waved happily to the crowds; his eyes twinkling in his swarthy face.

To understand this joy, you have to remember what Britain had endured for the past decade with Cromwell. Now it was a time to rejoice with the return of the monarchy and with them, the return of age-old traditions and customs. It marked a new historical period about to unfold and no other time in history was more important since William the Conqueror and the Normans arrived in 1066.

As the Stuarts made their way bemusedly through London, every window, every rooftop and every doorway was occupied. There was an almost tangible feeling that anything was possible now that Charles Stuart was back and he waved happily to the crowds when he saw the cheering people leaning out of windows festooned with ribbons and flowers. There was even a fiddler playing a happy tune to the accompaniment of the clapping crowd. As blossoms showered down on him, the roaring of the crowd became deafening. There was even a celebratory firing of cannons from the Tower to add to the incredible noise. It all seemed too good to be true.

As we all know, if anything is too good to be true, it usually is.

Parliament had dangled the juicy carrot in front of Charles and he had snatched it willingly but what he soon came to realise was that the Divine Right of Kings no longer existed. Parliament was in charge now and everyone was taking it for granted that the king was just *their* instrument and *their* servant, not the other way around as he and his family still firmly believed. He could no longer levy taxes without their consent and during his absence because Parliament had decreed that they had the final authority on absolutely everything.

As Parliament dispersed the army of over 40,000 men, Charles took a big deep breath to make sure he understood their meaning. It was pretty obvious. *They* were in control of everything. They were also hoping, for the sake of the country, that Charles would not take them up on their concession to allow him to punish his father's murderers. Revenge had no place in this new system.

They would find that Charles had no such thought. It wasn't revenge he was after. Revenge is an act of passion. What he wanted was vengeance.

Vengeance is an act of justice.

Almost immediately, Charles began dishing out punishments with zeal in his enthusiasm for vengeance. Of the men who had signed the death warrant, only 30 remained to be punished: a third were dead and the rest had fled the country before his arrival. They would have had a fair idea of what was in store for them.

Within the first year of trials, nine were hung, drawn and quartered and in the next year, another three received the same punishment. A few were spared, but not many, and the remaining nineteen were told that they were to spend the rest of their lives in prison as a guest of His Majesty the King.

Even in death, Oliver Cromwell did not escape Charles' punishment. He and the other two men who had initiated the sentencing were immediately exhumed, hanged for 24 hours on Tyburn Tree near Marble Arch, and then beheaded. Their decomposing bodies were then thrown into a dung pit and the heads were placed on spikes at the end of Westminster Hall, where his own father had been executed. Their heads were boiled first, of course.

For some, being locked behind the ponderous walls of Old Bailey Prison with its enormous ironclad door leading into a cobbled courtyard would have been punishment enough. They were shuffled around in chains led by grim, armed guards and the foul stench that filled the air would have been hard to tolerate. It would have been a mixture of waste, vomit, blood, rotting food and death. As they sat in the darkness of their cell the night before their death, they would have been trying to image a worse hell but it would have been hard to come up with one.

As prisoner after prisoner was executed, it almost seemed like a blood thirst seized London. The crowds were just as heavy as when Charles had arrived a few months earlier but the mood had changed to something almost savage. The brutal executions seemed to unleash something primal in London.

Enterprising men began erecting spectator stands so that as many people could view the hangings as possible – for a fee of course. On one occasion, the stands were so overcrowded they collapsed, killing and injuring hundreds of people. Not that it was a deterrent to anyone. It seemed to only add to the carnival atmosphere.

Most people swarmed to Tyburn Tree excitedly to watch and jeer, sometimes throwing mud, as prisoners were brought to their execution point. By then, the prisoners were almost thankful to be out of Old Bailey, even though they knew there was a noose waiting for them among the other 23 nooses that had swinging corpses attached.

Some prisoners knew their punishment was to be hanged. Others knew they would not be so lucky. Some knew their punishment was to be hung, drawn and quartered and then left for either the carrion eaters or the weather to decompose their bodies. Their last few moments on earth would have been spent watching guards with stubbly cheeks and rotting teeth wipe the backs of their grimy hands across their running noses. They would have watched the guards stuff their greasy hair under their caps then pull out their swords to use as prod while the crowd cheered them on. They would have noticed everything and there would have been panic in their hearts knowing the pain that was about to engulf them. In the end, it would have almost been a relief to walk up to the scaffold and get it over and done with.

Almost at the same time as Charles was notified that the executions had begun, another message reached him and his happy mood suddenly vanished. On a beautiful bright September morning, Charles' young brother Henry awoke with a fever. Two days later, when the physicians noticed that a nasty rash had appeared on his forehead and body, fear gripped their hearts. Within days, pustules had bubbled up on his skin. They knew exactly what that rash meant. Smallpox.

Charles was immediately notified and more physicians were summoned to Henry's bedside in Somerset House. Both older brothers had already faced smallpox and survived, the scars were still evident on their skin, so they knew they were immune to the highly contagious disease.

Both brothers sat by his bedside through the next day and night willing him to live. Henry was young, active and strong and he had barely ever been ill. Surely he would pull through. He had survived Cromwell's cold, dank prison for ten years so how could he *not* survive? Would Fate be so cruel as to take him away now, after everything he'd already been put through?

But sometimes, even with the best of care available, nothing can be done. On 13th September, at the age of 20, Henry died. Then, three months later, their sister Mary contracted the same disease and succumbed as well. For all the dreams Charles would have had of his first year as the King of England, this would certainly not have been one of them.

By December 1660, Charles had settled in and the old Parliament was finally dissolved. By April the next year, he was crowned King of England at Westminster Abbey and he had assembled his new Parliament, dubbed the Cavalier Parliament.

After years of waiting for that day to arrive, Charles was more than ready to begin ruling in earnest. As he stood in front of his Parliament, he told them he had a few ideas of how to begin his reign. First of all, he decreed that Christmas could once again be celebrated. Then, he stated, theatres would reopen, licences would now be granted to women to play female roles on stage and maypoles were back in business.

It was a great start and his people loved him for it.

But if Charles thought his troubles were finally over, he was terribly wrong. Europe was still in turmoil. France and Spain were bickering again and the Dutch were flexing their muscles and looking hungrily over the sea at England. With everything at boiling point, Charles realised he needed to strengthen his kingdom... just in case. It was time to find a suitable wife, and Parliament wholeheartedly agreed.

But with all of the choices available to him, what they hadn't expected was that he would find a Catholic one.

Negotiations for a marriage with Catherine of Braganza of Portugal had begun during his father's reign but to Parliament's relief, all discussions had been put on hold at news of the execution. During Charles' restoration to the throne, he renewed negotiations again with fervour, despite Parliament's objections and protests.

Parliament couldn't believe what they were hearing. Of course they wanted Charles to marry... but to a Catholic? With so many eligible young princesses champing at the bit hoping that the handsome English king would notice them, they were astounded that he couldn't find one who was more suitable. That is, until Charles informed them that marrying Catherine seemed like a pretty good opportunity. A golden one even. She came with a sizeable dowry that included Tangier, seven islands of India, £300,000 and an annual income of £30,000. When they heard *that* little piece of information, there was never any doubt that Parliament would agree to the marriage, despite her religion.

Catherine landed in Portsmouth on 20th May 1662 and Charles informed her that they would be married the next day in two separate ceremonies. The first one, the Catholic service, would be held in private. But the Protestant service would be a glorious occasion, celebrated by the whole nation.

Throughout the day and night, church bells rang and bonfires blazed. Torches were lit across London Bridge and were reflected brilliantly across the Thames to welcome their new queen. The whole city seemed to be ablaze. But while England gathered eagerly for the first peek of their new queen, Charles was keeping a secret. Tucked away, out of sight, was his tempestuous mistress, Barbara Villiers, soon to be Lady Castlemaine, and he had no intention of giving her up.

From the very first glimpse of Catherine, England was a little disappointed. As she walked with her head held high towards her future husband, people turned and whispered. Considering the reputation that Charles and James had for beautiful women, both of them had chosen rather plain wives to marry. And why didn't she smile? Wasn't she just a little too aloof for their 'Merry Monarch' who was always so charming, outrageous and cheerful? The fact that Catherine couldn't speak English made it even worse for her.

Still, Catherine looked content while Charles seemed pleased enough and their early days of marriage were... well... *satisfying* for him.

Catherine had not expected much from the marriage. From her point of view, marriage and all that went with it, was an unavoidable duty. Her job was to be 'available' for her husband and it was a bonus if he was kind to her and the resulting childbirth didn't kill her. But when she met Charles, she was surprised at how much she actually liked him. He was thoughtful, considerate, even amusing, and yet iron-willed and shrewd with an understanding of how to get the most out of people. She loved his silent strength and she quickly fell in love with him.

Unfortunately for Catherine, things didn't go smoothly for too long and she soon found that sexually, Charles was not very Puritan… or faithful. Barbara Villiers was pregnant with her second child and once the son was born, Barbara demanded that she be named 'Lady of the Bedchamber' to the queen. Charles duly placed her name on the list and Catherine instantly and petulantly crossed it off.

Both argued incessantly but in the end, there was no doubt that Charles would win. Catherine duly surrendered and Barbara was given the post. After the dust settled, an actress by the name of Moll Davis appeared on the scene as well, followed by Hortense Mancini, Catherine Pegge, Elizabeth Killigrew, Louise de Keroulle, Winifred Wells and Nell Gwynn. By then, I should imagine, it would have been standing room only in the 'Bedchamber'.

For a girl who had been sheltered for most of her childhood in a Catholic convent close to the palace, Catherine just wasn't prepared at all for the life Charles offered her. It was so contradicting. One day he would be very attentive and caring and the next day, from her chambers high in the castle, she would look down and see him walking idly, arm in arm, laughing with one of his mistresses far below. Catherine would watch, eyes wide and breath held, as he drew the brazen woman close, whispered in her ear and smiled widely before she laughed coquettishly at their private joke before continuing their walk to the river. A couple of times, when seeing Charles with one of these women, she was so distressed that her nose bled and she had to be physically carried to her bedroom. To make matters worse, unlike fertile Barbara, Catherine had trouble producing an heir. This was not her dream of how she would spend the rest of her life at all.

While Charles went from mistress to mistress, the rivalry between England and Holland was growing more intense with the increase of Dutch trade. The Dutch was catching herrings off the coast of Scotland and they were amassing a sizeable income for themselves as well as gathering more wealth from dealings in the Orient. It all came to a head when the Governor of Bombay refused to give up the seven islands promised to Charles in Catherine's dowry.

As we know, the main reason that Charles married Catherine in the first place was the income she brought with her. Without the seven islands, England was missing out on a huge amount of money while Dutch fleets could barely stay afloat carrying heavy loads as they travelled several times a year around the West African coast of Good Hope. While Parliament raged at Charles, he and his brother James began making plans for war.

150 new ships were built, armed with 5,000 new and heavier cannons, and former Cavalier and Cromwellians joined together to receive their orders. While Charles gathered his army together and the people's fear of war grew, England was staggered by something far worse than they had ever imagined. It arrived in the form of the worst outbreak of bubonic plague in English history.

It seems that every time a tragic and momentous time in history is about to occur, a comet streaks across the sky. To superstitious England, it was sometimes seen as a sign of good fortune but most times, as when Edward the Martyr came to the throne and just before Bloody Mary died, it had ended up as a prediction of evil. During the winter of 1664, Londoners were to see a brilliant red comet flash through the clouds and instantly the people were terrified. And they had every right to be.

Reports of the plague from Europe had begun to filter into London in 1660s. As a means of preventing it crossing into England, ships were quarantined and naval ships were assigned to stop any vessels entering the Thames estuary. Ships from infected ports were required to moor on Canvey Island for a period of 30 days before travelling upriver. By 1664, as the continental plague worsened, that duration was extended to forty days. With these restrictions in trade, tempers flared as countries, in particular the Dutch, objected heatedly, even though their own death rate was being reported at around 50,000 due to the dreaded disease.

Somehow, and it's possible that it happened during a relaxation of quarantine restrictions with an angry Dutch trader, the disease was allowed to enter London from an infected ship.

London at the time consisted of 448 acres surrounded by a city wall built originally to keep out raiders. This city contained houses ranging from ones as rich as Whitehall and Covent Gardens to town houses and timber-framed Tudor houses overhanging the streets. But there were also tenement houses where the poor lived and in these derelict houses, there was no sanitation. Waste was still being thrown out the windows and open drains still flowed along the winding streets that were slippery with animal and human waste. Rubbish and slops were simply tossed out and the air was full of flies buzzing around the sewage. The stench was overwhelming and most people used handkerchiefs over their noses to mask the pungent smell. Some noblemen even cut an orange in half and held it to their noses as they travelled through the filth but there weren't many who could afford that exorbitant luxury. Like everyone else, they had to suffer the reeking smell.

In this busy city, everything London needed came by road. Carts, carriages and people crowded the streets making it sometimes difficult to cross over the nineteen-arch London Bridge into the city. The well-off were carried in litters supported on the shoulders of a dozen or more men so the filth didn't touch their clothes. The poor could only walk through it, splashed by carriages or drenched by the slops being thrown from windows above them. Black, choking smoke, belching from factories would have only added to the discomfort and distress.

But if people thought it was bad in London, outside the city limits, half a million destitute people lived in makeshift shantytowns that were rat and flea infested. Life would already have been unbearable without adding a dose of the plague to top it all off.

The plague, called the Black Death, had always been a hazard of life in Britain making its first appearance in 1347. To understand how severe this particular outbreak was, we need to know how big the population was. There was no official census at the time but the best estimate of those times is around 384,000 people. In 1563, a thousand people were reportedly dying in London every week with a total of 15,000 having died in that year alone. By 1625, the number had climbed to 41,310. This outbreak surpassed all previous horrendous figures.

It all started with the freezing winter of 1664 when the river traffic on the Thames was blocked twice by ice. The ice was so thick that people could actually walk from one side of the river to the other without fearing that the ice would crack under their weight. Everyone knew that once that happened, any dip into the icy depths of the Thames would certainly result in an agonising death. People were cautious and they were very careful.

But it wasn't the ice they should have been careful about. The only thing the unusually cold weather did was to delay the spread of the disease for a short while. With the arrival of warmer weather, the disease began to take a firmer hold. By July 1665, the plague was rampant.

As Charles and James, together with their families, packed up everything and moved to Oxford to try and outrun it, businesses were closing and merchants were fleeing. But ordinary people did not have that luxury. They had to stay put and wait it out since they could not abandon their tiny homes and already meagre livelihood for an uncertain future elsewhere. All they could do was walk quickly through the narrow streets with their mouths covered so they might not breathe the foul air and keep their eyes diverted from the doors with tragic red crosses marked on them.

As the plague raged through London in the summer months, only a small number of clergy and physicians remained to cope with the increasingly large number of victims. One to remain was General Monck with all the readiness of a man accustomed to obeying without thinking of the risk. Over the years he had been rewarded suitably for his part in restoring Charles to the throne. He was Gentleman of the Bedchamber, Knight of the Garter, Master of the Horse and Charles had raised him to peerage by making him Baron Monck, Baron Beauchamp, Baron of Teyes, Earl of Torrington and Duke of Albemarle. He also received an annual pension of £7,000 and was one of eight Lords Proprietors given title to a huge tract of land in North America, which became the Province of Carolina. Already in charge of the Admiralty while James commanded the fleet, there was never any doubt in his mind that he would remain in charge of the government while Charles and his family left London for cleaner air.

Most people who opted to flee were ultimately turned away from villages outside of London and were forced to steal and scavenge from fields and paddocks. Many simply died of starvation and thirst in the unusually hot summer that had followed the cruel winter. Burial grounds became overfilled and enormous pits were dug to bury the dead. Drivers of 'dead-carts' travelled the streets calling out *'Bring out your dead'* and the ponderous carts, full of dead bodies, lumbered away to the pits. As time went on, there were too many victims and too few drivers to remove the accumulating decomposing bodies. They were simply stacked up against the walls of houses. Bonfires burned day and night in the hope of cleansing the air of the stench.

By August one year later, Charles and his family had returned but 7,000 were still dying every week and some historians consider this a vast underestimation as many parish clerks who kept the records were dead themselves. In the space of six months, the plague had claimed around 50% of the population. There seemed no way to stop the disease from spreading.

In 1665, London was still essentially medieval. It was still overcrowded with warrens of winding, cobbled alleys and as summer turned to autumn, there was no rain, only oppressive heat, and London's wooden buildings, packed tightly together and leaning closely to one another, turned tinder dry in the drought. Unpaved roads cracked and a hot dry wind stirred up clouds of dust throughout the city. Rain barrels and animal troughs dried up and the usually muddy slopes of the Thames baked to hard clay. Still it grew hotter and thoughts of a worse outbreak of the plague filled people with abject terror. As bad as life seemed with the everyday threat of the plague encompassing their lives, they were totally unaware of yet another tragedy that was about to be unleashed on them.

In the early hours of Sunday 2nd September, lanterns glowed a ghostly orb on the dark streets of London. The city smog had settled but pale plumes of smoke still drifted in the moonlight and rose upwards forming a grey cloud covering London. The clip clop of horse hooves echoed down the streets as the carriages splashed through puddles of excrement and urine. The stink hung heavily in the air and as the streets slowly emptied, the buzzing of voices began to quieten. For the people who had managed to survive the plague, they must have imagined that things could not possibly be worse.

Suddenly, a little before midnight, a fire broke out at a bakery and London would never be the same again.

Fires were quite common in those days and Londoners were used to fires. In the past, they were soon quelled. Even the Lord Mayor of London's reply, after having been woken up and informed about the fire, was *"Pish. A woman might piss it out!"* But despite dousing it with precious water, neighbours were unable to prevent the fire from spreading. The fire soon took hold as flames began to jump from house to house.

The problem was with so many wooden houses closely packed together, they fell outwards, spilling fire in all directions. The fire soon consumed adjoining houses as it swept towards the paper warehouses and flammable stores full of oil, pitch, tar and resin on the riverfront. Instead of the strong east winds extinguishing the fire, the wind fanned the fire further into a firestorm as it supplied fresh oxygen to the flames creating a chimney effect with burning embers floating hungrily in the air. In the rapidly expanding sheet of flame, sparks and burning ashes lodged on thatched roofs and in wooden gutters as people ran screaming into the streets with their clothes smouldering and glowing. By evening on 2nd September, 300 houses had collapsed as the fire continued through the warren of streets lined with wooden houses.

It would have been the noise that woke Charles in the pre-dawn hours on 3rd September. Then, as he looked down at the streets of London from his bedroom window high in the castle, the sight he saw would have jolted his heart and tightened his throat. He would have been stunned to see the city blazing out of control like a fiery oven below him. Showers of hot ash would have filled the night skies and in the distance, he would have heard the roar and crackle of the fire intermingled with a hissing sound as ash hit the Thames. From his lofty viewpoint, he would have been able to see boats filled with people, clinging to bits of furniture, musical instruments, rugs and chests of money. And he certainly would have heard the screams of people as the ground burnt through the soles of their shoes. He would have seen the steeples of dozens of churches, including St Paul's Cathedral, silhouetted by the colossal flame and he would have felt the intense heat. By then he would have recognised the smell of burning bodies. It was probably as he stared down in shock at the chaos, that another reality would have crossed his mind. The date was September 3rd, and all hell had broken loose again, just as it had on that exact same date during battles at Drogheda, Dunbar and Worcester.

As the fire raged unchecked, looting began and the upper class were growing desperate to remove their belongings from the city. People tried to evacuate by boat but were ultimately cut off, as the only exits were the eight city gates. The need to get beyond the city walls caused near panic as distraught refugees pushed and shoved their way with their meagre bundles of possessions loaded on horses and wagons. In their terror, they would have missed seeing the thousands of rats scurrying to escape as well. Instead of people manning buckets full of water from the river to the fire, they fled. As they fled screaming in panic, they would have stumbled and fallen over the bodies of the dead as well as others who had fallen in their panic to escape the flames. Embers were burning along the streets like a river of fire.

By the next day, half of London was still in flames and the fire had spread through most of the city. Charles and James had attempted to help by working in the bucket brigade but by then, the fire was well and truly out of control. It threatened Charles' court at Whitehall as the financial heart of the city began to burn. St Paul's Cathedral roared into flame, covered in wooden scaffolding due to restorations, and the lead roof began to melt and run down the streets in a glowing stream. The pavements shone with fiery redness.

By late afternoon, the Royal Exchange caught fire and was a smoking shell within a few hours. The fashionable wealthy areas were already charred ash and Baynard's Castle in Blackfriars was completely consumed, burning long into the night. Oil, pitch, coal, wood, turpentine and gunpowder had fuelled the fire which melted steel lying along the wharves and the iron chains and locks on the city gates. Hotter than an ordinary house fire, it was hot enough to consume bodies fully and only leave skull fragments.

Two things saved London from being wiped out completely. Firstly, the strong east winds mercifully died down and secondly, the garrison at the Tower of London used what gunpowder was left to blow up whole streets in the effort to create firebreaks to halt further spread. The sound of the explosions however created fresh panic when a French invasion was suspected.

By 6th September, the firebreaks had begun to take effect. The city was still smouldering and the streets glowed with heat but the worst was over.

Small fires still burned but they were burning themselves out.

During the fire, 13,500 houses, 87 parish churches, six chapels, four prisons, livery stables, public buildings, markets and 57 halls, as well as three city gates, were just burnt-out shells and totally destroyed. The devastated area was 436 acres and the monetary value was estimated at a staggering £10 million (over £1 billion by today's standards). In the utter mayhem, 80,000 people lost everything and were left homeless, forced to camp on the sides of the roads.

In the chaos after the fire, Charles did not want to delay rebuilding the gutted city and if the fire had been an astonishing spectacle, his rebuilding was extraordinary. His people already had few possessions but now they were destitute and what Charles knew beyond a doubt was that with desperation came rebellion.

Charles' plan was to build a new city with improved hygiene and fire safety. He wanted wider streets and open wharves more accessible along the length of the Thames with no houses obstructing access. Most importantly, buildings were to be constructed of brick and stone, not wood and the rooves were to be tile or slate. And there were to be four categories of dwellings. The smallest would be two storeys each at least 9ft high with an attic and a cellar intended for alleys and lanes. The next category was meant for streets and main lanes and would be three storeys plus an attic and with the ground level being 9ft and the second storey 10ft. The third would be four storeys and all these houses were to have the same height of roofline. The fourth category would be 'mansions for persons of extraordinary quality' but still limited to four storeys.

It would seem that out of two terrible disasters came a rebirth.

While Charles planned his new city, creating a hive of activity, war with Holland was proving to be a costly business and it dragged on endlessly as Charles procrastinated over signing a peace treaty with the Dutch. In the back of his mind was the hope that his cousin Louis XIV in France would do the right thing and offer assistance. What Charles didn't know was that in France, Louis was having problems of his own.

France was basically bankrupt and Louis was in the process of charging his Controller-General of Finances with embezzlement. By the time Louis first became aware of his financial problems, things were already out of hand. What Louis found was that his Minister had been skimming from the royal treasury for years and was privately spending lavishly on luxuries for himself and his family. It was only when the General indiscreetly purchased a private island that something twigged in Louis' brain that something wasn't quite right and figures just weren't adding up correctly.

While Louis struggled with his own finances, the Dutch had grown impatient waiting for Charles to sign the treaty. Through the years, they firmly believed they'd been forgiving, even magnanimous, as England went from turmoil to chaos. But enough was enough. It was during a dense, heavy fog one warm night in July, the Dutch decided to put an end to the dithering and attack.

In the darkness, the ominous sound of cannons suddenly boomed deafeningly up the Thames. When the thick fog cleared, England realised with shock that the Dutch had taken advantage of the weather conditions and sailed unopposed into the mouth of the Thames. Thirty Dutch ships had abruptly appeared like ghosts through the fog and a landing party of a thousand Dutchmen had captured the town of Sheerness. From there, they'd sailed further up the Thames and on to Chatham, where England's naval base was situated. They burned three main ships and ten lesser vessels and towed away the *Unity* and the *Royal Charles* before England even knew what was happening.

The question on everyone's lips was *'How could the Dutch have gotten that far without alerting the guard ships in the harbour?'* Then it all became clear. Charles' brother James, due to a lack of funds, had discharged most of the crews from the prize vessels, leaving the ships almost unattended. It seems that most of the money had been spent on rebuilding the city after the fire not on maintaining the navy and as a consequence, only three guard ships were left to defend the harbour.

When the rumour began that the Dutch were in the process of bringing a French army across from Dunkirk for a full-scale invasion, the people of London flew into a mad panic. Wealthy people rushed to gather their few valuable possessions together again while the poorer people fled with what they could carry in their arms. On top of the plague, then the fire, England was stretched to breaking point.

As the Dutch advanced, English crews abandoned their half-flooded ships without a fight, making it easy for the Dutch demolition teams to row unobstructed to any ship they could reach. As they boarded ship after ship, the Dutch burned and plundered without mercy. With adrenaline rushing through their bodies, they fully intended to continue on to Gravesend and finish what they'd started.

They didn't know that Charles had been watching intently and hoping for that exact move. As they surged into Gravesend, he gave the order that the harbour was to be blocked by five 'fire' ships. These old wooden ships were to be filled with combustibles and steered towards the enemy fleet. Once the enemy was in sight and impact was inevitable, the unlucky person chosen for the job secured the tiller, lit the fire, and then quickly jumped from the abandoned ship, mercifully before they caught on fire as well. If all went to plan, the fire ship would hit the target and send it roaring up in flames. The strategy was to destroy as many Dutch ships as possible and create such a panic that they would break the Dutch formation, send them into disarray, and give the English a sorely needed advantage. It had worked for the Greeks and it had worked during medieval times. Charles was not about to let it fail for him now.

It was the order that stopped the carnage. Although the raid had cost England around £200,000 plus 1,200 soldiers killed and the replacement costs for the four lost ships, it was the Dutch who suffered the most with an estimated 5,000 men dead.

The raid had been a serious blow to England and Charles was furious at the Dutch's underhanded attack while peace negotiations had been taking place, no matter how lengthy they may have been. In the resulting indignation, Cavaliers remarked that nothing had ever happened like this under Cromwell. Charles retaliated by demanding to know how he was supposed to protect England when he was so short of money. Parliament retorted that he was supplied with plenty of money but if he didn't spend so much on his mistresses and luxuries, he would have had plenty of spare cash to spend on his navy.

It was fortunate for England that as Charles and Parliament ranted at each other, the Dutch had backed down and reluctantly signed the peace treaty. They may have signed the treaty and believed that all was forgiven: but we all know better. Charles may have forgiven them but be damned if he was going to forget what they'd done. He had already proven that he was a patient man but he was going to show them that he also had a long memory.

During the years of their marriage, Catherine suffered miscarriage after miscarriage. By June 1669, after three heart-breaking miscarriages, she and Charles were both forced to accept the fact that Catherine had suffered her last pregnancy and there would be no children. When news arrived that Charles' mother had died as well, Catherine crumbled. Amid rumours of a divorce, she moved into Somerset House just as she fell seriously ill and collapsed.

As Catherine struggled with her health, the last thing Charles needed was the government putting pressure on him regarding an heir, on top of everything else. As far as Parliament was concerned, the only way around the problem was for him to divorce Catherine and legalise his first illegitimate son, James Crofts, born in Rotterdam in the Netherlands to Lucy Walker.

Six years before, in February 1663 at the age of 14, young James had been brought to England, along with his grandmother, from his school in Le Chesney near Paris, called Petit Ecoles. Two months after that, a marriage was arranged for him to wed the 12-year-old Scottish heiress Anne Scott, daughter of Frances Scott, 2nd Earl of Buccleuch, then he was created Duke of Monmouth with the subsidiary titles of Earl of Doncaster and Baron Scott of Tyndale to top it off. His new name, Charles declared, would be James Scott, 1st Duke of Monmouth, and the impressive array of titles were meant for his son to fit neatly into the English society and the Peerage of England.

And he didn't disappoint Charles. At 16, he had served in the English fleet under his uncle James Duke of York in the Second Anglo-Dutch War and he had returned to England as captain of a troop of cavalry. One year later, in September 1668, he was made colonel of His Majesty's Own Troop of Horse Guards and less than another year after that, he acquired Moor Park in Hertfordshire in readiness to start a family with his wife Anne, now 18.

He was well known, popular and charismatic, much like his father, and he was highly regarded as one of Britain's finest soldiers. He was even a Protestant. But he lacked one vital ingredient. And that was legitimacy. Because of that, the official heir presumptive to the throne was the king's brother, James Duke of York.

We all know Charles had his faults but to give him his due, a lack of loyalty was not one of them. He refused all requests to divorce Catherine continuously and fervently, and through Catherine's years of illnesses and depression, Charles refused to *'get rid of her'* as Parliament had requested. Catherine was family and you didn't just *'get rid'* of family.

Behind everything Charles did was the issue of money, or more precisely, the lack of it. He owed a lot of money to William of Orange for the eight years when he and his family had lived in The Hague during Cromwell's rule. He had exorbitant costs with his many mistresses and he regarded the allowance given to him by Parliament as meagre, barely enough to cover half of his expenses. With hands out every way he turned, Charles was willing to agree to almost anything if there was more money in his pocket at the end of it all. And once again, he turned to Louis XIV, his cousin through their grandfather Henry IV of France.

There have been fewer men in history who have outshone Louis XIV. By 1670, he was in his prime and France was by far the strongest nation in Europe. France's population was 20 million, four times that of England, and they had some of the most valuable and fertile regions in the globe. They were at the head of learning and art, they had a powerful army and Charles' youngest sister Henrietta had married Louis' only brother, Philippe. But apart from all of that, they both hated the Dutch. It was almost inevitable that they would join together and sign a pact.

But as always, there were conditions.

In Dover 1670, the two kings put their heads together and agreed that they would declare war on the Dutch Republic. Louis would attack by land with the help of 6,000 soldiers from England as well as 50 ships, all under the command of Charles' brother James. For this, Charles would secretly receive 2,000,000 gold crowns in the course of six months – money he desperately needed if he was to even consider repaying any of his debts.

The only catch was Charles had to become a Catholic.

At this time in history, most Englishmen had begun to despair of ever being able to 'beat the Dutch'. With that in mind, Charles tried to explain to Parliament that to do that, he needed the backing of France. Only with their support did England have any sort of a chance. He produced the treaty that Louis had given him and even though Parliament was very unenthusiastic about the expense of a new war, five members of Parliament co-signed without too much of a fuss.

Charles was amazed at how smoothly it had all gone but then again, the clause stating he would declare himself a Roman Catholic had been conveniently absent from the document. Charles knew full well that if it had appeared, there would be complete outrage and there would have been no money at all from England. So *that* somewhat vital part of the treaty remained his little secret. That and the amount of money he was about to receive from Louis, of course.

While negotiations were being finalised in Dover with Louis, Charles' nephew William III of Orange, had obtained permission to travel and enter England. And Charles knew exactly what he was after. Money.

William was the son of Charles' sister Mary who had lost her husband years before to smallpox when she was heavily pregnant. While she was still in mourning, she had given birth prematurely to William and no one had expected him to live long in an age of high child mortality, especially as the child was very feeble anyway.

William's whole life was plagued with bad health and chronic asthma. The illness had almost claimed his life on several occasions during his young life. Along with his frailty, his coldness and aloofness was legendary, although that trait could be accredited to the fact that his mother had virtually deserted him and left for England when his uncle Charles had been offered his throne back. As a result, from an early age, he had grown up in a circle of men who took over the job of raising him and caring for him.

Back in the Netherlands, William was having problems, not just with England, but also with a Dutch Republican by the name of Johann De Witt. De Witt had been the Dutch political leader since 1650 when Cromwell had co-signed an agreement forbidding the Dutch to ever appoint William III, the one-month-old grandson of Charles I, as their ruler. De Witt had been happy enough to comply since it gave him the leadership but seventeen years later, William of Orange was not a baby anymore and he was demanding his throne back.

To do that, William needed money so he could stake his claim to the throne and oust De Witt from Holland. That money, he reasoned, was to come from Charles who had run up a huge bill while staying in The Hague with his family during Cromwell's rule.

All William wanted was for Charles to pay back at least part of the 2,800,000 guilder debt the House of Stuart owed the House of Orange. After all, they were family. William's mother was a Stuart. His grandfather was a Stuart. And his great grandfather had been a Stuart. The House of Orange had supported the Stuarts when they'd been exiled from England and now it was time to pay back that debt. Family did the right thing when it came to family. Right?

When William arrived in England and made his claim for expenses, Charles stated that sadly he was unable to pay. William grudgingly agreed to reduce the amount owed to 1,800,000 guilders, but the answer was still the same. Again Charles said sorry, he just didn't have the money.

William couldn't believe what he was hearing. *Everything* depended on him getting this money. This money, *his* money, was needed to buy an army. It was needed to buy weapons and support and ultimately it was needed to buy back his kingdom. And then he had a look around. What he saw was a lifestyle that differed dramatically from his own. Charles seemed more concerned with drinking, gambling, and cavorting with mistresses than ruling and of course with those vices, money slipped through his fingers like water. And it wasn't just Charles. James was no better. Understandably, William was furious.

Charles knew he was playing a dangerous game with both William and England. He had hoped that an attack on the Dutch Republic would have already been under way, but it had to be delayed because the French needed to establish secure diplomatic relations with Munster and Cologne, two key German principalities, first. With the debt to William still hanging over his head, Charles could not see any other way out but to make his nephew part of the conspiracy with Louis.

The more Charles thought about it, the clearer his thinking became. He would promise William that if he signed the treaty, William would be made the Sovereign Prince of Holland after the war was won. Of course, Charles did not want William to know how much money was coming his way from signing the treaty so he simply left that part out. Again. The catch was, to achieve that, William had to agree to become a Roman Catholic as well.

William was horrified by the proposal. Becoming a Catholic was the *very* last thing he would consider and of course, he flatly and hotly refused. Charles was all apologies but in the end, he told William it was become a Catholic or nothing. He just didn't have the money. Sorry.

In fury, William packed up and returned home empty-handed.

William wasn't Charles' only problem. He needed Parliament to give him more money to build a stronger fleet of ships since he had promised so many of them to Louis. He needed 82 ships to fulfil his side of the agreement and that would cost a lot of money that he just didn't have. To get that money he had to convince Parliament that if they wanted to defeat the Dutch, England needed to increase their navy. And that took money.

Lots of money. England could surely not expect to be involved in a war with such a weak navy.

By this time, Charles was digging himself deeper into a hole. He was receiving considerable payments from Louis, about £225,000 a year, but because he wanted to keep these payments a secret, they couldn't be directed to building a fleet. Not that he wanted to contribute anyway. It was *his* money and he much preferred to spend the money on his mistresses and his quality of life. After all, hadn't Parliament told him to live off his own money?

To most of England who were suffering terribly and slowly going bankrupt, Charles looked like he had won the lotto. On one hand, Charles was asking for more money but on the other hand, Parliament and bankers were incredulously watching Charles on a spending spree. Not surprisingly, they came to a rather quick decision. There would be no loan to finance the fleet. If Charles had so much money to spend on himself, then he could find a little bit more to spend on the security of his country.

Charles should have seen it coming but still he held back. With the realisation that Parliament would not be handing over any money, determination stepped in and he took matters into his own hands. In his resolve to get money any way he could, he made a monumental mistake. He declared he would only pay back the *interest* on his existing loans to the banks, with no payment forthcoming at all on the principal for the duration of one whole year. Effective immediately.

Charles had never intended England to suffer the terrible repercussions of his decision. His only thought was the size of the windfall he would be receiving. Doing the math, he was looking at an extra £1.3 million (around £100 million by today's standards), and with this money, he could build his ships. But the short-term consequences of the decision were disastrous for England. Many bankers went bankrupt and the multitudes who had put their life savings in those banks lost everything as well.

But it wasn't just England who was having a disastrous year. The year was 1672 and the Dutch were having a devastating year as well. Louis declared war on them on 6th April and Charles followed suit the next day.

Suddenly, and without further warning, Louis struck with terrible force on 5th May with 120,000 cavalry and 12,500 horses mobilised and armed for the first time with a bayonet fitted to the muzzle of the musket. As France savagely advanced through the country, Holland was both panicked and furious that De Witt had let this disaster happen.

Considering William of Orange's past dealings and disappointments with Charles in England, he could be considered a patient man. But patience is one thing and indecisiveness is another and indecisiveness was not one of his faults. He had been watching intently and keeping up to date with Louis' movements as his men reported back to him constantly on Louis' progress. He was waiting for his big chance and he didn't have to wait long for the day to arrive.

On that fateful day, Johann De Witt had walked the few steps from his house to the prison where his brother Cornelis was being held, accused of plotting to kill William. The two men sat huddled together in the filth of the dingy cell and you can believe they were working on a plan to release Cornelis from his jail. While they talked, the guard disappeared to supposedly stop a group outside from pilfering. Without any forewarning, both brothers were dragged from the prison by an angry mob, shot and brutally murdered. Their naked bodies were strung up on the nearby public gibbet and their fingers, toes and *'other body parts'* were cut off and allegedly taken away, cooked and eaten.

The question whether William had hand in the murders will always remain unanswered. The fact that he had ordered the withdrawal of his cavalry detachment, that would otherwise have prevented the lynching and butchery, has always raised eyebrows but nothing was ever proven. The fact is though, the very next day William stepped back into the picture to restore public order.

Charles was never one to let an opportunity slip by. With France still rampaging and William now on the throne, he saw a chance that could send some more booty his way.

Lord Arlington and the Duke of Buckingham were two of Charles' most staunch supporters who had reputations for getting the job done, no matter what the circumstances. With that in mind, they were given the job of heading to Holland to give William the good news that England wholeheartedly supported him.

All the way, Dutch crowds cheered them on, thinking that England had come to save them from the French. They were almost right.

When Arlington confronted William, the Dutch ruler said nothing at first. From experience, it was always best to let the new arrivals start the conversation. Then, in a strained voice, William asked Arlington to state his business.

Arlington cleared his throat and spoke in an imperturbably calm voice that was a sharp contrast to William's visible anger. He announced that England would indeed support him and all it would cost him would be 10,000,000 guilders for their efforts, payable in yearly payments of £10,000.

If William was angry before, now he was apoplectic. All semblance of patience and fortitude flew out the window and an intense fury shook William to the core. Buckingham and Arlington witnessed an uncharacteristic display of temper as William raged at them publicly, screaming and yelling that he would rather *"die a thousand times than accept them"*. Arlington quietly threatened annihilation if William didn't comply and William screamed at him to go ahead and bring it on. It all became rather messy.

Far from pouring oil on troubled waters, the situation had turned volatile. In Parliament's mind, the only way out was to pressure Charles to offer his consent for William to marry his niece, James' daughter Mary. Mary was of marriageable age and the union would put an end to all the hostilities.

As risky as it was, Charles could see the logic in the suggestion. He would still have money coming in from France and he wouldn't have to pay back the debt to Holland anymore. Plus the war with Holland would be put on hold. The only side effect was that it would probably inflame Louis. Despite that, it would certainly settle things down a bit with William. With the added bonus that William was a Protestant, Charles agreed to talk to his brother James about it.

James was not happy about the new arrangement. Not happy at all. Mary was his eldest and favourite daughter and she was still in mourning after the recent death of her mother. Apart from that, she was barely 15 years old.

The two brothers argued incessantly while Mary sobbed hysterically. But Charles was adamant: Mary would have to marry William.

While Charles negotiated with William, his brother James was headed down another more dangerous path. He had decided to remarry after the recent death of his first wife.

The fact that he had decided to marry so soon after her death wasn't the problem. Nor was it that his choice of a bride was a beautiful Italian girl only one year older than his daughter Mary. What tipped Parliament over the edge was the fact that Mary of Modena was a Roman Catholic. To make matters even worse, James converted to Catholicism himself in support of his new wife.

England erupted. When you consider that Charles did not have any children and James was the heir presumptive, it's easy to see why everyone was in such an uproar. It would mean that England would once again have a Catholic ruler on the throne with lots of Catholic rulers in the future. The last one had been Bloody Mary and we all know how that had turned out. All they could do was pray that Catherine would fall pregnant and carry the child to full term.

It was 1677 and the day of Mary's wedding dawned cold and damp. It matched her mood exactly. An evening wedding had been scheduled and all of England was gathering for the occasion. While royal courtiers busied themselves with preparations during the day, Mary wept quietly in her room and waited for the sun to set.

She hated William with a passion. He was twelve years older than her, much shorter and thinner, with legs as thin as a bird. His back was hunched, his nose was large, his eyes were small and his face was a pale as a ghost. But she knew there was no getting out of it. By evening, the sky glowed with blazing bonfires as people began celebrating with enthusiasm.

Mary cried throughout the entire ceremony while outside the cathedral people clapped and cheered. Weeks later she was still crying as she leaned on the guardrail of a ship, waving a forlorn goodbye to her father as she set sail for the Netherlands with her new husband.

Almost like a bad omen, the crossing was rough with choppy seas and incredible winds, which caused a further delay of two weeks due to the bad weather. Rotterdam had been William's desired destination but the port became inaccessible due to ice and they were forced to land elsewhere and make their way ponderously through the frosty countryside to a small nearly village. Thankfully, once they reached the village, they were met by coaches that then took them to Huis Honselaarsdjik, the country residence of the Dutch Stadtholders, 2.6kms southwest of the border. During the tedious trip, Mary cried harder and William grew angrier.

It is about this time in history when two political parties were becoming prominent in Parliament: the Tories, who supported Charles and James, and the Whigs who wanted to disinherit James and exclude him and his Catholic family from ever becoming rulers of England. Once again, there was talk of legitimising Charles' illegitimate son, the Duke of Monmouth and once again, Charles refused.

Looking at the mess his father and uncle were making of things, it was no wonder the Duke of Monmouth was feeling exasperated. In history, it had taken a lot less than this to infuriate ambitious relatives to make them finally take a stand. He was, after all, Chancellor of Cambridge University, Master of the Horse and Lord Lieutenant of Staffordshire and Charles had stated that all military orders were to be brought to him first to examine, giving him effective command of the forces. His reputation as a distinguished soldier had increased along with his popularity and to top it off, he and his wife had produced three healthy children, two boys and a girl. He had expected more from his father, considering his rank and position.

What Monmouth needed was to somehow prove that his father and his mother had in actual fact been married. This, above all else, would prove his legitimacy and put him in the front of the queue as the heir apparent, before his uncle Duke of York and before his uncle's Catholic offspring with his new fertile Italian bride.

When Monmouth produced a 'black box' containing a certificate of marriage between Charles and Lucy Walker, at the height of anti-Catholic sentiment, all hell broke loose. Of course, the claim of a marriage was totally false and Charles denied it vehemently. It was a hard thing for him to do, loving his son as much as he did, knowing that public opinion would have readily accepted Monmouth if he suddenly declared him the legitimate heir. But it was obvious Monmouth had a vain streak, and was easily led. And of course, he'd been indulged over the years since Charles' restoration and had been allowed to get away with reprehensible behaviour. He had been entitled in every way but not this.

The damage had been done and it was open war between Monmouth and his uncle James. The resulting antagonism resulted in James being sent to Brussels for his own safety and to keep things fair, Monmouth was banished to Holland and stripped of his military titles.

Now we all know Charles had his shortcomings. Heaven knows he had proved time and again that he was no angel. In his fifteen years on the throne, he was always in conflict with someone. First the Dutch, then the Spanish, and always with Parliament. He was constantly in need of money and there was a long line of women queuing up outside his bedchamber with their hands out for money. Most times, he did whatever he had to do to get it, whether it was the right way or the wrong way.

But for all his blunders there was always one thing he was consistent in:

his belief in the Divine Right of Kings. His father had died because of that belief and he had endured many harsh years of his life in exile because of it. Cromwell had taken that 'right' away from him and it was because of that same belief that Cromwell had plunged the country into rebellion and civil war. There was no exception to this rule and he wasn't about to fawn or kowtow to a Parliament who thought differently. If he shirked that belief now, he would be nothing but a fraud. He had stood by Catherine when Parliament had almost ordered him to find a new fertile wife and he stood by his brother James then. He had made bad decisions in the past but there would be no faltering on this subject. In this, he showed a depth of character.

It was 1680 and Charles knew what he had to do. He had already called Parliament twice before over the past three years and both times he'd dissolved it when the subject of his heir was brought up for discussion. This time, as Charles walked into the room, there was a ripple of excitement and expectation. As he sat on the throne, he was so motionless; he could have been made of stone. He looked silently around at the members before him and a hush came over the room as his eyes swept the chamber.

His eyes said everything. They glittered with anger and his whole countenance implied pent-up rage that might at any moment erupt. The unease was palpable and everyone seemed to hold their breath in the hush. When he spoke, his deep voice was firm, strong and controlled and if there was anyone who doubted the importance of the meeting, the crescendo of his voice was enough for them to understand. He told them in no uncertain terms that the exclusion of his brother, the Duke of York, was treason. Anyone who spoke of it set themselves against legitimate authority. There was to be no confusion over the matter. His brother was his heir and would remain so as God had ordained it and no man could alter that fact. Anyone who denied that truth made himself an enemy of God, king and country. He then said, 'I declare Parliament dissolved. I will not trouble you again.' In the silence, he stood up and walked out.

It was a moving speech and it was meant to be definite and final. True to his word, for the remainder of his reign, Charles ruled without Parliament.

But this passionate speech put both their lives in jeopardy and it's probably the straw that broke Monmouth's back. He could not wait any longer and he defiantly returned from exile to England, without Charles' permission. Within an hour or two, the church bells were ringing to announce the arrival of their favourite idol and bonfires blazed in the streets.

Charles, however, was not so delighted and he refused to receive his son at court.

Instead of keeping his head down, Monmouth toured the West Country, blatantly raising support for the Whig party while continuing to try and win back favour with his father. While Monmouth toured, the Duke of York petitioned his brother to return to England as well and permission was happily granted.

But while the two brothers were catching up after their long separation, the 'Rye House Plot' was being hatched and Monmouth's accomplices were plentiful. He was just a ticking time bomb.

Rye House was a fortified mediaeval mansion leased by a Civil War veteran, Richard Rumbold. The plan was to conceal a force of men in the grounds of the house and ambush Charles and James as they passed by on their way back to London from the horse races at Newmarket. The tactical advantages were abundant and could be carried out from good cover with a relatively small force operating with guns.

What saved Charles' life, oddly enough, was a fire. The two brothers were expected to make the journey to the races on 1st April 1683 but there was a major fire in Newmarket on 22nd March, which destroyed half the town. The races were cancelled and Charles and James returned to London early. As a result, the planned attack never took place.

A plot this big couldn't be kept quiet for too long and news soon leaked of a conspiracy where the Earl of Essex and three others from the Whig side of Parliament were implicated: Lord Russell, Member of Parliament for Bedfordshire, Lord Algernon Sidney, former Lord Warden of the Cinque Ports and Charles' own illegitimate son, Duke of Monmouth. The form it took was uncertain and discussions of seizing control of the throne and cities other than London, murdering the King and Duke of York, along with a Scottish uprising, were implied. Archibald Campbell, 9th Earl of Argyll, had rather conveniently left London for the Netherlands before anyone could point an accusing finger at him.

Once the plot was leaked, it started a lengthy process of incriminated persons confessing, in the hope of clemency. And the list was long.

Treason held a penalty of death and there was no doubt about it any which way you looked at it. It had been the punishment since medieval times and it would continue to be the penalty for another couple of centuries to come. And Essex knew that for his part in the plot, he could expect the book to be thrown at him. It wouldn't be pretty and it would definitely be painful, which is probably why he slit his own throat while he was imprisoned in the Tower. Sidney and Russell were given the expected punishments and both were beheaded for high treason. Seven more were hanged, drawn and quartered, two more were simply hanged and a woman by the name of Elizabeth Gaunt was burnt at the stake. Of the other twenty or more, at least ten were imprisoned or fined and a further ten were lucky enough to have fled to the Netherlands before they were captured.

Monmouth, however, was given a certain degree of leniency, being Charles' son. He was sent into exile again to the court of William of Orange in Holland. He would leave behind his estranged wife and family and he would leave behind his mistress Lady Henrietta Wentworth living in Hertfordshire where Monmouth had been hiding while waiting to hear the verdict of his conspiracy. He had survived the beheading but he was far from happy about the conditions of his exile.

It was 1684 and a time in history aptly named The Long Frost. During December 1683 and February 1684, England was experiencing the coldest three-month period ever recorded. The Thames froze for almost two months and in Kent, the ground was frozen to a depth of three feet. Inside country homes, indoor temperatures were so cold that the water in ewers in bedchambers froze as well as milk in dairies and ink in inkwells. Across the country, snow glistened in the eerie stillness as water wheels remained still in the freezing sunlight and people huddled down in their beds by the light of a flickering candle.

Charles had already been sick several times with a supposed kidney condition and James, as Lord High Commissioner of Scotland living in Edinburgh, had returned on every occasion to visit his brother. Charles may have been called the 'Merry Monarch' but it seems he was a pretty miserable man towards the end of his life.

One of Charles' passions was alchemy and that passion led him to dabble in science, specifically attempting to turn the base metal mercury into gold. In later life, Charles spent long hours in his private laboratory in Whitehall where he ran experiments on Mercury by heating and distillation.

At the time, Mercury featured prominently in the manufacture of felt hats and up to 40% of hatters were afflicted with chronic mercury poisoning, displaying symptoms such as irritability, paranoia and strange behaviour.

Hence the phrase 'mad as a hatter'.

Experimental science was apparently popular among the aristocracy of 17th century and Charles was no different from many others. He used large amounts of mercury without knowing that there were safety precautions to be taken and as a result his health began to fail. He became distinctly depressed, peevish and irritable, glowering at people he once would have had a good laugh with and so unlike the 'Merry Monarch' the people knew and loved.

In the first few days of February 1685, Charles complained of feeling unwell and had no appetite for dinner although supposedly, it was his favourite – goose egg omelette. His attendants noticed that his speech was slurred and his thoughts disorganised. He cried out, staggered, then fainted. James was called again and remained by his side through the last days of his brother's life.

Charles had the best medical men at his disposal and each one applied their own personal remedies. Most used leeches to bleed him while some used hot irons applied to his head (although for the life of me I can't imagine what that was going to achieve). He was given quinine and finally salt extracted from human skulls was administered orally. Not surprisingly, nothing worked. A couple of days later, he had a convulsion and was bled again. He seemed to recover for a day or so but was found on the morning of Friday 6th February speechless. By noon he was dead.

The words used in 17th century are 'possible', 'doubtful' and 'uncertain' and most of them applied to Charles' illness. No one seemed to know what had actually happened to him. He had been complaining of pain around his kidneys and this could have been the beginning of kidney failure due to the colour of his urine. His grandfather, James I, had the exact same symptoms and he had suffered from porphyria.

What we know now is that due to exposure to mercury vapours, his blood would almost certainly have contained high amounts of urea. His pain would have been acute as the kidney damage increased, resulting in convulsions. The bloodletting would have been a temporary fix as it removed some of the circulating toxins but it would have been only a short-term treatment. In the end, no one knew the cause of his death. Because of this, and sadly for his brother James, many people were pointing their suspicious fingers at him.

At the time of Charles' death, Monmouth was living it up, dancing and enjoying life with another mistress in Holland, waiting to step back into the limelight in England at the right moment. The Earl of Argyll had already begun planning a rebellion in Scotland as early as 1684 using money donated by the Rye House exiles in Holland. Argyll had ordered 400 sets of armour, including breastplates, backplates and steel caps, from an Amsterdam armoury along with other equipment for mounted and foot soldiers and had concealed them as a purchase for the Venetian Republic. Even the government of Scotland seemed to be very aware of Argyll's plans. They took the precaution of appointing the Marquess of Atholl as Lord Lieutenant of Argyllshire and had ordered him to march there with a strong force where Argyll could count on his support when it was needed.

Monmouth spent two years in exile in William of Orange's court, but as soon as news arrived of his father's death, William showed Monmouth the door and sent messages back to James, his father-in-law, offering his support.

With no further prompting needed, Monmouth left The Hague for Scotland. The right time had finally arrived.

Monmouth must have been wearing his rose-coloured glasses when he thought that three ships would be enough to shift James off the throne. He may have been popular with the English people but the fact remained he was illegitimate and had no right to sit on the throne anyway. But then again, William the Conqueror had a shaky claim when he invaded and he had pulled it off. So had Henry Tudor. Both of them had wobbly claims so why shouldn't Monmouth give it a go too?

What he didn't know was that William of Orange also wanted the throne for himself and he had begun making plans of his own.

JAMES II

Born 1633
Reign 1685 – 1688

Although there was a slight resemblance between James and Charles, they could not have been more different. While Charles had been tall, James was more of medium height. Charles spoke fluently and eloquently with a natural, easy charm while James stuttered slightly and was more serious. James was also not so open about his scandalous liaisons with his mistresses like his elder brother. But while Charles had succeeded in winning everyone's affection without even trying, James tried hard but never quite succeeded.

When Oliver Cromwell died, James had been serving in the Spanish army and had been doubtful of his brother's chances of ever regaining the throne. He had been considering a Spanish offer to become an admiral in their navy when news came of Cromwell's death but he chose to support his brother instead and declined the position. The next year, Charles was proclaimed king and the Stuarts began their return trip to England.

Although James was the heir presumptive, it seemed highly unlikely that he would inherit the Crown since Charles was still a young man more than capable and willing to father children. Following Charles' restoration, James was created Duke of Albany in Scotland adding to his title of Duke of York. And that's when James made his first mistake.

They'd only just returned to England. Charles had only just begun his vengeance by punishing the men who had signed his father's death warrant and James was still finding his way around the court. That was when Anne Hyde, the daughter of Charles' chief minister, Edward Hyde, chose to tell James that she was pregnant with his child. At that moment, everything changed.

James had met Anne when she was employed as his sister Mary's maid-of-honour in Holland. She was attractive and popular and had an eye for the men long before she met James. She'd already been in and out of love with Spencer Compton, a son of the Earl of Northampton and she'd quickly fallen in love with Henry Jermyn, who returned her feelings. But Anne dismissed Jermyn just as quickly as the others when she met James. Six months before Charles was restored to the English throne, James promised he would marry Anne and they sealed their love with many nights of passion.

When Anne arrived back in England, she was visibly pregnant and not wanting to create a scandal when he'd only just arrived, the couple were obliged to marry. The marriage took place one night between 11pm and 2am in the morning at her father's house in the Strand barely two months before she gave birth to their first child. The date? You guessed it: 3rd September.

It was a terrible start, to say the least, and unfortunately the child died soon after the birth. But despite the shaky beginning, James and Anne appeared to be in love, kissing and leaning against each other, considered improper behaviour from a man and his wife during the seventeenth century. Three further sons and four daughters were born over the years but sadly only two daughters would eventually survive: Mary and Anne.

Despite this, and very like his brother Charles, James proved to be a philanderer with younger mistresses, one of whom was Arbella Churchill.

Arbella was the child of Sir Winston Churchill, an ancestor of the Prime Minister of the same name, and her brother, the first Duke of Marlborough, would soon step into the limelight later on in history. The Churchill's loyalty to the royal household was beyond reproach and their only feeling about Arbella's seduction by James *"seems to have been a joyful surprise that so plain a girl had attained such high preferment."* Arbella became the duchess's lady-in-waiting and gave birth to two children during Anne's lifetime and two afterwards, and was often described as *"a tall creature, pale-faced, and nothing but skin and bone."*

James' time in France and Spain had exposed him to Catholicism and he had secretly been drawn to the faith, as was his wife Anne. Obviously it was not something that he could be open about considering the only reason he was back in England at all was because of Charles' assurance that he, and his family, would uphold Protestantism.

Although his two surviving daughters became staunch Protestants, James and his wife had secretly begun practicing their new faith and although they were never obvious about it, something must have given Parliament reason to doubt their sincerity. Suspicious rumours had begun to circulate that James was a closet Catholic but when he and his wife refused to receive the Eucharist in the Church of England, the suspicions became a reality and England knew for certain. James couldn't hide it anymore. That was his second big mistake.

When his wife Anne died of breast cancer in 1671, it was not surprising that he would remarry. James was after all, only 38 years old and he still needed a male heir. But what he did was unthinkable to the nation and to his position. He married a 15-year-old Italian girl who was 25 years younger than him. And she was a Catholic. His third huge mistake.

To England, her age had nothing to do with their anger. If she had been a Protestant, England would have been over the moon with joy and they would have opened their arms wide to her. She was young and presumably fertile and the possibility of producing many heirs was welcomed. The fact that she was a Catholic was their main gripe and a hysteria of accusations followed. She was an agent of a Popish plot. She had bewitched him. James would force Catholicism on England. Through it all, James remained stoic.

As Parliament watched in consternation, Mary did indeed prove to be very fertile. Within two years, she had delivered two girls, then a son who died one month later. Within three years, there would be another two more girls. With four lively girls in the nursery, it seemed only a matter of time before a new Catholic heir would be born.

James had been aware of his brother's ill health for quite some time but no one seemed to know what actually was wrong with him. Charles had the best medical men at his disposal and each one applied their own personal remedies. Leeches, hot irons applied to his head, even bloodletting was tried. Nothing worked. Finally, on the morning of Friday 6th February, he had a convulsion and was bled yet again. By noon, he was dead.

After his brother's death, James ascended the throne with the announcement that he would not be vindictive or arbitrary. He stated he would be fair and he would not push Catholicism on the country and his first Parliament grudgingly trusted him enough to give him a revenue of nearly £2 million a year. In return, James told them he would make no changes to the ministry. Everything looked rosy.

Then four months later, in the early days of July, a mysterious ship appeared off the coast of Dorset. Aboard was the young ambitious Duke of Monmouth ready to take on his uncle and remove him from the throne. With him was a small arsenal of weapons, 82 companions and in his pocket was £230. With this small amount of assets to his name, he was very aware that if he had any chance of winning, he needed the people of England to rise up and join him.

His landing at Lyme Regis had been chosen carefully and when he stepped ashore, most of the 3,000 residents cheered. He stepped off the boat and like many usurpers before him; he kissed the ground before marching joyously into the town centre with a banner that read 'Fear nothing but God'. Inside those pretty country cottages, a blood lust was brewing against the hated Catholic king.

It only took three days for the locals to flock to him, more than ready to join his army and fight. The 82 men soon grew to 1500. Rebel leaders were chosen and volunteers were given whatever handy farm tools had been lying around their farms at the time to use as a weapon, while basic training was devised to help them transform into a credible army.

Despite their enthusiasm, what Monmouth would find was that these men were just inexperienced local farmers preparing to stand up and fight as their ancestors had fought before them. It was all very romantic but most of them would have had a fair idea that they would probably die on the battlefield. What they were hoping for was that their pitchforks and scythes would do a lot of damage before they died because soldiers still took 25 seconds to reload their muskets once they'd been discharged. You didn't have to reload a pitchfork and that was their presumed advantage.

James was in the first glow of a successful Parliament when a messenger arrived at full gallop at Whitehall with news that Monmouth had entered the harbour and he was proclaiming James was a usurper who had murdered his brother in order to get to the throne. The messenger handed James a letter stating that in just one day, 1500 people had signed up to join his army and he had been sent by Monmouth to inform James that he was to stand down. Immediately.

James was astounded. The accusation that he had killed Charles for the throne was astonishing. He knew that Monmouth had always felt that he had been robbed of his inheritance, even though he had been given titles and land, but the fact remained: he was illegitimate and that had always been the reason why he had been overlooked.

What worried James more than anything was that he had no army at all to speak of, except for two paltry infantry regiments. With 1500 angry men marching towards him, things were looking pretty grim. He quickly passed an Act of Attainder convicting Monmouth of high treason and a reward of £5000 was offered for his capture – dead or alive.

For a while it was touch and go as Parliament considered what they would do. As with most instances in history, the fight was over religion so the appeal of having Monmouth on the throne was uppermost in everyone's minds. Monmouth *was* a Protestant after all whereas James was a Catholic and because of that, most of James' subjects wanted to simply sit back and wait for Monmouth to do the job for them without them having to lift a finger. It would save them a lot of time and trouble, not to mention money. Then, sanity prevailed and Parliament reluctantly decided to stand by him as Charles II had stipulated. As the militia was being rounded up and marched north, Monmouth marched resolutely south, declaring himself the rightful king at various places en-route.

The numbers on both sides were incredible. By then, Monmouth's army had swollen to around 7,000 passionate men following behind him. As for James, he had the backing of the Grenadier Guards, The Second Regiment of Guards, five companies of the Queen Consort Regiments, the Horse and Foot Brigade, the Royal Cavalry, The Kings Regiment of Horse and thousands of troops from royal supporters and earls. And as promised, his son-in-law William of Orange sent three regiments of infantry to help as well.

William even offered to come in person to command them, an offer graciously refused by James.

To say William had an ulterior motive goes without saying. On one hand, if James lost, there would be a young, arrogant, Protestant king on the throne who would be easy to remove at a later date. The fact that Monmouth was illegitimate was beside the point. William the Conqueror's claim to fame was that he was the illegitimate son of the Duke of Normandy whose sister was married to the King of England. You can't get much iffier than that.

But if Monmouth lost, William planned to take the throne from James anyway. England *did* owe him money after all and he had the rabbit in the hat with his Protestant wife, James' eldest daughter Mary, by his side. Either way, he came out a winner.

With his mind fixed on the big prize, William settled back patiently and waited.

As Monmouth's army resolutely marched south, dark thunderclouds started to mass in the sky above them. Soon the first drops of rain began to fall and by the time the army had reached Somerset, the heavens had opened up and it was bucketing down. The men who had been filled with confidence only hours before were soon a miserable dripping group, up to their ankles in mud and soaked through by the downpour. Feeling more miserable as the days progressed, they continued for three more weeks until 6th July.

James and Monmouth's armies finally met near Bridgwater in Somerset. But by then, Monmouth's men were thoroughly exhausted and thousands had already deserted him. Along the way, their patriotism had dwindled and the enormity of what they were about to do suddenly hit them.

Perhaps they'd had a glimpse of the future because this last battle of the Monmouth Rebellion, named the Battle of Sedgemoor, was the climax of one of the bloodiest events in English history as the beautiful Somerset countryside was soaked with the blood of thousands of men.

From Monmouth's lookout in the town, he saw the army approaching late in the afternoon as the sun began to set. It was probably then that he decided to attack James' weary soldiers in the dead of the night as they slept. Monmouth was hoping for one main advantage: surprise.

But at 10pm, about a mile from the English army, the eerie silence was broken by a single gunshot that had been fired accidentally by one of the rebels as they crept forward. In the time it took for James' army to realise what was happening, Monmouth had lost the only advantage he had.

On either side of a ditch, the vicious battle began. When the early light of dawn finally arrived, they were still fighting and Monmouth had run out of ammunition. By the time the royal cavalry crossed the ditch and attacked, there was only one direction for Monmouth's army to run: backwards.

Needless to say, Monmouth's men were slaughtered but it would be the day after the battle that the real slaughter took place. Hiding in trees, ditches and hedges, the rebels were cut down as they ran for their lives. In the end, 1500 rebels were dead as opposed to only 50 of the James' men.

When news came of the victory, James sent supporters out to Bridgwater to bring Monmouth back to London. He had plans for Monmouth and he could barely wait to see the young man he'd been fighting with for ten years standing crushed before him.

James waited for days. Still his men had not returned with Monmouth. When they finally arrived empty handed, it was with news that Monmouth had escaped the battlefield, disguised as a peasant hoping to hightail it to the nearest port and escape back to the continent. James desperately sent every available man out to scour the southeast looking for him and two days later, only a couple of hours from reaching the coast, Monmouth was arrested, lying asleep in a ditch.

For weeks, James had been anticipating the moment when Monmouth was finally brought before him. He lived and relived the moment in his head, memorising what he would say and predicting Monmouth's total submission. By the time he was told Monmouth was in the castle, he could barely contain himself. But when he finally set sight on the young man, he couldn't believe his eyes. Standing in front of him, beaten and humiliated, was someone he barely recognised. Only a couple of years before when Charles had banished him to The Hague, Monmouth had been a dapper young man full of life and vitality with the world at his feet. The man standing before him was thin, unshaven and shabbily dressed, begging and sobbing for mercy. James had to look hard beneath the filth to see the face of his frightened nephew.

Perhaps most of us would have remembered the child, not the adult. We would have remembered the laughter and the playful romps of a tiny boy without a care in the world. We would have perhaps even remembered how much he had been loved as a cherished little boy and how brave he had been in battle when he grew to manhood. Perhaps being the romantic underdog or even being a self-sabotaging, handsome young man would have had something to do with our emotions and again, perhaps, we would have been lenient.

James was not that person. He resolutely sent Monmouth to the Tower of London and on that day, his fate was sealed.

Given the circumstances, Monmouth was not given access to defence, nor did he offer one. He was charged and convicted of high treason and sentenced to death by beheading.

It was all done in somewhat of a rush. From capture to death, barely five days had passed. The night before his execution, Monmouth would have heard the crowds gathering beyond the tower walls and he would have known what was happening. The execution of a royal duke was a massive event. People would be getting up early to get a good seat on the wooden stands and with food and drinks available, it had the makings of being a great family day outing.

As expected, an immense crowd had gathered on Tower Hill to witness the execution. At ten o'clock in the morning, Monmouth arrived accompanied by two bishops. He was heavily guarded by soldiers carrying pistols and they all ascended the scaffold with him, which was already decked out in black for mourning. Jack Ketch, the king's executioner was waiting and Monmouth's last words to him are well known.

As Monmouth knew, Jack Ketch was not a man noted for his expertise. There were few experienced executioners available at such short notice and with that inexperience; chances were something would go wrong. The axes were heavy and as the blade was brought down, it could twist and instead of slicing, it would crush its way through the sinews and muscles of the neck.

On presenting Ketch with six guineas, Monmouth said he didn't want to be butchered as badly as the late Lord Russell, who received multiple blows from Ketch before being killed. Ketch would receive six more guineas from his servants, Monmouth told him, if he performed his service well. After being undressed, he asked to test the axe blade and was concerned that it was *"not sharp enough"*. Ketch contradicted this criticism.

As Monmouth laid his head on the block, Ketch stepped forward and the crowd cheered. The first chop was off target and only caused a flesh wound, causing Monmouth to rise up and turn. Two more strokes were then delivered just as ineffectively. As the boos of the crowd were heard, Ketch tried twice more. When those failed, he brought out his hunting knife to sever the last remaining sinews that were still connecting Monmouth's head to his body.

Ketch left the scaffold surrounded by guards to prevent the crowd from tearing him to pieces.

Days later, when it was realised that no official portrait existed of the Duke, James exhumed Monmouth's body. He had his head stitched back on to his body and he was propped up for the portrait to be painted.

While Monmouth was being painted, his men were being hunted down and made to pay for their part in the rebellion with their own blood. They would have had some idea of how barbaric that punishment would be. Beheading was supposed to be a quick and painless death, a privilege only for the nobility, but for most of the rebels, they had something much worse waiting for them. They would be locked up in makeshift prisons awaiting hanging in the trees outside and their dangling bodies would be left to rot as the flies swarmed around them, showing that rebellion just wasn't worth it.

James' revenge was methodical and meticulous. It took nine days to sentence 1400 men, with 514 sentenced in one day alone. In the end, 330 were executed and another 849 were transported to Barbados. What happened to them when they got there was of no interest to James. Getting rid of the rebels had been his prime concern.

In the end, the punishments rivalled anything the Tudors had ever done and in just four weeks, England had lost the best part of a generation.

It was a colossal mistake on James' part to execute Monmouth. He would have been much better off to show leniency by simply keeping him locked away in the Tower indefinitely. The result of Monmouth's death was that the Whigs gained strength and popularity and ultimately, it was the Whigs who were responsible for overthrowing James later on. He'd proven he was a bully and he should have understood that Englishmen would not tolerate such arrogance. Especially after Cromwell.

So instead of things settling down for James, things heated up.

Flush with success, James walked into a meeting in the House of Lords and informed the members that instead of disbanding his army, he would be keeping it operational.

Warning bells must have been clanging madly in their heads. Not only was keeping an army active an expense they could not afford, but it was against every tradition they held. You just did *not* keep an army active during peacetime – unless you had an ulterior motive in mind, that is. The thought had barely taken shape when James told them he would be making his Catholic friend Richard Talbot the Lord Deputy in Ireland and his viceroy.

That's when they knew they were in trouble.

There were certain things concerning James that had never sat well with Parliament. One, of course, was that he was a Catholic. Placing so much power in Catholic hands was not just unwelcome: it was downright risky. Going back on his word and appointing a Catholic to such a high position in Ireland was another worry and it was beyond forgiveness. They were also well aware that his recent viceroy appointment would strengthen the Irish army adding support to the already large one James had. Catholic loyalty to James in Ireland would be unquestionable and it would be easy to find new recruits in Ireland.

It was everything and more that they had feared when they had given him the army in the first place.

By now, James was on a roll and nothing was going to stand in his way, much less a bunch of pompous nobles who thought he would do what they told him to do. Their objections fell on deaf ears and arguments became more heated until James did what every member of his family had done before him. He dissolved Parliament.

In hindsight, this was probably the worst thing he could have done. English people still had memories of the days when Charles I had done exactly the same thing after he couldn't get his own way. Cromwell had stepped into the picture and had ruled with an iron hand and things had gone from bad to worse. They had seen Charles II dissolve Parliament on many occasions but they had grudgingly forgiven him because life had become a bit more tolerable after the Cromwell debacle. But this was something else entirely. This was unforgivable. Their worst nightmare was becoming a reality as Catholic after Catholic stepped into prominent positions of power. Even James' most faithful supporter, his dead wife's brother Laurence Hyde, Earl of Rochester, turned against him.

Parliamentary ministers sent heated letters to James and he sent equally heated ones back to them. Backwards and forwards the letters continued until James finally put his foot down and declared that the Protestant religion was false and he would not promise to support them in any way. To prove his point, he went on a rampage of promotions, replacing Protestant office-holders at court with his own Catholic favourites. By May 1686, he was in full swing and had begun to dismiss judges in the Common law courts who disagreed with him as well.

Things seemed like they couldn't get any worse for England. When James' Italian wife gave birth to a healthy baby boy two years later, they knew their nightmare was only just beginning. Where James' only two possible successors had been his two Protestant daughters, Mary and Anne from his first marriage, this new birth opened up the possibility of a permanent Catholic dynasty.

It was the final straw. They wanted James out and the most likely candidate was James' eldest daughter Mary, married to William of Orange. In their minds, Parliament could see James aligning himself with Louis XIV in France in a 'holy league' to destroy Protestantism and as the idea took root, it grew at an amazing rate. While James revelled in the birth of his son, seven nobles, later known as the 'Immortal Seven', were on their way to Holland to invite William to invade.

It was all working out exactly as William had planned.

Parliament didn't have to ask him twice. Unbeknownst to the English, William had already begun assembling an army. It was perfect timing really. France was occupied with campaigns in both Germany and Italy, which meant it would be impossible for Louis to drop everything and rush to James' aid and with nobody available to try and stop him, William fully intended to take advantage of the situation. They actually hadn't needed to ask him at all.

By November, James finally realised what was happening but by then it was way too late. As expected, his first thought was to ask his cousin Louis for help but Louis was already overextended with problems of his own in Germany. As James received the refusal for help from Louis, William was already landing in Brixham, in southeast England, with an army of 11,000 foot soldiers and 4,000 cavalry.

In reality, James' army should have been adequate to keep the invaders out. He had the numbers and he had the advantage of the home ground. What he didn't have was support from his most trusted officers. As William stepped off his ship '*Brill*', officer after officer left James' side and defected to William. When Lord Churchill left as well, declaring support for William, followed by James' own daughter Anne, he lost his nerve and fled, throwing the 'Great Seal' of London in the Thames on his way out of the country.

It was a feeble attempt at escape and within days he was caught by local fisherman and returned to London. Fortunately for James, William had no desire to make a martyr of his father-in-law. He had what he wanted. Two days before Christmas, William allowed James to escape the country and of course, he went straight to Louis in France.

The jury is still out on James. Was he an egotistical bigot and a tyrant who rode roughshod over the will of the vast majority of his subjects? Was he simply naïve? Was he perhaps just plain stupid? Perhaps he was only doing what he thought was best and he was actually an intelligent, clear-thinking strategically motivated monarch? After all, English taxes had remained low during James' reign, at only about 4% of the national income. This would suggest that he had no intention of modelling England after France, whose taxes were at least twice as high.

But no one will ever know the truth. What we do know is that as William and Mary settled themselves in, James was plotting his revenge. He wasn't finished yet. Not by a long shot.

WILLIAM AND MARY

1689–1702

Things were looking pretty good for William for a while.

Within a month after James fled, Parliament had declared that James' flight meant he had abdicated and the throne was vacant. It was good news for William since he had been the one asked to invade and remove James in the first place.

Feeling pretty buoyant that his patience had paid off and had been rewarded, he began to take stock of his resume. He would be the ruler of Holland as well as the King of England, Ireland and Scotland. He could retrieve the money owed to him by Charles II and he could put it back into his own personal treasury and reinforce his struggle against Louis XIV to contain French expansion. All in all, a good month's work. The world was his oyster.

The only thing that dampened his outlook was the absence of an heir. Mary had miscarried a child in the early days after their marriage but there had been no pregnancy since then. Not that that presented a problem to him at all. He fully believed there was still plenty of time for her to conceive.

After all, she was only 27 years old.

It was while he was taking stock of his new kingdom that his newfound confidence began to slowly dissipate. Parliament was beginning to make it increasingly obvious that it was *Mary* who was to be regarded as the queen, ranked first in the line of succession to the throne. She was James' eldest daughter and as such, it was *she* who was the next in line for the throne, not him. It was only then that it finally dawned on him that after everything he'd done, he was only going to be her consort. With that realisation, all of his dreams flew out the window.

William was a smart man. He knew that the only precedent for a joint monarchy in England dated back to the sixteenth century when Queen Mary I had married Philip of Spain. Philip had only remained king while Mary I lived and even then, restrictions were in place. William was also a proud man and he was not about to be pushed aside after all he had achieved so far. His dream was right there within his grasp and he was going to reach out and grab it. So when the majority of the Tory Lords proposed that Mary should be sole ruler, William threw a wobbler.

William hadn't ousted James from the throne simply to lose it to his own wife. For him, that was unimaginable. After all, Charles I was *his* grandfather as well and he wasn't about to let Parliament forget that little piece of information. He threatened to leave the country immediately and for a while it looked like he was truly intending to do just that. It was at that very moment that Mary intervened.

Mary was in a difficult situation. On one hand, there was her husband. Sure, he was a cold reserved man, but who could blame him? He had been deserted by his mother almost at birth and raised by old men. For most of his life he'd had no idea of what it was like to feel a woman's gentle touch and love. And after a rather shaky start – all right, downright *terrible* start – to their marriage (and what young girl wasn't scared of the unknown), she had grown to love him. On the other hand, there was her father whom she dearly loved but who was repeatedly sending her angry letters, berating and scolding her for the loyalty she showed to her husband instead of the father who had loved and raised her. She was torn between loyalty and concern for her husband and unbearable distress of the circumstances surrounding the deposition of her father. No matter what she did, someone would be hurt. And when it came down to the crunch, she didn't even *want* the throne. She'd *never* wanted it.

Then, like a lightning bolt, everything seemed clear to her. She didn't want the throne just for herself. It was William's just as surely as it was hers. He was the one who could make a difference and he was the one who had put everything aside for her. The least she could do was to repay him for his reliability and dependability. She would only rule if William was by her side as an equal.

The statement certainly had the desired effect on Parliament and they were more than a little stunned. William on the other hand was mollified and once Parliament realised that Mary would not change her mind, they reluctantly agreed to the joint rule. But it had been touch and go for William for two uncertain months.

For centuries, kings and queens had been set apart from the rest. They were almost god-like warriors. Traditionally, the birth of a son was cause for celebration and James had succeeded where so many of his predecessors had failed. He had produced a son. A royal *legitimate* heir. But while James revelled in the birth of his son, it was the trigger to his downfall.

Parliament had no doubt that James' child would undoubtedly be Catholic and Catholicism meant absolute rule, almost tyranny, as in the continent. And James hadn't helped things along with his autocratic manner. He'd acted as if he was semi-divine and he actually believed that God had appointed him. Parliament was determined to put a stop to all that sort of nonsense by showing the world that the Protestant religion had precedence over family and family loyalty. And they were going to keep William and Mary's feet planted firmly on the ground. Realising how close it had been, they decided they were going to make sure that William and Mary knew their place in things. Putting their heads together, they drew up a document designed to ensure that they could function without interference from any royal family. Ever. If William and Mary wanted the throne, they were to be made aware that there would be a few stipulations to go along with it.

This was the Golden Age of Parliament where debates were alive and passionate. On one side were the Whigs, standing enemies of the Stuart kings. The word 'Whigs' was a term applied to those who wanted to exclude James from the throne because of his religion and originally came from the Scots, meaning 'cattle driver'. On the other side were the Tories who believed in tradition and they were fiercely loyal to the British monarchy and gentry. Their name itself derived from the Irish word meaning 'outlaw'. And the two parties butted heads endlessly. But they agreed on one thing. Putting William and Mary in their place.

The 'Bill of Rights' Parliament handed William and Mary stated that no sovereign was allowed to interfere with elections or freedom of speech and Parliament was to be summoned frequently and not to be questioned outside of Parliament itself. No sovereign could suspend or dispense with laws passed by Parliament or impose taxes without Parliamentary consent and no sovereign could maintain a standing army in time of peace without Parliament's consent. Parliament could, however, declare war if everyone agreed. Parliament would control expenditure and the financial settlement given to William and Mary, deliberately making them dependent upon Parliament. Monarchs were forbidden to establish their own court or act as judges and they were forbidden to impose cruel and unusual punishments. More importantly, Catholics were absolutely excluded from becoming monarchs. This last, but very important item, effectively excluded James and his Catholic heirs from ever succeeding to the throne. As a final point, an oath was required to be sworn to maintain the Protestant religion before any coronation took place.

Parliament had thought of everything. No crises, as in the past, were going to recur, that was for sure. In no uncertain terms, Parliament was letting the couple know that they hadn't assumed the throne. They had been *given* the right to reign by Parliament and as such, they were to be held accountable for their actions by the people. They would be judged like never before.

They handed the document to William and Mary, if a little tremulously, then stood back and waited to see their reaction. To their utter astonishment, the Bill was signed without hesitation and history was made.

When William and Mary walked down Westminster Abbey to be crowned, a hush fell as people turned to gawk at their new king and queen. Mary walked with grace as if she was gliding on ice and despite wearing a tightly-bodiced dress; she stood erect and seemed unconcerned that she was towering over her husband.

Though Mary was a robust 5 foot 11 inches tall, William was considerably smaller and had always suffered from chronic ill health. He had been a small sickly child who suffered continuously from asthma and his entire life had been spent wearing a body brace to support his hunched back due to scoliosis. In England, his health deteriorated further and his doctors advised him to move out of the capital. Hampton Court seemed the most likely place so they moved into the countryside to set up home and began redecorating.

Over the next few years, the rambling Tudor palace was transformed into a palace much like their home in Holland. While they happily redecorated, James was putting the finishing touches to his invasion plans.

James wanted the throne back at any cost and the best way he saw to do that was to take control of Ireland before moving on to England. But standing in his way were the Protestants in Ulster, in particular Derry. He knew if he did not have control of Derry, he would never have control of Ireland and therefore England.

In Ireland itself, tension was mounting. James' friend, Richard Talbot, still holding the position of Viceroy in Ireland, knew that the Protestants in Ulster could not be trusted to support the Jacobites, a Latinised name given to James supporters. From the Protestant side of it, they saw Talbot as the one responsible for disrupting their power base. As for Talbot, he was determined that they would remain under Jacobite rule, whether they liked it or not.

Central to this disturbance was Derry, a strategic city full of supporters loyal to Scotland. Desperate to avoid trouble at all costs with the Scots, Talbot arranged for the military garrison to be replaced by a regiment of Scottish highlanders and clansmen, known as Redshanks. As Catholics, their loyalty to James was unquestionable.

Arguments raged throughout the city at the decision. The Protestants thought that once the Redshanks were in, they would never leave, even though the Anglican bishop urged them to be allowed to enter the city. They were, after all, James' soldiers and he was still their king. But the Presbyterian bishop thought otherwise. He stated that the gates to Derry should be locked immediately and they shouldn't waste any time dithering about it if they valued their lives. If they delayed, all would certainly be lost.

It was a critical moment. Eight or nine young men, acting on the impulse of the moment, ran to Ferry-Quay gate, drew their swords and raised the drawbridge. They seized the keys and locked the gate against the Redshanks when they were only 60 yards from the spot. They literally slammed the gate shut in their faces. Three or four others joined in and with no time to lose, the other gates were secured as well.

It was a major step to take and one that left no allowances for going back. They had taken matters into their own hands and had started a rebellion that was inviting the king's anger. Soon after, when the garrison at Enniskillen heard what had happened, they followed suit by shutting their gates against the Scots as well, knowing full well that their show of solidarity could bring the whole of the English army down on them.

In Dublin, Talbot was furious by the turn of events but in France James was simply stunned. It was all going terribly wrong. Ireland was a Catholic nation, just as he was a Catholic. This wasn't how it was supposed to be.

Knowing that word was probably on its way to William, and with time running out, the siege in Derry forced James to put his plan into action sooner than he had hoped.

It was not a complicated plan. All James hoped for was for the support of Catholics in Ireland. He also hoped that if he could hold out, he could use Ireland as a launch pad to take back Scotland and England. Then he would march on to London and seize his throne. And there was no time to waste. William and Mary were about to be crowned king and queen of England. But if worst came to worst and they actually pulled it off, James was determined that it would be the shortest reign in history, daughter or no daughter. But the fly in the ointment was the Ulster Protestants.

On the 12th March, James landed in Kinsale, along with several French generals and 6,000 of their men, ready to start his fight-back. Together, they would join another 5,000 loyal Catholics under Commander Richard Hamilton who was already on his way north to subdue Derry's rebels. What James didn't realise was that there were just as many Protestants in Ireland who supported William and they were already taking up arms and preparing to attack James and his supporters.

James advanced north, taking town after town, until he finally reached Ulster. By April, he was at the gates of Derry, hoping that his tremendous show of strength would force them to surrender. James had thought that the mere sight of his soldiers would shock and awe Derry into submission.

It never occurred to him that this might never happen.

What James didn't know was his commander, Richard Hamilton, had already spoken to the leaders in Derry and he had guaranteed that Jacobites would not approach the city.

It was inevitable that there would be confusion on James' part. Part of that confusion was that he had no idea that there had been any sort agreement made. When the guards saw James and his army standing outside the gates demanding entry, there was no doubt in their minds that it as an act of duplicity. Derry had been offered an agreement, and they had accepted, and yet here was the king himself breaking that very agreement.

Before James knew it, the guards on duty were firing at him and his troops. He had ridden straight into a storm of anger as the city prepared themselves to fight against him to the death.

Outside the walls, James was in no mood to hang around for the fight. Talbot had already sent word that 4,000 Dutch troops had arrived in Belfast to help William, which meant James was needed in Dublin. Leaving the French generals in charge until the additional 6,000 troops promised by Louis in France arrived to help, he left to make plans with Talbot. He gave the generals clear orders. Take Derry at any cost. He left before the smell of smoke reached his nostrils and women's screams filled the air.

You would think that 17,000 men would be invincible but from the very beginning, the lack of armament and the lack of discipline were evident. Cannonballs crashed into the rooves of houses and smashed into their walls but it was the Williamites who made the important strikes and in the chaos, two of James' French generals were killed.

But as bad as it was on the outside, inside the walls of Derry was worse. They were suffering from malnutrition and starvation, forced to eat rats, horseflesh and even their own dogs. It was a slow death for some in the bitter cold and due to the unavailability of fresh water; the streets ran with faeces and urine. Soon, disease was rampant.

It was an epic power struggle to decide, not only who would control England and Ireland, but also the balance of power in Europe and it shaped the course of our history to the present day. It was a remarkable 105 days where the people of Derry defied James and refused to surrender the city to his Catholic army. The words 'No surrender' are as meaningful today as they were when they were first shouted three centuries ago.

On 26th July, starving and rife with disease, the remaining citizens of Derry were just about to give in and begin negotiations when reinforcements from London arrived. At the 11th hour, Derry was saved.

What *they* hadn't known was that six weeks earlier, on 14th June, William had arrived in Ulster, pale and asthmatic, but ready for a fight. Although his face was lined with constant pain and fighting ill health, he had marched south at the same time that James was marching north from Dublin. As Derry was struggling to survive, the two armies had met on 1st July at the River Boyne, 30 miles north of Dublin on the outskirts of Drogheda.

No year in Irish history is better known than 1690 and no Irish battle is more famous than William III's victory over James II at the River Boyne.

It would be the last time in history that a king would fight on a battlefield.

On one side, there was James who had fought with his brother Charles in Europe and although he was prone to panicking under pressure and making rash decisions, that was 1658 and a lot had changed in 30 years. Still, he was a man in his late fifties and his best years as a military leader were behind him.

On the other side, there was 40-year-old William, a fragile man but a battle-hardened commander known for his reckless courage in countless campaigns who was yet to win a major battle. But William had one advantage over James. William had 36,000 strong, composed troops gathered from all over Europe and all of them were better trained and better equipped than James' 23,500 troops.

On the night before the battle, soldiers on both sides prepared themselves nervously for the day ahead. On the march down, both armies had taken whatever metal and lead they could find, mostly from churches along the way, and they were sitting by their campfires, melting it all down to make bullets for their muskets. After the lead had melted, they prepared cartridges with rolls of paper in which they poured gunpowder and then dropped the bullets on top. In battle, the soldiers would bite the top off the cartridges to release the bullet, literally biting the bullet.

As his men worked, William walked around his soldiers with his arm in a sling after a near miss earlier on in the day. He believed that his presence would encourage his men and he'd even bought with him a portable house so he could sleep among his men.

On the other side of the river, it was a different story. James sat alone in his tent, never showing his face.

The fight started in the early hours of dawn as the sky became a watercolour of pinks, reds and oranges but after four hours of fighting, neither side could say they were ahead. By noon, William decided he had to do something and the only possible option was for his army of Dutch and English cavalry to go down to the riverside and cross over to the south side, meeting the Jacobites head on. But in making that decision, he had chosen the most difficult place to cross where the banks were deep and muddy and for a frail king, getting across the river was going to be more than a little bit difficult.

Sure enough, his horse got stuck in the mud halfway across and as he tried to move his horse forward, he had an asthma attack. One of his men saw that he was in trouble and waded back across the river and threw William over his shoulder, carrying him to safety on the south bank. Behind him, 2,000 cavalrymen were still struggling to cross the river and face the Jacobites along the mile and a half stretch of mud.

By early afternoon, William's vast number of men were beginning to make progress. With the Jacobites heavily outnumbered and worn down by the relentless attacks, their only chance for survival was to make a stand on high ground. Ahead of them, they saw a church on top of a hill and they desperately ran towards it with the Williamites hot on their heels. But by doing that, they'd actually allowed themselves to be surrounded on three sides and by late afternoon, it was all over. They simply couldn't hold out any longer.

Throughout the battle, William fought bravely alongside his men. James however was nowhere to be seen. Instead, James had remained behind in a ravine where he could see the battle raging on the hill three miles away. When it was obvious that his wearying army could not possibly win, James sped down the road to Dublin ahead of his men.

He was unaware that his men had seen him running and they already knew he was miles ahead, having deserted them in a cowardly attempt to get himself to safety. Two days after his victory, William triumphantly marched into Dublin as James was making a speedy retreat back to Louis in France. His cowardly behaviour would earn James the title *Seamus an Chaca* or 'James the Shit'.

William was jubilant when he returned to London. He rode through the streets, waving happily and was greeted with cheers by people who had come out and lined the streets to see him. Even Parliament praised him. He had fulfilled his promise as a Protestant monarch to defend the country against Catholicism and in doing so, he had secured the throne for himself and his family.

But as successful as he was, he hadn't finished yet. Not by a long shot. There were still the Scots to deal with for their complicity in the Jacobite uprising in Ireland and there were many Highland clans who were still loyal, and as such, a possible threat to William, despite James' recent spineless behaviour at The Battle of Boyne. Many of them had sworn allegiance to James and William wasn't about to forget about it. What he wanted was for the clans to pledge alliance to *him*, and he didn't think it would be too hard considering the Derry debacle either. With that out of the way, he could continue his own war with Louis.

Knowing William's history for patience, it's not surprising he took his time in thinking long and hard about what to do. It took him a year to come up with a plan but by August 1691, he was ready to put the plan into action. He would offer the Highland clans a pardon for their part in the Jacobite rising, but only if they took an oath before a magistrate and agreed to pledge allegiance to him before New Year's Day. That date was four months away and it would give them plenty of time to take affirmative action. It was also a symbolic date for William representing the beginning of a new reign and the start of new era.

Of all the clans in Scotland, the clan Donald was a huge force in the Highland system and the MacDonalds of Glencoe were only a small segment. Glencoe had a rugged beauty and it had been their home since the early 14th century when they had supported Robert the Bruce. It was one of the most magnificent areas of natural wilderness in all of Britain with Loch Leven to the north and the vast empty spaces of Rannoch Moor to the south. Skirted on both sides by huge imposing mountains was the Glencoe pass.

Alasdair MacLain was not a man who could hide in a crowd. The head of the MacDonald clan was a huge man with flowing white hair, beard and a well-respected leader and very much old school. His clan were constantly involved in trouble with both the law and with neighbouring clans for consistently raiding, pillaging and cattle rustling. Unfortunately, they also had a dislike for the nearby Campbell clan. And the feeling was entirely mutual.

William's order came through with promises of money and land for the clans who signed the oath but by the time it was circulated publicly, the terms had changed and were much more threatening. The clans would sign the agreement or be punished with the utmost extremity of the law.

One of the problems for the clans was that many of them were already bound by an oath to James now back in France. James had promised to return to Britain to reclaim his throne and the Highlanders were not-so patiently waiting for him to fulfil that promise. James' delay put them in a difficult spot. While they *wanted* to wait for his return, and had promised to stand by him and fight with him and beside him when he *did* return, they had William's dire threat hanging over their heads if they didn't sign allegiance to him. If James didn't come back soon, their families' safety would be at risk. That meant signing the allegiance to William, like it or not. According to Williams's instructions, their lives depended on it.

They sent urgent word to James of their predicament, outlining the importance and speediness of his reply and informing him that the deadline was 1st January.

Weeks turned into months and still James dithered with a reply, convinced that he was close to returning. It wasn't until 12th December that it became apparent this wasn't going to happen before the deadline so reluctantly James sent orders back to Scotland releasing the clans from their oath. The problem was that due to his prolonged delay, his messenger only arrived back in the Highlands during dreadful winter conditions and with only three days before the deadline.

Cruel winter winds swept through Glencoe on 31st December as MacLain arrived at Fort William ready to sign the oath, fearful for his clan's safety. When he arrived, Colonel Hill told him that the oath had to be taken before a sheriff, which involved another 60-mile trek further on to Inverary.

And Inverary was the hometown of his enemies, the Campbells.

Colonel Hill knew about the friction between the Campbells and the MacDonalds, which is why he gave MacLain a letter of protection and a letter for the sheriff, Sir Colin Campbell, requesting that he receive MacLain's late oath since he had come to him within the allotted time. Hill assured MacLain that no action would be taken against him but he urged MacLain to make haste to Inverary in any case.

MacLain could have met the deadline had Campbell soldiers, commanded by Captain Drummond serving with the Earl of Argyll's regiment, not captured him along the way. They detained him for a full day and then finally sent him on to Inverary where he was held for several more days due to the absence of the sheriff, who was visiting his family across the waters of Loch Fyne. When Sir Colin returned, MacLain pleaded with him to accept the late oath. He gave him the letter from Colonel Hill and explained the reasons why he had been delayed. Reluctantly, the sheriff accepted the late oath.

But other forces were already in play as MacLain headed back to Glencoe, sure that his signed oath was on its way to London.

In Edinburgh, the Secretary of State, John Dalrymple and John Campbell, 1st Earl of Breadalbane and Holland, had other things in mind. John Campbell, a senior member of the Campbell clan, saw an opportunity for revenge for the decades of raids on Campbell lands and the tradition of sheep and cattle rustling by the MacDonalds. As such, he had a strong dislike for the MacDonalds and he'd already decided to decline the late-delivered oath. Together with his cousin, Archibald Campbell, 10th Earl of Argyll, they found a willing accomplice in John Dalrymple who had been disappointed in the fact that the clan leaders were taking the oath of allegiance at all. He was rather hoping they would have declined. Together, the three men sent an order to London for William to sign, stating that MacLain and his den of thieves had not signed within the allotted time and they should be punished severely.

I suppose we should give William some credit for not knowing the full circumstances surrounding the late oath. He had given a specific order and his commanders in Scotland had informed him that that order had not been carried out. They'd just omitted a small, rather important, part of the story but William didn't know that. As a result, he had to show that he meant what he said. If you make a threat, you had to carry through with it.

He signed the order and sent it to Sir Thomas Livingstone, commander of the forces in Scotland. With the order, he gave explicit instructions to John Dalrymple: the MacDonalds were to be slaughtered. From there, the order was sent to a Major Duncanson who then sent three of his commanders, two from the Campbell-dominated Argyll regiment and lastly, Colonel Hill from Fort William, with an infamous letter.

"You are hereby ordered *to fall upon the rebels, the McDonalds of Glenco, and put all to the sword under seventy. You are to have a special care that the old Fox and his sones doe upon no account escape your hands, you are to secure all the avenues that no men escape. This you are to putt in execution att fyve of the clock precisely; and by that time, or very shortly after it, I'll strive to be att you with a stronger party: if I doe not come to you att fyve, you are not to tarry for me, but to fall on. This is by the King's special command, for the good and safety of the Country, that these miscreants be cut off root and branch. See that this be putt in execution without feud or favour, else you may expect to be dealt with as one not true to King nor Government, nor a man fit to carry Commissione in the King's service. Expecting you will not faill in the full-filling hereof, as you love your selfe, I subscribe these with my hand att Balicholis Feb: 12, 1692. For their Majesties service. (signed) R. Duncanson."*

Unaware of what was happening in Edinburgh and London, the MacDonald clan were billeting 120 English soldiers hospitably in Glencoe. The soldiers were under the command of a Captain Robert Campbell of Glenlyon but most of the regiment was recruited from the Argyll estates and only a minority bore the Campbell name.

Captain Campbell was actually related by marriage to MacLain and so it was natural that he should be given special treatment and billeted in the old chief's house. Each morning for the past two weeks, Captain Campbell had visited the home of MacLain's youngest son, Alexander, who was married to Campbell's niece. This niece had a brother by the name of Rob Roy McGregor.

During the day on 12th February, the sky was a seething cauldron of clouds and a light dusting of snow had fallen, making all the paths cold and slippery. The feeble afternoon sun had only persisted occasionally through the thick dark clouds and in the winter light, there seemed to be no colours except grey, white and black. Captain Drummond arrived in Glencoe and due to his role in detaining MacLain and ensuring that he was late giving his oath, he would not have been welcomed at all. What they didn't know was he was bringing a letter from Major Duncanson bearing fateful instructions to give to Captain Campbell.

In his heart, Drummond must have known what he was about to do was wrong. He'd eaten their food and accepted their hospitality. He even spent the evening playing cards with them before retiring, wishing them a good night and accepting an invitation to dine with MacLain the following day. Still, he continued with his instructions.

By evening, a blizzard howled through Glencoe and snow blanketed the rugged landscape as the MacDonald clan slept restlessly. As they slept, the soldiers were preparing to carry out their instructions to systematically kill everyone they could.

In the early hours of 13th February, MacLain had woken from his fitful sleep to the sound of muffled cries. Before he could rise from his bed, he was killed along with thirty-eight others. Forty women and children managed to flee the massacre but they would soon be dead of exposure after their homes were set alight and burnt to the ground. A few survivors had managed to escape into the hills finding makeshift shelters but they would lose their lives as well in the relentless blizzard. Among the death was MacLain's elderly wife who died on the mountainside just outside of the town.

The survivors told stories of how a few of Captain Campbell's soldiers had alerted the families and given them time to rug up and escape. Two lieutenants had even broken their swords rather than carry out the orders. In addition to the soldiers who were actually in Glencoe that night, two other detachments, each with 400 men, were to have converged on the possible escape routes. But both were late in taking up their positions, and it was suggested that the lateness of the two other companies was not purely because of the snowstorm, but a ploy *not* to be involved in the atrocity. What they *did* know was that Colonel Hill from Fort William had brought the orders for the massacre.

An inquiry was held under the category 'murder under trust' but nothing would ever come of it. The King himself had signed the orders and he could not be held responsible. The conclusion of the enquiry was that William was to be exonerated and the blame placed firmly upon Secretary Dalrymple's shoulders. Not long after the enquiry, Dalrymple resigned his position but no other action was taken. A few years later, he was back on the Privy Council of Scotland and created 1st Earl of Stair by Queen Anne in 1703. Apparently all would be forgiven.

William did not wait for the verdict from the enquiry. Europe was waiting for him to deal with, more specifically France, and he left immediately.

While he was away fighting on the continent, Mary was left as regent during his long absences but it was not what she wanted at all. She had never felt confident and she was always scared of making a mistake. In the past, with every mistake, William had been angry with her, which made her make even more mistakes. Whenever he was in England, he constantly reminded her of her inadequacies as a barren wife, not to mention as a daughter who had utterly betrayed her own father. Mary would have preferred to be someone else living somewhere else. Her role was a task to be endured.

As she sat on the throne and waited for William to come back, she had tremendous difficulty dealing with the curses from her angry father who constantly sent her seething letters berating her for her role in the invasion. She had broken one of the Ten Commandments that stated she should respect her parents and she lived in fear of never being forgiven by God. It was a difficult situation for her and it put her under constant psychological stress as her husband and her father jockeyed for her loyalty.

Despite William's physical frailties and Mary's mental fragility, they were good monarchs together. Although it was with trepidation at the beginning, Mary proved to be a firm ruler while William was away, ordering the arrest of her own uncle (her mother's brother) Henry Hyde, 2nd Earl of Clarendon for plotting to restore her father to the throne. In January 1692, the influential John Churchill, who had been made Earl of Marlborough by William at the insistent requests of her sister-in-law Anne, was dismissed from his post on similar charges. The dismissal however diminished Mary's popularity somewhat and further harmed her relationship with her sister Anne, who was strongly influenced by

Churchill's wife, Sarah. By then, Anne had suffered quite a few miscarriages and Sarah had staunchly supported her through every last one of them.

The severe tension between the two sisters was the talk of England and Europe. Everyone watched and waited as Anne publicly defied Mary and appeared at court with Sarah by her side. Anne was making a deliberate stand and obviously supported the disgraced Churchills, which led to Mary angrily demanding that Anne dismiss Sarah and vacate her lodgings.

In April, there was a temporary truce as Mary fell ill with a fever and missed Sunday church service for the first time in twelve years. She was to recover but during her recovery, Anne delivered another stillborn child.

Mary's visit to Anne was meant to console her sister, perhaps even to offer an olive branch, but it turned into another spat as Mary picked up where she left off and chose the opportunity to once again berate Anne for her friendship with Sarah Churchill. She just couldn't help herself. After a visit that ended in the two sisters openly raging at each other, Mary left, never to see Anne again.

Throughout the years, William never lost his hatred of France, more specifically, Louis XIV. By then, Louis had become a remarkable monarch. With his guidance, France had changed drastically from its savage medieval ways to become a refined country. French culture had become one of the most appealing in the world and the world associated that greatness with Louis. In his lifetime, Louis never once doubted his divine right to be the king. Many had tried unsuccessfully to live up to his standards but most had failed. Even his army was incredible. His infantry and artillery in times of war added up to 400,000 men. Added to that, he had 220,000 cavalry and navy: an amazing total of around 620,00 loyal and devoted troops. No one could match it and William hated him for it.

Then in December 1694, England went into shock.

At 32, even though in good health, Mary contracted smallpox. Trying to prevent the further spread, she sent away anyone who had not previously had the disease. Her sister Anne, who was having continued difficulties of her own carrying children, was sent a letter telling her to stay well away, even though the sisters were still estranged and Anne had survived the disease when she was a child. By then, the sisters' strained relationship was over money and Anne had been of little or no comfort during William's long absences away on his campaigns. Still Mary did not want her sister to suffer yet another miscarriage because of her.

There was, of course, no sign of a cure for smallpox in those days. There was however a degree of understanding of the infection. It was generally well known that you did not touch the sick, you did not breath in close proximity of them and you certainly did not touch garments from anyone who had smallpox. Little help was offered by any treatments and most people knew that all you could do was to let it run its course.

It was the explorers who were spreading smallpox around the world, along with armies and migrants. England's population had roughly doubled between 1520 and 1680 with migrants roaming from town to town searching for work. London's population had risen by 60,000 in 1520, and by 1700, it had grown to 575,000 people. As London grew, new industries established themselves and merchants were travelling around the country carrying infections wherever they went.

For weeks, the concerned nation waited for news that Mary had overcome the dreaded disease. When the news came, it was not good. Mary had died at Kensington Palace and the nation began to grieve in earnest.

William was distraught. Their marriage had been arranged and had started off badly but over the years, Mary had fulfilled every responsibility as his dutiful wife and they had grown to love each other. William had come to rely immensely on his wife during his absences on the continent and he had no idea who he could rely on to fill her place.

War with France took a back seat to this new problem that England faced. The subject on everyone's mind now was the lack of an heir. For a long time there had been rumours that Mary had not conceived any children because William much preferred the company of men. It was noted that he had grown up in the company of men and gossip was rife regarding William's newest young protégé. This young man, a strikingly handsome man 20 years younger than William, had risen from a royal page to an earl in a remarkable, even suspicious, amount of time. William was seen constantly in his company but he was never seen in the company of women, which gave the rumours even more credibility.

Parliament however weren't too concerned that William would remarry and produce an heir. If he did remarry, any children would not be seen as the next heir to the throne anyway. Mary Stuart had been the monarch: she had just chosen to share the throne with her husband. So up until then, with no children from their marriage, it had been taken for granted that the heir apparent, after both William and Mary died, would be Anne followed by her only surviving child, Henry. What concerned them was one major detail. Would Anne's delicate, frail child be strong enough for the difficult job ahead of him?

Up until then, Anne had endured six pregnancies resulting in two miscarriages, two stillbirths but two surviving daughters. Then in 1687, both girls contracted smallpox and died within six days of each other. When everyone believed there would be no more children, she finally gave birth to a son two years later, a sickly boy, who was quickly baptised William Henry. After the death of his aunt Mary, it became evident that this rather delicate five-year-old would follow his mother to the throne as second in line.

With war still raging on their borders, by 1696, France found themselves in the grip of an economic crisis. But they weren't the only ones. England was being crippled by the huge expense of the war and Parliament was completely fed up with it all. Apart from financially ruining England, the death toll was incredible. You can see why Parliament were at their wits end to know how to finish it. And France was having the same thoughts. The only solution they could see was to sign a peace treaty.

Reluctantly, the Treaty of Rijswijk was put together and signed, giving both sides a semblance of victory even though reluctantly, Louis had to make a humiliating concession and recognise William as the King of England. Despite the treaty and despite this mortifying allowance from Louis, William would never consider Louis anything else but his lifelong enemy.

With the treaty signed, everything seemed to settle down for a while. That is, until 1700 when disaster once again shook the nation.

Anne's fragile son, William, had been cherished and coddled and at the first sign of any sniffle, doctors were called urgently to attend him. He was never allowed to play with other children in case of a stray germ contaminated him, making him quite a lonely child. Even so, with the extra care surrounding him, William celebrated his 11th birthday at Windsor Castle but had complained a little the next day of a sore throat. Within two days, he had a fever and was delirious. On 30th July, he died.

It wasn't just Anne and George who were devastated. Surprisingly,

William, a man who had been ridiculed for his coldness and his rudeness, and heaven knows he was probably not the easiest man to live with, was inconsolable at the death of his nephew and his anguish took England by surprise. In the back of his mind was the fact that there were no more heirs to his throne.

While the royal family mourned the child's death, England was reeling as well. With no heir from William and Mary, and Anne's last surviving child dead, James Stuart's name was thrown into the ring again as the person in the front of the long queue. The idea took root and grew at a frightening rate. In the minds of Parliament, they could see the Stuarts returning in droves and with them they would bring back Catholicism and destroy Protestantism. Almost with a shudder, the idea was scrapped immediately.

As Parliament went into overdrive, James had a stroke in France and died.

England seemed to be going from one disaster to another and while they'd already discarded James as the possible heir to the throne, his death left an even worse option. Waiting in France to take up his father's cause was James' son and Anne's half-brother, 13-year-old James Francis Edward Stuart. A young boy and yet another Catholic.

While England reeled over the loss of their frail heir, Spain was also suffering from the loss of their 39-year-old king, Charles II, who had become the King of Spain following the death of his father Philip IV in 1665.

At 35, Charles had been short, lame, epileptic and completely bald. His lower jaw had grown abnormally larger than the upper jaw resulting in an extended chin and the inability to chew. This trait, known colloquially as the 'Hapsburg jaw', was common to royal families where there had been acute inbreeding through royal intermarriages. To add to his problems, his tongue was so large that his speech could hardly be understood and he frequently drooled. After he had demanded at one point that the bodies of his family should be exhumed so he could look at their corpses, his mental health became a serious issue, as had many of his ancestors in the past.

As bad as his mental health was, his physical health was even worse. His autopsy report stated that his heart was the size of a peppercorn, his lungs corroded, his intestines rotten and gangrenous, his head was full of water and he had one testicle black as coal. Needless to say, he died childless. He was the last of the Hapsburgs and he had survived longer than anyone had ever expected.

Unlike the French throne, a female was permitted to inherit the Spanish throne so next in line, after Charles, were his two half-sisters, Marie Theresa and Margaret Theresa. The elder sister Maria had married Louis XIV of France in 1660 and had delivered a son she had named Louis, called 'the Dauphin'. However, Charles had passed the Dauphin over in his will and had named his 16-year-old grandnephew, Philip of Anjou, the Dauphin's son, as his successor.

All sorted, you would think, and all still absolutely acceptable to the French. And if it was just a simple matter of hereditary rights, then the heir presumptive should rightfully have been Philip of Anjou anyway, being the only remaining male. But one year after Maria had married Louis, her younger sister Margaret had married Leopold I of Austria who also thought *his* younger son should inherit the Spanish throne. Leopold announced that Maria had renounced her claim to succession to the Spanish throne in return for the payment of a dowry to the tune of half a million gold crowns when she married Louis. Therefore, Leopold argued, it was the children of *his* wife, the younger half-sister Margaret, who should be the next in line. He stated that *his* grandson Charles, Archduke of Austria, was by rights the new king of Spain, not Philip of Anjou.

Louis had never been shy about letting the world know what he was thinking and he wasn't about to start now. Louis entered the ring and stated that the dowry promised to Maria had never actually been paid and he demanded that Charles' last will and testament be honoured and his wife's renunciation of the throne be classed as invalid. If he chose, he threatened, he could willingly assert his will by force of arms.

Louis had thrown down the gauntlet and Leopold willing picked it up. And so the war began between the two cousins, Charles of Austria and Philip Duke of Anjou, and it was the spark that ignited the powder keg under England. Because of the hatred between William and Louis, France's growing strength made continued war inevitable and England became unwittingly involved in the War of the Spanish Succession that would continue for another 13 years.

England was still staggering from the shock of young William's death but the unanswered question now was, if Parliament were so strongly opposed to young James Francis Edward Stuart in France, who else was eligible? Princess Anne was the only eligible one left in line of succession established by the Bill of Rights, signed by William in 1689. That stated that there would be no more Catholic monarchs on the throne, and it was pretty evident that she would not be having any more children to carry on the Stuart dynasty. When suggestions began to surface regarding the restoration of James' line, Parliament became absolutely desperate to find a family member who was a Protestant to take over after Anne. And then, like a light shining down from heaven, they saw a solution. There *was* a relative. Sophia Electress of Hanover was the granddaughter of James I through his daughter Elizabeth and as such, she had Stuart blood running through her veins. And she was a Protestant. In their desperate attempt to find a Protestant heir, Parliament had overlooked up to fifty of Anne's other relatives, many who had a better claim to the throne than Sophia, on the grounds that they were Catholic. That, they stated, would have been absolutely unacceptable.

In something bordering on panic, they quickly passed an Act of Settlement stating that if Anne died without issue, Sophia would inherit the crown and with the Act duly signed by both Parliament and William, they breathed a sigh of relief. That relief would be short lived.

As usual in England, February is traditionally bitterly cold and that morning was no different than any other except the sun was shining gloriously. William, not willing to pass up an excuse to ride in the sunshine, took his horse out for a gallop. Suddenly, his horse stumbled in a molehill and he was thrown violently to the ground, instantly breaking his collarbone.

It could have been worse. He could have broken his neck or could have been paralysed but William's health had never been very good to start with so his injuries were cause for serious concern. His collarbone was set and he requested that he be taken to Kensington Palace, which was around 12 miles away.

The carriage ride was horrendous and the bone had to be reset when he arrived. Afterwards, he retired exhausted to bed. The next morning, he awoke feverish and over the next few days, his condition worsened. By the beginning of March, he was seriously ill with pneumonia and by 8th March, he was dead.

With very little fanfare, he was buried beside his wife Mary in Westminster Abbey as Anne stepped up to the throne.

Anne had never liked her brother-in-law. She had even called him 'the Dutch abortion' on a few occasions. So when William died, she was quietly delighted. She had outlived her uncle Charles, her father James, her son Henry, her sister Mary and her sister's husband William. She had outlived everyone. Overnight, Anne, aged 37 and childless, had become Queen of England.

Parliament's decision to pass the Act of Settlement barely one year before William's death had proved to be timely indeed.

ANNE

Born 1665
Reign 1702 – 1714

When it comes to tragic lives, Queen Anne undoubtedly wins the competition hands down, mainly due to her horrific gynaecological record. In sixteen years, she had seventeen pregnancies: twelve were either miscarried or stillborn, having died weeks before in her womb. Of all her children, only one survived to 11 years of age before he died as well. There was nothing more heart-breaking than seeing Anne and her husband mourning together over a tiny empty cot. Sometimes they would weep uncontrollably together. Other times they would just sit in silence, staring at nothing. It was unimaginably awful.

By the time Anne came to the throne, she was sick with grief after losing so many children and she took the throne knowing she was the last of her line.

No one had ever called Anne glamorous. She had very poor vision, she was not highly intelligent, and she suffered from polyarthritis, blotchy skin and gout. From birth, she was plagued with numerous health problems and no one had ever really expected her to live to adulthood. In any case, England was not too concerned. She was the second of James' two daughters and her uncle, Charles II, seemed more than willing to produce a large family, if you know what I mean. Anne was so far down the line, she was almost forgotten.

You'd think that being a royal would mean that your mortality rate would be considerably lower than most, but that doesn't seem to be the case at all. Anne grew up in a world full of controversy and death. In 1669, at only 4 years old, she was sent to France for some medical treatment where she lived with her paternal grandmother Queen Henrietta Maria at a chateau outside of Paris. Within a year, her grandmother was dead and she was hurriedly sent to live with her aunt, Henrietta Duchess of Orleans, who had been married for ten years to Louis XIV's younger brother Philippe.

Henrietta had been having problems with her own health at this stage. For two years, she had been complaining of an intermittent, intense pain in her side and shortly before Anne arrived, the pain had progressed and she was having digestive problems so severe, she could only drink milk. Then one morning late in June, she drank a glass of chicory water to relieve the colic and immediately, she felt the all-familiar pain in her side again and days later, she was dead.

With the sudden death of her aunt, 4-year-old Anne was hurriedly rushed back to the family home in England. In two years, Anne had lost two close family members and had already lived in four different homes.

But there were even more changes for her in the future.

In the space of seven years, Anne's mother had delivered six children but she had been ill for around fifteen months after the birth of her youngest son Edgar. By then, she had already lost two small boys within a month of each other just before Edgar's birth, and at a time when Anne would have been a lively 4-year-old, Anne's mother was heavily pregnant again, which is perhaps part of the reason why Anne was sent to live with relatives in France in the first place. Her elder sister Mary was 7 years old and could look after herself in a fashion with the help of a nanny but we all know how much attention a 4-year-old toddler requires. To make matters worse, Anne and her mother were both suffering from ill health, so with a sickly baby to look after and another child on the way, Anne's mother would never have been able to cope.

While Anne was away on the continent, her mother delivered a daughter she named Henrietta and by the time Anne returned home, her mother was heavily pregnant yet again. But within months of Anne's return, Henrietta was dead as well. You'd think that things could not get any worse but one month after giving birth to her last child Catherine, yet another sickly daughter, Anne's mother was diagnosed with breast cancer. After receiving the diagnosis, she simply gave up.

There didn't seem a time in Anne's short life when someone wasn't dying. In the space of nine months, Anne's mother died, her young brother Edgar died and in December of the same year, her youngest baby sister Catherine died as well. Of her seven brothers and sisters, the only sibling left was her elder sister Mary.

Her world at 6 years old must have been so full of confusion and death. On top of everything else that had happened in her short life, she and Mary were only one year away from being sent to live at Richmond in the care of Colonel Edward Villiers and his wife Frances. After their mother's death, they would be separated from their father who was starting a new chapter in his life by marrying an Italian princess only seven years older than Anne herself. On the bright side however, she was also only one year away from meeting the charismatic Sarah Jennings. Not too far in the future, Sarah Jennings would become Sarah Churchill after marrying John Churchill, a promising young officer in the English army and the brother of her father's former mistress, and she would be destined to become Anne's closest friend and advisor for most of Anne's reign, although somewhat controversially.

The next few years were even more monumental for Anne. Life seemed to settle down at the home of the Villiers for a short while although there was a rather wobbly health scare for her at the age of 12 when she contracted smallpox. With her health always fragile, and so many robust people succumbing to the disease, no one really expected her to live through the illness. To their utmost astonishment, she did.

Almost at the same time as she was recuperating, her sister Mary was betrothed, then quickly married off to William of Orange, leaving England soon after to begin her new life in Holland. A year later, Frances Villiers contracted smallpox and was dead as well.

To have had so many changes in her young life must have left the 14-year-old almost numb with shock. Her mother, grandmother and aunt were all dead and her father had little to do with her. She had lost all but one of her siblings and that one had left the country to live with her new husband in Europe. Even her guardian had died. She was utterly alone.

To all intents and purposes, Anne must have been a lost little girl, isolated and alone. It helps to explain why Sarah Jennings was able to step in and cement their relationship with such ease in a world full of upheaval and it's easy to understand why Anne clung desperately to the one constant in her life.

At 15, Anne was still unbetrothed and her uncle Charles II had begun looking for an eligible match who would be welcomed by his Catholic ally, Louis XIV of France. Her sister Mary had been living in Holland for six years by this time and even though both William and Louis hated each other with a passion, Louis was keen on an Anglo-Danish alliance to help contain the growing power the Dutch seemed to be amassing. Prince George of Denmark, the younger brother of King Christian V, seemed the ideal match to appease Louis and Anne's uncle on her mother's side, Laurence Hyde Earl of Rochester, made the negotiations while Anne's father James eagerly consented. It was the ideal solution to diminish William of Orange's influence.

William's enemies seemed to be gathering together under his very nose and there was very little he could do about it. So naturally, when the betrothal was announced, William was very concerned. But despite this, or perhaps *because* of it, the marriage went ahead in July 1683 and Anne moved to her new residence at the Palace of Whitehall. With her, she took her best friend Sarah Churchill.

Although an arranged marriage, both Anne and George seemed devoted to each other and England breathed a sigh of relief. Within a couple of months, Anne fell pregnant and England celebrated joyously with the news. But the revelries did not go on for very long: Anne miscarried soon after the announcement and sadly for her, it would be the first of many.

Year after year, pregnancy after pregnancy, miscarriage after miscarriage, Anne began to lean more heavily on Sarah for support and companionship. When babies died, Sarah was the one by her side comforting her. When Anne's uncle Charles died and her father James became king, it was Sarah who fully understood the implications.

The year 1687 was particularly devastating for Anne. In January, she suffered a miscarriage and barely two weeks later in the first two weeks of

February, her only two surviving children, Mary and Anna Sophia aged two and one, died of smallpox within six days of each other. In October the same year, Anne delivered a stillborn son when she was seven and a half months pregnant and in April of the following year, she miscarried yet again. Through all of it, Anne became more dependent and emotionally fragile and Sarah seemed to be Anne's most loyal companion. As for the smart, young, ambitious Sarah, it was the perfect arrangement.

The House of Stuart desperately needed an heir for its survival and England was beginning to feel nervous. That nervousness escalated when James and her stepmother finally produced a son in 1688 and a Catholic succession seemed more than likely. That is, until Parliament stepped in and invited her brother-in-law, William of Orange, to invade and the Glorious Revolution began.

On the advice of Sarah and John Churchill, Anne refused to side with her father after William landed in England on 23rd November 1688. She even sent a letter to William offering him her support and the next day, Churchill withdrew his support from James. Prince George followed the same night.

At a time when James' head must have been spinning from the number of changes in his life, it seems surprising that he took the time to single out his youngest daughter for punishment. After all, his young wife had just delivered the long sort-after heir. But James had to take his anger and frustration out on someone and his daughters became the recipients of his rage. Parliament was constantly berating him concerning both his religion and his overspending, and his son-in-law William had done the unthinkable and taken up Parliament's offer and invaded England to overthrow him. Despite having sent endless angry letters to Mary, it seemed she even condoned her husband's invasion.

So to say James was angry at Anne's lack of loyalty as well is an understatement. He was livid and he took his anger out on her by issuing orders to have both her and Sarah put under arrest at St James Palace.

With grim visions in their minds of years spent cowering in the forbidding Tower of London, Anne and Sarah panicked. They fled Whitehall by a back staircase and in the nick of time made it to Bishop Compton's house. It would be two weeks before Anne was reunited with her husband in Oxford and it was only when she returned to London a week later that she heard that her father had fled to France and William had taken over. As if nothing had happened at all, Anne simply resumed her life, almost callously and disinterestedly.

I'd like to do a little sidestep here for just a short time and talk about Anne's reaction. We know she suffered tremendous losses in her life and they would surely have had a major impact on her personality. As such, we can almost understand that she was unable to show a certain level of emotion at her father's departure considering he was just the last in a long line of people who had deserted her. It could even be said that her mother had deserted her in a fashion because she had simply 'given up' after being diagnosed with breast cancer at a time when Anne would have needed her most.

Psychologists today say that most girls are the product of their mother's love, either aloof or smothering. But what if the child had never experienced that love at all? What if that same child had never experienced a structure of stability, shelter or nurturing? Could a tiny child, who'd never experienced that unconditional love, be expected to evolve emotionally when the very components of that love had never been a part of her life at all? And let's not forget that it wasn't her father who had sat by her bed, miscarriage after miscarriage. He'd been distracted by his new family and there was never a time when Anne had felt close to him anyway. It was her friend Sarah Churchill who had comforted and consoled her. And it was Sarah and her husband who had whispered that perhaps James was just not the right person for the job. He was, after all, a Catholic and everyone knew what *they* were capable of. So perhaps we can forgive Anne for listening to the one person in her life who had remained steadfastly by her side. Her rock and her only friend. The one who she could not even bear to consider losing. Sarah Churchill.

Sorry... back to William.

For their devotion, Anne beseeched William to give the honour of Earl of Marlborough to John Churchill and both William and Mary agreed. Then Anne asked that her husband should be made Duke of Cumberland and they agreed to that as well. Anne should have stopped there. Instead, she went one step too far and requested the use of Richmond Palace plus a considerable parliamentary allowance to boot. It would mean that Anne would be financially independent and *that* William and Mary would never consider. They flatly refused and it marked the beginning of a fight between the sisters that would last for years.

While Anne bickered endlessly with her sister, it seemed she could not get along without Sarah. When Sarah was absent from court attending to her own family, they would send letters to each other using playful pseudonyms. Anne would sign her letters 'Mrs Morley' and Sarah would sign her name as 'Mrs Freeman'. Soon they began addressing each other by these pet names in public and while Sarah's impudence stunned everyone at court, it infuriated and enraged Mary at her sister's stupidity.

And then, on 24th July, 1689 at Hampton Court Palace, Anne gave birth to a live baby boy. The child was baptised William Henry three days later and his godfather King William III declared that the title of Duke of Gloucester would be his. After William's birth, Anne would eventually go on to have more unsuccessful pregnancies: two premature babies who lived for about two hours, four stillbirths, and four miscarriages.

When William was born, he seemed to be a bright healthy little boy. But shortly afterwards, he suffered from a series of convulsions and his doctors feared the worst. Anne and George were inconsolable and never left his side, wringing their hands and crying softly throughout the night. Almost miraculously, he pulled through, although weaker and less lively than before. When he was stronger and given the all clear by his doctors to be moved, he was given his own household at Campden House near the Kensington gravel pits because of the purer air. There he could be taken outside every day for exercise in a tiny coach pulled by Shetland ponies.

The little boy did not walk or talk until the age of three and as he grew older, it became more apparent that there was something terribly wrong with the child. Still, Anne and George seemed oblivious and glowed with happiness.

The year 1692 was unsettling to say the least for William and Mary. The Whigs and the Tories were playing a push and shove game and at the head of it all was Sarah's husband, John Churchill. Mary had never trusted Churchill, or Sarah, and she suspected that Churchill was secretly conspiring with the Jacobites to overthrow her and her husband and place her father back on the throne. It was a rather strange thought to have had since it was John and Sarah who'd convinced Anne to side with William instead of James in the first place.

When looking at it now, it seems highly likely that the reason behind the lack of trust on Mary's part was due to Sarah's influence over Anne. Her distrust of Sarah had filtered down to Sarah's husband and the seed of doubt began to grow. In the end, it was a suspicion Mary acted upon. She ordered Churchill dismissed from his office and demanded that Sarah be removed from Anne's household.

It was Anne's turn now to be furious and there is no better way to retaliate than a public show of contempt. But defiance is one thing. Defiance against a monarch's order, sister or no sister, is something else entirely and it was something no one had even dared to consider. No one that is, except Anne. Not only did Anne openly refuse to remove Sarah from the household, she also insisted that Sarah accompany her to a social event at the palace. It was Anne's turn to throw down a gauntlet and of course, Mary was all too ready to pick it up.

Anne must have felt confident that her sister would not react adversely. They were, after all, sisters and she must have considered her friendship with Sarah as a strictly personal relationship. But if she thought Mary would just let it slide, she was very mistaken. Mary upped the ante by having Sarah *physically* removed by the Lord Chamberlain. And the squabble escalated further.

By then, Anne was apoplectic. She told George to pack their things and that they were taking up residence at Syon House, the home of the Duke of Northumberland, where Mary had no control of her. Sarah could live with them there.

For George, normally a quiet man, he must have felt caught in the middle of a terrible family squabble that had the potential of utter disaster. Being the queen, Mary would always win and sure enough, when Mary heard the news, she was livid. There was nothing she could do but show her sister that no one embarrassed the queen. No one. She stripped Anne of her guard of honour, courtiers were forbidden to visit her and authorities were instructed to totally ignore her. Even William's guards were instructed not to salute George any more.

A month later, Anne gave birth to a son who died within minutes of birth.

Give Mary her due, she did go to visit Anne to sympathise with her but before long, the two sisters were at it again. Sarah's name was angrily mentioned and Mary berated Anne over the friendship yet again. When Anne remained indignantly stubborn, Mary left in a fury.

The sisters never saw each other again.

Within a couple of months, Anne was pregnant again and had decided to move to Berkeley House in Piccadilly where she began to take every precaution to deliver a healthy child. By then, she had lost eight babies, and William was the only child who had survived so far. In March, she had another stillborn daughter. Nine months later, she had another miscarriage.

It was during the month of December 1694 that England was shocked by the news that Mary had contracted smallpox. For days, the nation held their breath but in the end, Mary died.

With the terrible news, England began to realise that Anne was the only one left who could succeed to the throne after William's death, followed by her sickly 5-year-old son. Any children William may have to another bride in the future would be placed so far down on the list of claimants to the throne, they would be almost non-existent.

It wasn't just England who was realising this fact. Anne had begun to grasp the point as well that her status had been somewhat elevated as the future queen. With that dawning in her mind, she began to feel that she deserved a little recognition of that detail. With Mary all but forgotten in her mind, it was then she repeated her request to William that she and George be allowed to move into St James Palace with an increase in allowance since she was the heir apparent.

William was too distraught over the death of his wife to argue. His past decision had been not to allow the move but that was when Mary was alive and everything had changed since then. Somehow the move seemed unimportant in the scheme of things so he relented and allowed it. As an afterthought, he restored Anne's honours and even gave her Mary's jewels although he stopped short of allotting her a place in government or appointing her as regent during his absences abroad. Within three months, he had also restored John Churchill to his offices at Anne's request, which was more or less due to Sarah's quiet insistence.

Things were moving at a very fast pace for Anne. She was getting used to her new status, moving house and organising her new household. And then it suddenly hit her. When she died, her son would be the next in line to the throne and she hadn't seen him for quite a while. It was then that she and

George decided to make a hasty trip to visit him at Campden House and check on his progress.

What they saw appalled them. The little boy had to be held up by his servants when he attempted to walk and even then, he tottered. He could not even go up and down stairs without help. Although he seemed to have grown, although slowly, by 5 years old, his head was so round that his hat was big enough for most men. This was the dawning of awareness that William had hydrocephalus.

Anne and George were horrified. If the Jacobite faction discovered his affliction, cartoonists and comedians would poke so much fun at her family that her future crown would be jeopardised. None of them would stop at using their child's deformity as a weapon for brutal scorn. And so, young William was kept tucked away out of the public gaze to the intense sadness of both Anne and George.

Over the years, Anne had suffered from gout that rendered her lame and from 1698 onwards; she was being carried around in a sedan chair. And she'd developed quite a sweet tooth. As a result, she rapidly gained more and more weight and in Sarah's own words *"she grew exceedingly gross and corpulent"*. As she grew fatter, her face, already scarred from her childhood smallpox infection, grew even redder and more spotted and she was forced to bandage her gout-affected feet with poultices.

As for young William, he had days when his illness had no effect whatsoever and he would become an average high-spirited little boy who loved stories of war and had a troop of local boys called *"Horse Guards"* whom he loved to drill before his uncle William. Young William was close to his uncle who in turn loved showering him with gifts of toys. His education had been delayed due to his speech difficulties and occasional bouts of illness, but eventually a tutor was appointed to him so he could begin lessons in geography, mathematics, Latin, and French in an effort to prepare him for his future role as sovereign.

On his 7th birthday, William was installed as a Knight of the Order of the Garter at St George's Chapel and when he was 8, he began lessons in government and religion as well. His portrait was painted at ten but by then he already looked more like 17. Still, he was making good progress.

That is, until his 11th birthday.

William's birthday dawned bright and sunny. A party had been organised at Windsor Castle and Young William had celebrated the day with all of his favourite foods and a ton of new toys. There were jesters and music and he listened excitedly to the sounds of cannons being discharged in his honour. Even his friends, the 'Horse Guards' were there.

It wasn't until the next day that his servant, Jenkin Lewis, reported that William was complaining of a headache and a sore throat. Everyone assumed it was because of the excitement from his birthday so he was put to bed and left alone to rest. In the evening, his throat had worsened and he had chills. Two days later, he was no better and he'd developed a serious fever and was delirious.

At first, his doctor suspected scarlet fever and then smallpox, so they waited for the rash to appear. Nothing happened. They used the usual dreadful treatments of the time, bleeding and blistering, which no doubt made the boy's already fragile condition even worse.

It was as his mother and father were bent in anguish over his bed that William died in the morning of 30th July 1700 at Windsor Castle. And behind them stood the ever-present Sarah Churchill.

Of course, being a royal who had died with no symptoms except for a sore throat and a fever, there was bound to be an autopsy done on his body.

The day after his death a detailed post-mortem was performed.

The autopsy report was conclusive. It painstakingly described inflammation and infection in the throat and larynx, with a grossly swollen neck and evident pus expressed from his lymph nodes. The lungs were described as both being full of blood and pus Put in context with the clinical course of the illness, this is a picture of an acute bacterial infection of the throat with an associated pneumonia in both lungs. Interestingly, and probably for research due to his enlarged head, the surgeons opened the boy's head and found excessive fluid in the cavities within the brain. This would confirm the diagnosis of hydrocephalus.

Parliament was in a state of shock. With no heir from William and Mary, and with Anne's last surviving child dead, the idea of returning James and his new family to England was thrown into the ring once more. The idea took root and grew at an alarming rate. In the minds of Parliament, they could see James aligning himself with Louis in a 'holy league' to bring back Catholicism and destroy Protestantism. Almost with a shudder, the idea was scrapped immediately.

Parliament went into overdrive almost at the same time that James had a stroke and died in France. The only Stuart remaining was James' son and Anne's half-brother, a 13-year-old Catholic boy by the name of James Francis Edward Stuart. Or 'The Pretender' as he was being called.

Why 'The Pretender' you ask, when it seems obvious that James' son would certainly be the heir to the throne? Well, as we know, James and his 15-year-old bride, Mary of Modena, were married while Charles II was still alive but this is where the story gets juicy.

Mary of Modena's story is almost as tragic as Anne's. For the first four years of her marriage to James, she seems to have been pregnant almost the whole time. But the story is not a happy one. Her first pregnancy ended in a miscarriage, the next child died of convulsions at only nine months old and in the same month, she delivered a stillborn baby. Things began to look a little better for the happy couple when a healthy child, a daughter, was born ten months later. The happiness did not last however. Their next child born a year later died of smallpox at only one month old, followed by a daughter who died at birth, then another stillborn child two years later followed by the death of their only surviving daughter at not quite four years old, apparently of natural causes. One year later another child would die of convulsions at two months old followed by a stillborn child a year later and another miscarriage one year later again. In the space of ten years, she had lost ten children. And this is where it starts to become complicated.

James seems to have been more like his brother Charles than we thought when it comes to women. During his wife's pregnancies and childbirth horrors, he still felt the need for female 'companionship' and had continued an affair with a woman by the name of Catherine Sedley, Countess of Dorchester. Three years after the death of her last child, Mary became irritated by James' continued affair with Catherine and moved into new apartments of her own in Whitehall in February 1687.

Then towards the end of 1687, Mary visited the spa city of Bath, not yet the popular resort it would become later in the Georgian period, but a place that was said to have had 'healing waters'. When she returned shortly before Christmas, the jubilant couple announced happily that while she was on her retreat, Mary had discovered that she was pregnant.

To say feelings were mixed is an understatement. English Catholics were ecstatic but the English Protestants were seriously doubtful. Bath's PR people had credited the therapeutic spa for restoring her fertility but the Protestants were sceptical and openly suspicious that it was Bath's reputation for licentious behaviour that should be credited instead. Rumours spread that the baby was not James' child at all.

After the baby was born, an even wilder rumour took hold. James' enemies claimed that a male baby had been smuggled into the Queen's chamber in a warming pan to replace her own stillborn child. Witnesses to the birth were called but these witnesses were even doubted since they were themselves not of royal birth and hence not to be trusted. Everyone knew that money spoke volumes. It was mainly due to James' mismanagement, but the rumours had substance since he had excluded many from the birth whose testimony would have counted as valid and most of the witnesses were either Catholics or foreigners. When James' daughter Mary was alive, she had been convinced that it was just a plot to trick her out of her inheritance by replacing her and William with the boy from her father's second marriage. A male child was needed and indeed, a male child had been produced.

So when James Francis Edward Stuart declared himself to be the heir to the throne of England as King James III of England and Scotland, you can see how England was both infuriated and incensed at his audacity, considering no one was even sure if he was a Stuart at all. That he was immediately recognised as the King by France, Spain, Italy and Modena meant nothing to them whatsoever.

Parliament searched desperately through the Stuart family tree looking for a more suitable candidate but with fifty of Anne's Catholic relatives standing in a long queue to claim the throne, they needed to be quick. One by one they went through the list crossing names off as they went, even the names of those who had a legitimate claim to the throne were discarded in their frantic attempt to find a Protestant heir. Until the name Sophia Electress of Hanover finally popped up. She was the granddaughter of James I through his daughter Elizabeth and as such, she had Stuart blood running through her veins. And she was a Protestant.

Parliament breathed a sigh of relief. But the succession needed to be unequivocally definite. Almost before the ink had dried on James' death certificate, Parliament bought in the Act of Settlement stating that if Anne died without issue, her second cousin, Sophia Electress of Hanover, would inherit the crown and William willingly signed the document.

The Act came in the nick of time. The next year, while out riding, William fell off his horse after it had stepped into a mole hole and he broke his collarbone. Complications had followed and after weeks of intense and debilitating pain, William finally died of pneumonia.

At 37 years old, Anne was the queen and she let England know in no uncertain terms that she would do anything for the happiness and prosperity of England. As you can imagine, it made her immediately popular. She appointed her husband George as Lord High Admiral and gave him nominal control of the Navy. Then she gave control of the army to John Churchill and appointed him Captain-General. To Sarah, she gave the prestigious positions of Lady of the Bedchamber, Keeper of the Privy Purse, Mistress of the Robes and Groom of the Stole: all highly sought after positions of great importance that also paid very handsomely.

One month later, she was carried to her coronation at Westminster Abbey in a sedan chair with a low back to allow her train to flow behind her.

Though never credited with much intelligence, Ann was smart enough to know that the Act of Settlement, passed one year before, applied only to England, Ireland and Wales. Scotland had made it abundantly clear that they had the right to choose whoever they wanted to sit on their throne and *that* someone would be from the Stuart Dynasty, namely James Francis Edward Stuart, not a foreign one. The Scots had long memories and they had never forgotten the massacre at Glencoe. The butchery that William had conveniently overlooked and forgotten about would forever live in their hearts as an example of what could happen if you trusted a foreigner.

Anne was also smart enough to know that it was necessary to have a united England and in her first speech to Parliament in October, she began negotiations to do exactly that. Despite her good intentions, discussions were still continuing in February the next year, with no one able to agree on anything.

Scotland responded to the Act of Settlement with a law of their own they called The Act of Security. They stated that if the queen had no more children, they could choose a monarch of their own and that monarch would most certainly *not* be the same person sitting on the English throne. That was for sure. When Scotland threatened to withhold supplies from England if they did not agree to their Act, Anne grudgingly granted it but then bounced back with another one of her own she called the Alien Act. This one had worse repercussions as it threatened to impose economic sanctions on Scotland and also declared that Scottish subjects were to be regarded as aliens when in England.

It was a rather spiteful, vindictive thing to do and once again, anger bubbled to the surface. It didn't help matters at all when Anne then reappointed John Dalrymple, the man responsible for the Glencoe massacre, back on to the Privy Council of Scotland and then created him 1st Earl of Stair.

It seemed like yet another snide insult and a vicious thing to do and it reminded Parliament that William may have been aware of Anne's potential for biased judgement many years ago when he refused her request to hold a seat in Parliament. With anger mounting to a dangerous level, Anne was forced to listen to her advisers and she reluctantly repealed the Alien Act.

Dalrymple, she declared however, would remain an Earl.

For five years, insults were traded back and forth and negotiations continued slowly with a lot of finger-pointing and name-calling. Each had their own fears and as such, no one was willing to give in. Finally in March 1707, a compromise called the Act of Union was agreed upon. Scotland would receive a guarantee that they would have access to colonial markets and would be placed on an equal footing with England in terms of trade. In return England would have a guarantee that the Hanoverian dynasty would succeed Anne to the Scottish throne. With this Act, England and Scotland were united under a single kingdom with a single Parliament. Forever more, they would be called Great Britain.

Over the years, Anne's emotional dependence grew and extravagant gifts found their way to Sarah Churchill. Sarah and her husband had already been given the titles of Duke and Duchess of Marlborough by William, at Anne's request, followed by a gift of the Blenheim estate in return for her husband's military victory in the war with the Spanish. But for some reason, things were slowly changing and no one could put a finger on the reason why it was happening.

It wasn't that England was upset by the tension, because they weren't. On the whole, Sarah was a very disliked person. She was arrogant and conceited and it was all too obvious that she took advantage of her closeness to the queen in feathering her own nest. But in her overconfidence with her firm position in Anne life, Sarah went one step too far. She tried to influence Anne politically. It was a dangerous move in a relationship that had been precarious for a while, given Sarah's constant nagging and petty arguments with Anne. You could just see that eventually, it would come to a nasty end.

Although Anne had disliked William when he was alive, she knew he had been a clever king. He had seen most Tories as generally friendlier to royal authority and even though the Whigs had purged the Tories from all major positions in government, William had tried to balance the parties. Anne followed his policy as closely as she could and supported her moderate Tory ministers, John Churchill and Lord Godolphin. However, as the Spanish War of Succession went on and on, Anne became less and less tolerant and dissatisfied with the Whigs and even more supportive of the Tories. And as a staunch Whig supporter, Sarah was very vocal and critical of Anne's decisions. It seemed nothing Anne did suited Sarah and she had no qualms about letting Anne know about it, often quite rudely. It marked the beginning of Anne's souring relationship with Sarah.

For Anne, the final straw came in 1708 at a thanksgiving service after a battle victory. Sarah had been standing at the door to St Paul's Cathedral when she noticed that Anne was not wearing the jewels she had deliberately selected for her. Sarah indignantly questioned her about her bad choice of jewellery and demanded to know why Anne had disregarded her specific choice. They had a loud and heated argument on the steps in front of everyone and it ended with Sarah telling Anne to shut up and be quiet. The next day, Sarah was asked to remove her things from the palace and you can be certain she put up a good fight. All to no avail. Not too long after, it was Sarah's cousin Abigail Marsham who quickly replaced her and Sarah found herself evicted.

Through Anne and George's marriage and the deaths of all her children, George had always been her rock. He'd stood by her and supported her, whether he thought Anne was right or wrong. So his death in October 1708 marked the point when things became unglued for Anne. With her rock gone, what was the point anymore? Occasionally she would rouse herself but it was never with the same fervour as before.

The only commitment she clung to was the estrangement with the Marlboroughs. With the Spanish war all but over and a new ruler on the

Spanish throne as the Holy Roman Emperor, Britain no longer had any interest in the war and it was finally over. A treaty was signed with the ageing Louis XIV and with it, there seemed to be no need to have an army anymore, even less a commander to head that army. As a result, John Churchill was once again dismissed from his office.

The treaty with France meant more to England than just peace with Spain. By signing it, Louis recognised the Hanoverian succession in Britain. By then, Anne was unable to walk at all and by Christmas of 1713 there were constant rumours of her impending death. Her doctors blamed her failing health on the emotional strain and towards the last year of her life, she refused to even leave her bed.

It wasn't just Anne who was weakening. Louis XIV's health was steadily going downhill as well. He was 75 years old and despite the image of a healthy and virile king that Louis liked to project, his ailments varied from diabetes, dental abscesses, recurring boils, fainting spells, gout, dizziness, hot flushes and headaches.

With Louis' health deteriorating fast, Anne's own declining health frightened England even more. A new chapter was about to begin and although it was by far a more appealing chapter than the Stuart option, this one held many unknown factors. This chapter would be a German one. The prospect was openly discussed and Anne's constant refusal to allow Sophia of Hanover to visit England fuelled gossip that she secretly favoured the Stuarts rather than the Hanoverians. She publicly denied the rumours but she still refused Sophia's requests to enter England.

Although considerably older than Anne, Sophia of Hanover enjoyed much better health. But at 83 years old, Sophia knew her demise could come at any time. She constantly sent letters to Anne begging to be allowed to visit, but angrily, and rather rudely, Anne constantly refused. It was only after receiving yet another angry letter from Anne refusing her permission to enter the country that Sophia began feeling ill. Two days later she was walking in the gardens of Herrenhausen when she ran to shelter from a sudden downpour of rain. It was there, alone in the garden, that she collapsed and died.

One month later, at only 49 years of age, Anne suffered a stroke and died as well. After twelve months in bed, obesity, gout and seventeen pregnancies had finally taken its toll on her body and it finally caught up with her.

Her father, James II, had died on 16th September, 1701, at the Chateau of St Germain-en-Laye. Strangely, his body was placed in a coffin but was not then buried. Perhaps it lay in waiting for a formal burial at some point in England. Instead, for some reason, it was kept in a French chapel overseen by monks in Paris. These monks divided up his body, presumably as relics. His brain travelled to the Scots College in Paris, his intestines were sent in pieces to the English Church of St Omer and the parish church of St Germain-en-Laye, and his heart went to a convent in Paris.

And there his body rested in pieces until the French Revolution, when the sites of his various body parts were looted and nobody currently knows where any of them are.

Perhaps, like the English king Richard III (whose remains were discovered in 2012 under a parking lot in Leicester, England), various parts of James's body will eventually come to light and this problematic king will be buried with the full honour due to an English monarch.

It would be a new era for England and they were to find that their new king, George of Hanover, was a short, quiet German who could barely speak a word of English.

But at least he was a Protestant.

END OF THE STUART DYNASTY

No one can agree why Anne's health had been so bad for so long. She was, after all, only 49 years old. Sure she was overweight, which everyone knew caused difficulty during births. But lots of overweight women had children. Hughes syndrome, an autoimmune disease affecting the blood, has been suggested, even porphyria, which can potentially cause recurrent miscarriages and is also associated with other complications such as premature birth and stillbirth. And don't forget that James I more than likely suffered from porphyria.

But whether by bad health or bad luck, the Stuart dynasty had come to an end. There would still be Stuart blood pulsing through the veins of the coming generations: George I's great grandfather was James I after all. But it was the Stuart dynasty that had failed to continue with Anne's death. Historically, the poor health of a monarch may have had political importance, but it is the inability to produce a suitable heir that has been the usual cause for the end of a dynasty, as well as bad luck, I suppose.

The Stuart dynasty began with Robert II in 1371 and although we grow up with children's stories that give us a picture of kings, queens and fairy tale princesses in medieval Scotland, the reality was far from being a fairy tale. Their lives were constantly at risk from enemies within their kingdom and they had to keep watchful eyes out for ambitious nobles.

Many died 'mysteriously' and many died simply trying to protect themselves and their family, as with King James I of Scotland in 1437. He had been staying at the Blackfriars monastery in Perth with his wife and her ladies in waiting. As he prepared for bed, he heard armed men clattering through the monastery. The queen and the ladies tried to bar the door as James prised up the floorboards with tongs from the fireplace before dropping down into the sewer beneath the privy in an attempt to escape. Crashing above him were supporters of the Earl of Atholl who was next in line for the throne after James' son.

There was no way out for James. One by one the men, armed with swords, axes and knives, lowered themselves down into the sewer beneath the privy. James fought hard for his life with his bare hands but he was finally and inevitably slain. His wife, Queen Joan, survived the plot and escaped with her son but she would eventually have her own revenge. Her husband's murderers were hunted down and horrendously tortured before being executed.

Through the centuries the Stuarts had endured. They survived wars, crusades, bouts of the plague, smallpox, a great fire, murder and ill health. And they'd survived years of captivity, as we know with Mary Queen of Scots.

But when looking back over the last four generations of Stuart kings, each one seems to have been precarious. After Elizabeth I's death, it was Mary Queen of Scots' son James who would become James I of England in 1603 when he was 36 years old. His weak legs remain unexplained, as do episodes of jaundice, but a shrunken kidney containing stones at his post mortem explains the evidence of blood and tiny stones in his urine. From 1616 he was disabled from arthritis, and began showing dementia six years before he died. The possibility that his thyroid glands were not functioning properly has been a recent speculation.

Henry also seems to be an unfortunate name to be called if you were a Stuart. Firstly, the family name came originally from Henry Stuart Lord Darnley who lost his life after his wife Mary Queen of Scots took a lover and had him assassinated. James I's son Henry lost his life to typhoid and Charles I's son Henry died of smallpox – both at 18 years of age. If only Prince Henry had survived his bout of smallpox, there would have been a Protestant Stuart who would have been fit, well and acceptable to Parliament and the dynasty could very well still be with us today. The same would have happened if just one of Anne's children had survived to adulthood. Perhaps it was fate, not just ill health, that severed the line from future generations, given that the decapitation of Charles I was not truly a surgical procedure.

The story of James I's children does not make for easy reading. First there was Henry, Prince of Wales who was intellectually remarkable but died of typhoid in 1612 at 18-years-old. Four of James' children had died before they reached the age of two, and his daughter-in-law, Catherine of Braganza, had failed to produce a child despite the many illegitimate children that Charles II was able to father out of wedlock. It would be his daughter Elizabeth who would marry the Protestant Prince Elector of Hanover and of her two children, one would die of pleurisy while the only surviving daughter Sophia would live to give birth to the future King George I of England.

With each generation, it wasn't just producing an heir that was a problem. It was keeping the heirs alive as well. James I lost 5 children, as did his sons Charles I and James II. And then we know the horrors that Anne suffered.

So with Anne, the last of the Stuart dynasty died as well. Never again would there be a Stuart on the throne of England. That was reserved for the Hanovers.

But when saying that, there is one thing that we should consider. Charles left no legitimate children but we know of a dozen by his ten mistresses. The present Dukes of Buccleuch, Richmond, Grafton and St Albans descend from Charles in a direct male line and Diana, Princess of Wales, was descended from two of Charles's illegitimate sons: the Duke of Grafton and the Duke of Richmond. Also, through Charles II and his mistress Louise de Kerouaille, their son Charles Lennox Duke of Richmond would become the ancestor of Camilla, Duchess of Cornwall and Sarah, Duchess of York. Lady Diana's son, Prince William, second in line to the present British throne, is likely to be the first monarch descended from Charles II and Stuart blood will once more run through the veins of future kings and queens of England.

But let's not get too far ahead of ourselves. The Hanoverians are about to arrive on English soil and life would be very different from the one that Parliament had imagined. They would find that compared to the Tudors and the Stuarts, the Hanoverians would be something of a hard sell with England. The German kings seemed cold and remote and if you asked anyone to disclose their private opinion, they would have said they were barbarians.

Although Hanoverian Britain was the hub of slave trade and exploration, this era is barely etched in our minds. Of course, there are exceptions. Hollywood has immortalised The Madness of King George but let's not forget this era was also Jane Austen's era as well as the British Museum, the greatest architect Christopher Wren, Sir Isaac Newton, the cure for smallpox and the foundation of the press. It was an era for poets, painters, geniuses in Science, the arrival of tea and coffee, exotic fruit, fine wines, Indian silks and Chinese porcelain. Still, it is in danger of disappearing beyond our mental horizon even though it lasted longer than either the Tudor or the Stuart age.

It was an age when people experienced everything from passionate repulsion of some monarchs and delighted ardour for others. There were violent wars abroad and riots at home, expanding trade in the Far East and thankfully, the disappearance of the plague in Britain. London virtually glowed with increased capital and the middle class began to show itself with polished living standards.

Only one year after George I arrived from Hanover, an armed Jacobite uprising was threatening his throne and although the Hanoverians were very unpopular, England supported their new German king.

In the following chapters, you will read about George I, an unremarkable man who treated his wife cruelly. His son George II was incredibly obstinate and George III was... well... mad. Even George IV was unfit to rule and was widely hated while his brother William did what Charles I and Charles II had done: he dismissed a government simply because he disliked it.

But still England supported them.

If you disregarded the Catholic Stuarts in France, the Hanoverians were all England had left.

PART II

GEORGE I

Born 1660
Reign 1714 – 1727

George was born with a silver spoon in his mouth. For the first year of his life, he was the only heir to a vast German empire that belonged to his father and three childless uncles and things were looking pretty rosy for George's future. But then his brother Frederick Augustus was born, and in just four years, another four brothers and a sister followed in quick succession, which meant his inheritance was spread a little thin. If that wasn't bad enough for him, after the death of one childless uncle five years later, his two remaining uncles had married and his inheritance became shakier still with the prospect of future sons from both of them.

History books are full of feuding family members who battled mercilessly against each other for the right to sit on a throne and George's father would have been well aware of his son's uncertain future. At 15, probably mindful of this very fact, his father began coaching him in military matters and even took him on a campaign to train his son for battle.

Since the law in Germany restricted inheritance to the male line only, the uncertainty disappeared when one uncle unexpectedly died without sons and it looked extremely likely that the other one would not have any legitimate children. By then, his father had begun his reign as Duke of Calenberg-Gottingen, which meant George and his brothers had a secure future ahead of them. Things had certainly turned sunny side up for George.

Two things improved his future even more dramatically. Firstly, his family adopted primogeniture, the custom where the firstborn male child would inherit the family estate, and overnight he did not have to share the inheritance with his brothers anymore. Then secondly, George's father arranged for his niece, Sophia Dorothea of Celle, to marry George and she came with a healthy annual income to boot. With everything going so well for him, George must have thought he had the Midas touch.

His mother, Sophia Electress of Hanover, had been totally against the arranged marriage from the start and who could blame her? All you had to do was look at the Hapsburgs to make your heart skip a beat or two if you wanted evidence of inbreeding. On recent Hapsburg had been short, lame, epileptic and completely bald and he had only lived to 35 years of age. His lower jaw had grown abnormally larger than the upper jaw resulting in an extended chin and the inability to chew. To add to his problems, his tongue was so large that his speech could hardly be understood and he frequently drooled. No matter which way you looked at it, inbreeding could lead to eye-popping physical and mental faults.

But thankfully her daughter-in-law delivered a healthy, bouncing baby boy, arriving into the world with a full-throated indignant bellow two years later, and all doubts flew out the window. They called him George Augustus and after another couple of years, a somewhat quieter daughter arrived to complete the set. By 1682, life was looking pretty promising for George.

On the surface, everyone appeared happy enough in George's household. Until George's mistress delivered two daughters in quick succession and certain rumours began to bubble up to the surface. Taking a mistress and having children to her wasn't what everyone was concerned about, after all it wasn't an unusual practice for the men of many royal families throughout the world. Some of them indulged themselves further and took several mistresses at the same time. Look at Charles II for instance. What bothered everyone were the uncertain whispers that began circulating about George's wife. They inferred that Sophia Dorothea had taken a lover of her own, a rather handsome and dashing Swedish count and pretty soon, the rumours became an irrefutable fact.

To say that George was astounded and humiliated at his wife's audacity is an understatement. The scandal sent shock waves throughout the Hanoverian court and gossip soon spread that George much preferred the company of his mistress to his wife anyway. His mother and brothers tried to make Sophia see sense but in the inevitable wave of anger that followed, she steadfastly persisted in her own romance. Everything came to a nasty head when the body of the said Swedish count was found in the River Leine weighted down with stones and four German courtiers were suddenly and miraculously flush with money.

There was no coming back from a scandal of that proportion and George wanted nothing further to do with a wife who had disgraced him, abandoned him and ultimately committed adultery. No one felt inclined to mention the fact to George that he was doing the exact same thing. Still, on those grounds, the marriage was dissolved and for punishment for her indiscretion, she was sent back to Celle, imprisoned without access to her children, forbidden to remarry and only allowed to walk unaccompanied within the mansion courtyard until the day she died some thirty years later. It seemed a harsh punishment by any standards but if you're a king, most agreed there were no recriminations.

While George tried to live down the scandal in Hanover, Britain was facing their own huge problem. In a frantic attempt to produce an heir, Anne had endured 17 pregnancies only to have her last surviving child die.

Drastic action was needed and the idea of a ready-made family in Germany looked very appealing and promising to England. What they really wanted was an uncomplicated ruler and not an obstinate pig-headed Stuart. In their desperation to find a Protestant heir, Parliament went through the Stuart family tree with a fine-tooth comb, right back to James I, and came up with his daughter Elizabeth and her daughter Sophia, the current Electress of Hanover.

Sophia was a part of a very German tradition of women who led the social and intellectual scene unlike the British princesses who were quite badly educated. Sophia was rational and intelligent and even Louis XIV was heard to say that he was in love with her brilliance. The whole package appealed immensely to the English Parliament who stated that regrettably and unacceptably, the other 55 closer relatives, who just so happened to be Catholic, were definitely not eligible for the job.

The Act of Settlement in 1701 was one of the most important documents in the whole of British monarchy. It changed history and set out who could, and who could not, be their king or queen. First of all, you had to have *some* Stuart blood and secondly, you had to be a Protestant.

Sophia was delighted with her new windfall as the future Queen of England and she desperately wanted to pay London a visit. Anne however did not share the same enthusiasm. She had no want to have her rival queen coming over, especially since this new one was a whole lot smarter, prettier and better educated than her. Somewhat stubbornly, Sophia was repeatedly told that she would just have to sit back and wait for Anne to die.

With her new inheritance looming on the horizon, Sophia knew she had to expand her new dynasty if they were going to survive. She had only one son and he in turn had only one son, and there was no doubt at all in her mind that it was high time her grandson married and had children of his own. He was 19 years old, after all.

When Sophia told her son that she had commenced a search to find her grandson a bride, George objected strongly. He had no intention whatsoever of permitting his son to enter into a loveless marriage as he had. Everyone knew how *that* had turned out. Through countless and vocal arguments, Sophia stood firm and the search went on regardless of her son's opinion.

A couple of princesses were considered but frustratingly, negotiations came to nothing.

In the meantime, Prince George had taken things into his own hands after hearing of a young woman who was a ward of his aunt and uncle, the king and queen of Prussia, due to the death of both her parents. He had been pleased to hear that she had turned down an offer from Archduke Charles of Austria because it would have meant giving up her Protestant religion.

Caroline's story is like something out of a Walt Disney story. She was a beautiful woman, orphaned at a young age and rumour had it that her beauty and intelligence were unparalleled. As such, she had many suitors. Then one day in September, she received unexpected visitors, a Baron von Eltz and his manservant, who had stopped to supposedly present greetings from the Hanoverian Chief Minister on their way back to Hanover. This unknown visitor was in fact Prince George and when he met Caroline, he was thoroughly smitten. He rushed home and told his father he had met the woman he wanted to marry and proposals were drawn up immediately. Three months later, the couple were married and five rather short months later again, their first child Frederick arrived. Over the following seven years, three daughters would follow.

Throughout those years, Sophia continued to beseech Anne to be allowed to visit her future home but permission was repeatedly refused. It was only after an angry letter from Anne that arrived on 5th June in 1714 that the 83-year-old Sophia began feeling ill. Two days later she was running through the gardens of Herrenhausen to find shelter from a sudden downpour of rain when she collapsed and died. One month later in August, Queen Anne was also dead, due to a stroke, and on that day, George became the new King of England.

Unlike his mother, George did not come across as being very impressive. He was a rather shy man who preferred to avoid crowds and pageantry. What he *did* possess was the essential qualities that the Stuarts lacked – stability and permanence. When building a new dynasty, there is nothing more necessary.

What George didn't know was that before he even left Hanover for England, James II's son James Francis Edward Stuart, who was living in exile in France, was already plotting to take back his father's throne.

It was a beautiful autumn day in September when King George sailed up the Thames with his son. It had already been decided that Prince George's wife, Caroline, and their three daughters would come over in a couple of months' time while their son, seven-year-old Frederick, would stay behind permanently with tutors to show Hanover that they had not been forgotten.

George was expecting a wonderful welcome and what he saw pleased him. London was like nothing he had ever seen before. It was fifty times larger than Hanover and the crowd, estimated at around one and a half million people, were lined up along the river, pushing and shoving, eager for their first glimpse of their new king.

The English knew very little about him, not even what he looked like, and to most of England, being ruled by a German took some getting used to anyway. Their idea of Germany was a land full of yokels farming turnips and even at this early stage, before having even seen him, people were calling him their 'Turnip King'.

His son, Prince George, disembarked first to a riotous welcome, waving happily to the cheering crowds. George had been feeling nervous and unsure of what the reception would be, but when he heard the cheering, it heartened him considerably. But when George stepped out, he was greeted with silence. As he stood on the ship's deck open-mouthed, looking at the retreating backs of the crowd, he suddenly realised that the people had mistaken his son as their new king and were leaving.

The start was not as auspicious as he'd hoped nor was it the glorious one he had imagined. He was left to disembark alone with his eighteen German cooks and two mistresses, one very fat and the other very thin, earning them the nicknames 'the Elephant and the Maypole'. Even at this early stage of his reign, he was beginning to be just a little jealous of his son's popularity. Still he rallied and despite hearing that the people thought him awkward and clumsy, he persevered.

And then the English heard all about George's treatment of his wife. They heard the story of his mistresses and they heard the heart-wrenching story of how his wife's lover had turned up dead in the river after she had refused to give him up. They heard how George had cut her off without a second thought and then sent her away in exile never to see her family or children again, and never allowing her to leave her prison as long as she lived. And they didn't like it. Not one single bit. Where before they were sniggering at his uncouthness and woodenness in public, now it would seem that their new king was a hypocrite as well. The story became somewhat of a scandal in his early days as king and even before his coronation; riots were popping up all over the country.

Ultimately, it was George's English skills that let him down. But who could blame him? English was his fourth language after all and he had never expected to be the king of a country where the majority of his subjects could only speak one language, George's worst language at that. His difficulty with the language became more obvious at his coronation ceremony when he had to have a translator present to help him understand the proceedings. Even then, he'd looked a little bored and disinterested, choosing to gaze up at the ceiling instead of listening to the service. Along with the rioting in and around twenty towns on the day, one man was arrested for blatantly brandishing a turnip on the end of a stick outside Westminster Abbey.

From the beginning, George found he had to work very hard to win over his Parliament and the Whig ministers. In Hanover, he had been the absolute ruler but he was to find that was not going to happen in England. From his first Parliamentary meeting, England let him know in no uncertain terms that they had offered him the throne and they could take it away from him just as easily. It was almost word for word what they'd said to William and Mary and they were just as determined that George would understand that same message. He would be the kind of king *they* wanted.

Surprisingly, they were pleased to find that George was a lot more conciliatory than the Stuarts had been before him. But while Parliament were pleased with George's reaction, George was finding that life had not been quite so complicated for him in Hanover.

It didn't take very long for his first big crisis to arrive. It was barely four weeks after his coronation in October when an uprising of the Jacobites in Scotland took off, led by John Erskine, 6th Earl of Mar. They had already mustered highland chiefs in September and declared James Francis Edward Stuart as their rightful king but now they were determined to physically remove George from the throne if they had to and replace him with James as James III of England. With his army of about 12,000 men, Mar proceeded to take Perth. Some Tories had even joined the rebellion.

Since William's death and with Anne on the throne for the past twelve years, life in England had changed. Each political party had gained more strength and power because the monarch they had was more involved in trying to produce heirs and settle petty squabbles with her servants than with running a country. When Anne's husband died, she became even less interested and their power grew even more. In their complacency, they forgot that George was a German king who was certainly wasn't afraid to fight.

But things didn't go quite according to Mar's plan. There were still men who did not support the Jacobites and many of them were Campbells, in particular John Campbell 2nd Duke of Argyll, based in Stirling. This man was the son of Archibald Campbell: the very man who had been King William's chief Scottish advisor and who had been present when orders went through for the massacre of the MacDonalds at Glencoe. While Mar had been leading his army south, spies were informing John Campbell of Mar's actions and in an attempt to halt his progress, he moved his army of around 4,000 men to Sherriffmuir on 10th November 1715. Three days later, on a remote elevated plateau of heathland lying between Stirling and Auchterarder on the northern fringe of the Ochil Hills, their armies finally met head on.

Argyll knew he was seriously outnumbered but he surprisingly managed to halt the Jacobite advance. By evening, both armies were seriously reduced (the Jacobites had lost 800 while the government had lost 600) and not wanting to risk any more of his men, Mar allowed Campbell to withdraw.

Considering the size of Mar's army, it seems astonishing that the Jacobites failed and that both sides claimed it as their victory. An historian by the name of Neil Oliver has gone so far as to say that if Mar had not led his army like the leader of a parade instead of a campaign, the army could have easily bypassed Argyll and linked up with the English Jacobites and Catholics in the north of England. If Mar had decided to continue fighting instead of allowing Argyll to leave, history may be very different from what it is today.

It wasn't until 23rd December that James Francis Edward Stuart finally set foot on Scottish soil at Peterhead but by then, his cause was already largely lost. There was too little money and too few arms and he was disheartened and disappointed at the little show of support that was left for him.

As for the Scots, when they first saw James standing before them, they were more than a little disappointed themselves. This James Stuart was the son of James II who had captured and executed Monmouth after a bloody battle. His uncle Charles II had declared wars and defied Parliament time and time again almost until the day he died. His grandfather Charles I had been brutally beheaded for steadfastly standing up for his beliefs. The quiet, timid man standing before them who seemed almost uncomfortable with crowds, was not the leader they had imaged he would be. As he stood shyly before them, whispers of the warming pan' incident were muttered, arousing doubts of whether he really was a Stuart after all as the past rumours had insultingly suggested.

It wasn't just the cool reception from the Scotsmen that bothered James. He was unprepared for the bleakness of a Scottish winter as well. Howling icy winds blew constantly with persistent, bleak snowstorms unlike anything he had ever endured during a French winter and he soon fell ill with a fever that eventually worsened. By the time he recovered, the rebellion had all but fizzled out. He met with Mar at Perth but he could not find the means, or the words, to rouse the disheartened army. By 4th February, he had already decided to return dejectedly to France.

As James stood on the shores of Montrose, a coastal town in Angus 61 kms north of Dundee, ready to board his ship, the thought must have crossed his mind that it wasn't quite the glorious return that he had imagined it would be. He would have taken one last look around and remembered the swashbuckling stories his father had told him. The Danes had plundered Montrose in 980 and razed it to the ground, but they'd endured. William the Lion, King of the Scots in 1165, had built the Red Castle nearby where Edward I had visited with 30,000 of his men. Edward had stayed at the castle for three nights, humiliating John Balliol the whole time. The following year, William Wallace destroyed the garrison, slaying every soldier in sight. As James stood on board the ship his last night on English soil, he would have seen his own final chapter as something vastly different. It marked a failure that he had never imagined or foreseen. He knew his departure would be seen as abandonment and he fully understood the ill-feeling and disillusionment it would create. The shame it caused him was almost more than he could bear. He was returning to France disgraced and defeated.

His decision to return to France was one he would regret for the rest of his life. He arrived in Avignon to find that in September, during his absence, Louis XIV had died and he was not welcome in France anymore. Pope Clement XI eventually offered him a residence in Rome at the Palazzo Muti, which he gratefully accepted, plus a life annuity of 8,000 Roman scudi (large silver coins), and four years later, on 3rd September 1719 (doesn't that date keep popping up?) he married Maria Clementina Sobieska, the granddaughter of King John III Sobieski of Poland. One year later, his first son, Charles, was born.

Although the money given to him from Pope Clement XI helped him live in splendour and helped fund future attempts, future *failed* attempts, to restore the Stuarts to the British throne, he never emotionally recovered from his unequivocal defeat. He suffered from melancholy and depression for the rest of his life until he died on New Year's Day 1766. His claimed reign had lasted for 64 years, longer than any legitimate British monarch until Queen Elizabeth II's reign surpassed it in May 2016.

In Britain, after the failed Jacobite uprising in 1715, it was a very different story for George. He was jubilant at the news that James had left the country. It was his first victory and with it, after a few executions and land forfeitures along the way, the Whigs finally gained the upper hand over the Tories and the first thing they did was bring in the Riot Act.

This act declared that in future, any group of twelve or more who assembled unlawfully was liable for punitive action. If a group of people failed to disperse within one hour of the proclamation, the authorities could use force to disperse them. As most of the sheriffs were not averse to a little pushing and shoving, it also indemnified them against any consequences in the event of anybody being injured or killed. It made rioting a felony punishable by death and it virtually put a lid on many of the rumblings that had begun when George was crowned.

Britain didn't quite love their new shy king but they were in love with the idea of steadiness. That, above all, was what they craved after the constant upheavals caused by the Stuarts. But if things had finally settled down in Britain, it soon became apparent that all was not so harmonious in the royal household.

George's son, the Prince of Wales, had not seen his mother since he was 11 years old when she had been taken away and sent in exile to die alone in a German castle. Because of this, there was a huge gap in his life and he was never able to forgive his father for what he'd done. As such, this traumatic event caused a conflict that had a cataclysmic affect on the royal family. Not even the birth of George I's second grandson, George William (his first grandson was still living alone in Hanover with his tutors) could heal the rift. Instead, it led to a major quarrel that blew up between George and his son.

As was the English custom, the king was the person who appointed the godparents at the christening of any new royal member and for his youngest grandson, George chose Lord Chamberlain, Duke of Newcastle. What he didn't know was that his son carried an intense hatred for the duke. When the Prince of Wales saw Newcastle standing beside the baptismal font, ready to assume his role as godparent, it was like waving a red flag in front of a bull. The Prince demanded that the duke leave immediately.

As we know, neither George nor his son could speak English very well. Their manners were abrupt and both of them had thick German accents. So when the Prince of Wales told the duke to leave and he would *'find you later'*; the words came out sounding like *'fight you later'*. Those simple words were taken as a challenge to a duel and the ensuing argument that followed sent shock waves throughout the country.

When his father heard about the argument, he was beside himself with anger at his son's audacity to contradict his order. In a fit of fury, the Prince and Princess of Wales were told to vacate the premises of St James's Palace immediately and never return. As embarrassing as that was for them both, worse was to come. Their three daughters and their new baby son were to remain behind, virtually as hostages, ensuring the Prince of Wales' good behaviour in the future. In tears, Caroline pleaded with George not to separate her from her children but he stood firm. There was nothing else they could do but leave the children behind. They were physically escorted out of the palace after Caroline held her children tightly, sobbing her goodbyes.

As expected, the prince and princess missed their children immensely and on one occasion secretly visited the palace without George's approval. When Caroline fainted and the prince cried, George partially relented and permitted them to visit once a week. Later he would concede more and give Caroline unconditional access. Not so his son. The following February, the baby, George William, died and Caroline never forgave her father-in-law.

With the death of the child, as Caroline grieved, it was all out war between George and the Prince of Wales. The courts of Europe could talk about nothing else except the British royal scandal and Parliament watched appalled. With George, they had imagined a stable quiet reign unlike the Stuarts. What they got was a family squabble that surpassed anything the Stuarts had ever done, past or present. Eventually, nobles began taking sides and prolonged arguments over who was right and who was wrong filled the rooms in Parliament. Even the birth of another son did not quieten things down.

With the Prince of Wales still fuming at him, George turned his attention to the national debt and the stock market. It was this crazy speculation that plunged Britain into greater debt.

The scheme was called the South Sea Bubble in a time when the British Empire was becoming the big dog on the block. It was a time of increasing prosperity and a large section of the population had some money available to invest and they were looking for somewhere to put it. The South Sea Company had no problem attracting investors with an initial I.O.U. to the government worth £10,000,000 in return for a lucrative monopoly on trade in the South Seas. The company were enticing bondholders to convert their high-interest, irredeemable bonds to low-interest, easily tradeable stocks with huge financial gains at the end of the deal. The popular conception was that South American was just waiting for someone to introduce them to wool and fleece in exchange for mountains of jewels and gold.

The initial share sold for £128 on 1st January 1720 and shares disappeared in a heartbeat. Voracious speculators left no room for average investors who were being assured of the company's forthcoming dominance. By May, those same shares were valued at £500 and in June, they were £1050. Banks could barely keep up with the number of aristocrats begging for loans so they could buy more shares in the company.

Nobody questioned the repeated re-issue of stocks by the company in the rush to buy shares as fast as they were offered. And nobody questioned the fact that inexperienced management, who were basically just public relations directors, headed the company. The company set up shop in extravagant headquarters and as soon as investors saw the lavish offices they were occupying, they couldn't keep their money from gravitating towards the South Sea Company. With the spending, other companies appeared, some lunatic, some fraudulent and others merely optimistic. For example, one company wanted to buy Irish bogs, another wanted to manufacture a gun to fire square cannon balls and the most ludicrous of all *'For carrying-on an undertaking of great advantage but no one to know what it is!'* Unbelievably, £2000 was invested in this one.

The country was going wild But eventually, management took a big step backwards when they realised that the value of their personal shares in no way reflected the actual value of the company or its dismal earnings. Secretly, they sold their shares and hoped that no one would notice what was happening. But like all bad news it spread quickly but by then it was too late. Panic selling had begun and shares were down to £150 and falling fast.

A complete crash came in September as many banks folded when they couldn't collect on loans they had given to both recently bankrupted commoners as well as aristocrats. In the aftermath, many goldsmiths went bankrupt as well. Even Sir Isaac Newton lost £20,000 (equivalent to about £1.6 million in present day value) in South Sea Company shares. Suicides became a daily occurrence and even the Postmaster General took poison.

Investor outrage led Parliament to open an investigation and a proposal was even given to place all bankers in sacks filled with snakes and thrown into the Thames River. After the enquiry, reports came in that 462 members of the House of Commons and 112 peers had been involved in the crash. Even George's two mistresses were heavily involved and were blamed for being partly responsible for the whole thing. The fiasco severely damaged George's already poor reputation and would be one of the things that Britain remembered most about his reign. That and his wife being left to die in the German castle, that is.

When it became known that George had not personally invested any of his own money, many Parliamentarians sarcastically called him Lucky George. But I wonder if George thought of himself as lucky when his personal life was such a disaster, not to mention his terrible relationship with his son and his shattered reputation.

Things were just not going the way George had planned. His heart had always been in Hanover and he missed the clean, fresh smell of pine in the air wafting down from the lush mountains and he missed the small hamlets and towns nestled at the base of them. But most of all, he missed the people. They had never laughed at his crude manners or called him a 'turnip king' or snickered at his strange accent. He missed the people who had loved him so much before he had departed to start his new promising life in England. With his character in tatters in England, he returned many times over the years to the homeland that he never really wanted to leave in the first place.

It was the perfect place for George to die and it would be on one of his trips home that he was to have a stroke and die.

With his death, anti-German feeling subsided a little, just in time for his feisty son George Augustus to begin his own reign as George II.

GEORGE II

Born 1683
Reign 1727 – 1760

It was a warm summer's day in June 1727 when the Chief Minister, Robert Walpole, arrived unannounced at the country residence of the Prince and Princess of Wales. He was out of breath and in a panic. He had come to tell him that the man he had been locking horns with in a 'do or die' struggle for most of his life – his father King George I – was dead.

He received the news with barely a frown. His seething anger at the pain and suffering his father had caused was still so intense, it didn't cease at the news of father's death. To him, his father was an obstinate, self-indulgent, miserly tyrant and George decided not to even travel to Germany for the funeral, using the excuse that he was needed more in England than at the gravesite of the man he loathed.

As cold as that sounds, George I was not blameless in all of this. After all, he had exiled his wife to Ahlden House in Celle when his son was only 11 years old and he had denied his children the right to ever seen her again. It was the same story retold when George had alienated the prince and Princess of Wales from their children over the christening incident. Granted he has relented and allowed minimal visits but he had been arrogant enough not to listen to his son's side of the story. As far as the Prince was concerned, the incident should never have happened in the first place and as a result, his son had died without the comfort and love of his parents. It was something the prince could never forgive or forget.

When the will was read, it was pretty obvious there was anger on both sides. His father had stipulated that his succession in both England and Hanover was to be split between his future grandchildren, not given to his only son. It was a ridiculous will, even a spiteful one, and both England and Hanover disregarded it completely as George I had no right to pick and choose his successor in either country.

Four months later, 43-year-old George Augustus was crowned at Westminster Abbey as George II and the start of another long and turbulent reign began. Britain was headed into an uncertain new future at lightning speed.

It would have been difficult for any dynasty to step in to English society in this new age, but this particular one was still very new to England and the Hanoverians were still struggling with the customs and the language. They had been told in no uncertain terms that if any one of them made a mistake, they would be out as fast as they'd arrived.

England had already had a preview of what the Hanoverians were like. They had witnessed first hand the quarrelling between George I and his son and they were still a bit surprised at the intensity of the arguing. But within the first year of George II's reign, England were to find that this dynasty was actually more dysfunctional than even the Tudors had ever been.

Almost as soon as the coronation was over, George's son Frederick arrived from Hanover to take up the role of Prince of Wales as the heir inherent. The problem was that it had been 14 years since he'd last seen his family and he was still smarting seriously because of it.

21-year-old Frederick could be forgiven for thinking he had been abandoned at seven years old when his parents and sisters had left for London. He was left behind to be raised by tutors, even though there were good political reasons behind the decision. He was meant to be the representative for the family in Hanover so the German people wouldn't believe that they had been forgotten. But he had only been a small child and he had never forgotten this inconsolable anguish at seeing his family sail away while he remained, alone and lonely. He had always felt abandoned.

Anger clouded all judgment when he arrived in London in 1728. Not just had he lost touch with his parents over the 14 years, it soon turned out that no one could stand the sight of each other. He had acquired mistresses and large debts due to his fondness for gambling and he openly opposed his father's political beliefs while complaining of his own personal lack of influence in government. The open hostility was almost the undoing of the family.

Almost as soon as Frederick arrived in England, George began making preparations for a trip to Hanover. The question on everyone's lips was '*who is going to rule Britain while the king is away?*' Prince Frederick had only just arrived and he barely knew his way around the block much less running the whole country.

The question hardly mattered because George had his own ideas. When Parliament announced that it would not be the Prince of Wales but Queen Caroline who would reign as regent, it confirmed what everyone had been thinking. Caroline wore the pants in the family.

Although George and Caroline seemed like the happy royal couple on the outside, things were far from simple at home. Their love was not the fairy-tale story that we had imagined it would be when George first set eyes on Caroline and it was certainly not the sort of marriage that dreams are made of.

Behind closed doors, she knew how to manipulate him and he cheated unashamedly on her, even consulting her advice and opinion on his love affairs. But through every childbirth and even once when she collapsed, he was right there by her side, sleeping fitfully at the foot of her bed and kissing her hand repeatedly. She was his rock and he wanted *her* to reign as regent while he was away. He would have it no other way. And you can imagine how furious Frederick was about it. It was just another instance of being sidelined.

In English society, while the king was being called cold and prickly, Caroline was being called 'sociable'. She was always elegantly dressed in the latest fashion and her eyes sparkled with good humour. By then, Caroline's intellectual abilities far outshone her dull husband's and she had learnt how to cover up for George's poor social ineptitude with great skill. In her attempt to fit in, she struck up a friendship with the Prime Minister Robert Walpole and to complete the package, she became an avid reader and a keen supporter of the arts and science.

It was an age of endless possibilities for the self-made man and the English took full advantage of it. It was a time when there was a lot of new money from the middle classes and professional men such as doctors, lawyers and traders were popping up everywhere. It seemed they had money to burn on things they didn't really need. With this new money came new spending and new medical research.

Smallpox was still a virulent disease and it was killing up to 35% of people in some outbreaks. When Lady Mary Montagu, the wife of the Turkish ambassador, brought back news that the Turks had found a remedy, Caroline sat up and listened.

Lady Montagu told her that the Turks and the Africans had been rubbing powdered smallpox scabs, sometimes fluid from pustules, into superficial scratches made in the skin of patients who had not contracted the disease. The patient would develop pustules identical to those caused by smallpox but usually it produced a less severe outbreak than the naturally occurring one. After about two or three weeks, the symptoms subsided indicating a successful recovery. And as everyone knew, once you had smallpox, you were immune to future outbreaks.

Neither Caroline nor Lady Montague were strangers to smallpox. Caroline's father had died of smallpox when she was three years old. She and George had both contracted it but survived. Lady Montagu had lost her brother to the disease and had contracted it herself as well, although she was left with severe scarring. To show how much Lady Montagu believed in the remedy, she had allowed this practice of 'variolation' to be conducted on her five-year-old son Edward under the supervision of the embassy doctor, Charles Maitland. On her return to England, she had her four-year-old daughter inoculated as well in the presence of physicians in the royal court. To everyone's surprise, both variolations were successful. Later that year, Maitland conducted the same experiment on six prisoners in Newgate Prison with the promise of freedom if they survived. Again it was a success and Caroline took action by helping to promote the procedure throughout England.

As you can imagine, the remedy was received dubiously, to say the least. Rubbing powdered scabs into cuts and injecting the pussy fluid into your own body? Was she mad? You can see where this was going. No one believed her.

It was left to Caroline to show the people that she believed. Without hesitation, she had two of her daughters inoculated, and like a miracle, it worked. Caroline's faith in the remedy and the evident success assured Britain that the procedure was safe.

George's frequent trips back and forth to Hanover had become lengthier and lengthier ones and his absences only served to remind the British that he was foreign and he had another country to think about as well as theirs. To many of them, he became the king who was never there. What time he *did* spend in the country was spent with his mistresses, despite having a beautiful, happy, outgoing wife sitting at home. Not seeing any reason for discretion, George all but flaunted his affairs while Caroline remained silent.

Instead of Frederick being upset with his father's behaviour, he revelled in it. He had great satisfaction in showing the people that he was the opposite from his cold, grumpy, adulterous father. As for George, all he wanted was for Frederick to settle down. Negotiations had begun between George and his brother-in-law in Prussia for the hand of his daughter Wilhelmine to marry Frederick, despite the fact that the couple had never met. Plans came to an abrupt halt when Robert Walpole heard that after the marriage, Frederick would be expected to remain in Hanover with his new wife as the regent. *That* was something England would never agree to. And by the way, neither did Frederick. It was at this time that fresh negotiations began with the infamous Sarah Churchill, Duchess of Marlborough (Queen Anne's constant but eventually estranged companion) whose favourite granddaughter was a young lady by the name of Lady Diana Spencer.

Sarah's relationship with her children had always been strained although she'd managed to have a good rapport with one of her daughters, Anne, married to Charles Spencer, 3rd Earl of Sunderland. Anne was always quiet and steady so when she died at only 33 years of age, leaving three sons and one daughter, Sarah Churchill was heartbroken. It was no surprise that one year later, when Charles Spencer announced he was remarrying, that Sarah decided to take her 12-year-old granddaughter, Diana, under her wing.

With a grandmother as influential as Sarah Churchill, Lady Diana was at the top of the list of eligible high society brides. She had beauty and breeding and it was no wonder that she had many suitors. So when the first round of negotiations for a bride for Frederick fell through, Sarah Churchill pushed very hard for a proposed marriage between Frederick and Diana. Diana's early years had been spent in close contact with the children of George II, despite the initial aloof relationship between her grandmother and his family, so Sarah felt it was an almost given that the couple should marry since they already knew each other so well.

It's not such a stretch of the imagination to believe that Sarah still held a great deal of resentment over the supposed ill-treatment she had received from Queen Anne. With her granddaughter married to Frederick, she would have the last laugh and her family would reach the pinnacle of power when Diana finally became the queen. For someone like Sarah, whose humble beginnings were well known, it was a huge achievement and the idea almost consumed Sarah. As an added enticement, Diana's already massive dowry was raised to £100,000, which would undoubtedly help erase Frederick's huge gambling debts.

The ceremony was arranged to take place in secret in the lodge of the Windsor Great Park and the date was set and agreed upon.

Robert Walpole had an impressive spy system and once again, when he heard of the upcoming nuptials, he strongly vetoed them. Not only had Diana's father been involved in the South Sea Bubble, he had been implicated in what had become known as the Atterbury Plot of 1722 aimed at restoring the Stuarts to the throne. The Duke of Orleans, Regent of France, had made it known to Walpole's Secretary of State that the Jacobites had asked him to send 3,000 men in support of a coup d'état to take place in May of that year. Charles Spencer's papers had been seized and a letter of thanks addressed to him by 'The Pretender' had come to light. Besides all of that, Walpole much preferred a European match anyway.

So instead of marrying Lady Diana, 29-year-old Frederick married 16-year-old Augusta of Saxe-Gotha with a settlement from Parliament of £50,000. And instead of marrying Frederick, Lady Diana married the Duke of Bedford. A few years later, Lady Diana would die from tuberculosis and

Wimbledon House, her inheritance according to her grandmother's will, passed instead to her brother John. In 1961, her brother's descendant, Edward John Spencer, 8th Earl of Spencer and styled Viscount Althorp, became the father of a beautiful baby daughter whose name was chosen a week after her birth. The infant was christened Diana after her ancestor, Lady Diana, Duchess of Bedford. Through another of Sarah's grandchildren, a boy by the name of Charles Churchill, a son would be born in 1874 and he would be christened Winston Churchill.

In the past, Frederick had always been a womaniser and spendthrift but he compromised by having only one mistress following his marriage to Augusta, who had made a more than favourable impression on her future in-laws by throwing herself on the floor before them in a gesture of submission at her arrival, days before the wedding.

Standing beside his father, Frederick watched silently. It wasn't just his father who was crowing. His mother smiled widely as well, welcoming the compliant woman who she hoped would favourably influence their wayward son in the near future.

It was the last thing Frederick was going to let happen. Obedience was all well and good but that submissiveness should be directed solely to her husband and he fully intended informing his young wife of his expectations. There would be no more fawning to his parents and beginning the next day, she was to make sure she always arrived *after* his mother to court functions and church attendances so that she would be forced to push in front of the queen to reach her place. It put her in a terrible position from the very start because the queen in turn insisted that Augusta enter by another entrance in the future.

If England were hoping that the two men would bury the hatchet, they were being far too optimistic. There was still no love lost between the king and his son and an incident one month later made it all too clear to the country in no uncertain terms. George's ship had been caught in a storm while he was returning to England from Hanover, leading rumours to circulate that the king had been lost at sea and drowned. Although George later returned safe and sound many months later, Britain was very aware that Frederick had been hosting a great dinner party that night. As the smell of hot buttery rolls wafted through his dining room, the tinkling of glasses and laughter had stopped suddenly when the news of the storm and the possible consequences had arrived. All eyes were glued to Frederick's face. Never one for sentimentality, Frederick's face broke into a wide smile as he raised his glass and toasted to his own future as King Frederick, knowing full well that his father was presumed dead.

In June the following year, it all came to an explosive finale. Frederick had informed his parents that Augusta was pregnant and due to give birth in October and of course, George and Caroline were ecstatic. Plans were made and preparations began for the birth of their first grandchild.

In actual fact, the baby was due much earlier than that. She went into labour in July and it would have been a frightening night for Augusta. Instead of the usual procedure where the king and queen would be present to verify the birth, Frederick sneaked Augusta out of Hampton Court in the middle of the night and took her to St James Palace to ensure his family did not attend. It was a terrible trip for the young princess over bumpy ground in a rattling carriage while painful contractions grew closer and closer together.

St James Palace was far from ready to receive them, much less be prepared for the birth of the king's first grandchild. No bed was prepared, no sheets could be found and of course, the delivery was traumatic. In the final moments as Augusta screamed in agony, a tablecloth was produced for her to give birth on.

With something as important as a royal birth, there was no way it was going to remain a secret. All too soon for Frederick, news had travelled back to his father and mother that Frederick had left in the dead of night with his wife in labour and they were horrified. Eventually, Caroline found out where Frederick had taken Augusta and with two of her daughters, she arrived at St James Palace to discover to her relief, that Augusta had given birth to a *"poor, ugly little she-mouse"* rather than a *"large, fat, healthy boy"* and a worse scandal had been avoided. If the new heir-apparent had not been witnessed at his birth, (and let's not forget what had happened to James II when his second wife had delivered a boy with no royals present to witness the birth), who knew what stories George's enemies might concoct? James Francis Edward Stuart would forever have to live down the rumour of being the 'warming pan' baby and a 'Pretender' and Caroline had no want for *that* to happen to her family as well.

Needless to say, scandal or no scandal, the whole incident only made matters worse. Frederick was banished from court and sent to live in Leicester House with his new family, which seems to have been a repeating echo in the Hanoverian family.

It seems that history *does* repeat itself and their private war continued even the following year when Caroline undertook surgery for a hernia she had developed after the delivery of her last child ten years previously. The hernia had been left untreated but could not be ignored any longer. The operation was performed, without the use of anaesthetic by the way, and she bore the pain extremely well. In the end, it was not the operation that killed her: it was gangrene that set in afterwards. Through it all, George slept by her bed but refused to allow Frederick to see his mother, despite his frequent requests. It was only via a message sent through Robert Walpole that Frederick became aware that his mother had forgiven him on her deathbed. She was buried at Westminster Abbey on 17th December and Frederick was not invited, or allowed, to the funeral.

Everyone knew George loved a fight. If he wasn't fighting with Robert Walpole, he was fighting with his son Frederick. When he wasn't fighting with someone in England, he would go back to Hanover and fight to protect his borders against the Austrians. People were getting thoroughly sick and tired of it all. So when problems began again with the Spanish, they knew George would be completely delighted.

It all began when Spain began having suspicions that Britain was not honouring the Utrecht Treaty signed in 1711 after the War of the Spanish Succession. As part of the agreement, Britain had received a 30-year trade agreement from Spain, which permitted British merchants to trade up to 500 tons of goods per year in the Spanish colonies in America as well as selling an unlimited number of slaves. Britain had also granted Spain the right to stop British ships to ensure that they didn't go over that limit. Believing that the British were taking advantage of the agreement and smuggling, Spanish authorities began boarding and seizing British ships, as well as holding and torturing their crews.

When George heard, his first reaction was to declare war on Spain immediately, although Walpole knew that Britain could not afford another war like the last one. Instead of listening to George, he sent additional troops to Gibraltar as a show of support and to let the navy know that they were not being overlooked. As an afterthought, he dispatched a fleet to the West Indies as well to keep an eye on things.

Walpole had intended the move to be a cautious approach, but of course, when Philip of Spain saw more English ships arriving daily, it had the opposite affect. In an already tense atmosphere, he saw it as an act of aggression and he went into overdrive. He retaliated by suspending the agreement altogether and sent out orders for all British ships in Spanish ports to be confiscated. From there, it went downhill fast. An English admiral by the name of Vernon attacked Porto Bello in Panama with six English ships and quickly captured it, remaining there for three weeks.

By October 1739 it was getting so out of hand with both sides repeatedly violating the terms of the agreement that Walpole had no choice. He reluctantly declared war on Spain and by January the next year, both sides fully anticipated that France would enter the war as well, on the side of Spain.

If it was at all possible for things to worsen any further, it was when Charles of Austria died at the end of October 1742. Overnight England became embroiled in another succession issue with Charles' daughter Maria Theresa fighting to become the only female, and last ruler, of the House of Hapsburg. With war threatening the borders of his beloved Hanover, George and his youngest son, William Duke of Cumberland, left for Germany to protect their boundaries. It would be the beginning of a long military career for 21-year-old William.

Instead of fighting the Austrians, George should have been spending more time watching the Stuarts in Italy. James Francis Stuart and his son Charles were making preparations to take back what they saw as rightfully theirs. James had already made his son his regent and invested him with the title Charles III and by 1745 money had been raised with the help of France. Charles was basically an Italian who was challenging the Germans with the help of the French for the British throne.

When 'Bonnie Prince Charlie' set sail for Scotland, hoping for a warm welcome from the Highland clans once he'd landed, he must have been feeling more than a little nervous. With only two ships, it was always going to be difficult and he was going to need every bit of his charisma and leadership skills considering he only had seven companions with him as well.

Scotland can be bitterly cold in autumn but there is nowhere much colder than the small isolated island of Eriskay, north west of Scotland. If Charles had missed it, his next stop would have been Iceland. Today, ferries take 40 mins to cross the causeway to Barra, another equally isolated spot on the mainland, but for Charles, it would have taken him many days to make the crossing in the constant drenching rain.

When Charles landed, the sky was a steel grey and the winds were howling but despite the weather, and fortunately for him, he was to find that the Jacobites were in love with the past. They seemed to have forgotten about his father's failed attempt years before and were still intent on bringing the Stuarts back home along with their divine right to rule. With support from the Highland clans, both Catholic and Protestant, Charles gathered a force large enough to march on to Edinburgh. By early November, with his father's standard raised at Glenfinnan, Edinburgh surrendered to him.

The anxiety in the English court was palpable as news arrived that Charles had set up court at Holyrood Palace and had issued a public declaration. He'd stated that the Germans were engaging Britain in a personal, irrelevant foreign war that was a pointless drain on English money and that war was disrupting English trade. It wasn't King George who was suffering, it was the English people and they'd had enough.

England was certainly listening. Everything Bonnie Prince Charlie was saying was true. England *was* being run by barbaric foreigners who had no idea or care about the English people. Their king *was* spending so much time in Hanover. A satirical note had even been pinned to St James Palace decrying his absence. *'Lost or strayed out of the house'* the note quipped and it had been read by thousands of people before George had it ripped down from the gates. They were certainly in full agreement with Charles who then added, *'Who wanted to be ruled by a foreigner anyway?'*

It was a clever way to run down the Germans to the British public and you can see how this touched a raw nerve. Even the new Prime Minister, William Pitt, had stated that they needed more self-confidence as a nation and that the Georgians were treating the country like a province of Hanover not the formidable country that it was. *That* statement certainly did not win him any favours with George.

As Charles marched south at the head of approximately 10,000 men, tension mounted even more in the English court. George was busting for a fight as usual and he was ready to leap onto his horse and lead the charge. Ever the diplomat, Pitt tactfully reminded George of his advancing age and eventually convinced him to leave the fight to his youngest, and youngest and favourite son, William Duke of Cumberland, since Frederick had stated he would have nothing to do with it all.

There was no love lost between the two brothers. Frederick was well aware that his younger brother was in his father's good books and even without the added aggravation, they were like chalk and cheese. Frederick was busy trying to impress on the English that he was a much more gentle person than his overweight, obnoxious younger brother who had a penchant for picking fights and starting wars like their argumentative father.

It was probably the final straw for George. He had been thinking recently about his will and this fresh declaration only served to annoy him even more. He already regarded Frederick as the 'black sheep' of the family, and even his mother once famously described him as *'the greatest ass and the greatest liar... and the greatest beast in the whole world'*, adding *'and I heartily wish he were out of it.'* Frederick had just pushed George that one bit further to making a final decision. He came up with the idea to reshuffle the line of succession after his death by giving Frederick the role of Elector of Hanover while putting the crown of England firmly and squarely on the head of his favourite son William instead.

While the two brothers bickered endlessly with each other, as well as with their father, Charles was taking full advantage of the volatile situation and had been on the move again. He had taken Carlisle and Manchester comfortably and continued further on to Derby. But as he travelled further south, he found a totally unexpected and worrying lack of support for the Jacobites in England.

Bonnie Prince Charles was 30 years too late in his attempt to take back his throne. Though no one could say they particularly *liked* the Hanoverians, George and his family were firmly established in England by then and no one seemed interested in yet another monumental change. Sure, the English disliked the Germans. They were boorish and cold and could barely speak the language. And they fought callously and endlessly with each other. But England had not been happy with the arrogance of the Stuarts either.

Perhaps England was spot-on in their observation because arrogance seems to have been Charles' biggest downfall. Because of the lack of English support, Charles was given advice, good advice, from his colonels to return to Scotland to rethink their plans. Charles on the other hand didn't want to return. By returning to Scotland it would look like he was retreating and that was not his intention. It was so far from the actual truth it was laughable. He wanted England to know that he wasn't afraid of a battle. That's what he'd come for and that's what was going to happen.

As adamant as he was, his council wouldn't budge either. They'd heard that the English army was gathering force and as much as Charles tried to convince them that France was launching an invasion as well, no one wanted to listen.

In the end, Charles had no other choice but to reluctantly take the advice of his colonels and begin the long march back north. They withdrew on 6th December 1745, marching north through freezing snowstorms, taking whatever food and money they needed from the already cash-strapped towns. It was when they reached Glasgow that Charles' army made their fateful and worst mistake. They threatened to ransack the city if they weren't housed and fed. They even demanded all the boots and shoes of the townspeople of Dumfries since they'd worn their own out on the long trek.

It wasn't the way it should have been done and because of it, he lost even more valuable support from men who would have joined him willingly otherwise.

As Charles marched, George recalled William from Austria to act as his Commander at the head of the army to deal with the rebellion up north. By January, William had arrived in Scotland, taken control of the English army and made his first decision. They would wait out the cruel winter in Aberdeen until reinforcements from Prince Frederick of Hesse joined his rejuvenated army.

He waited until a rainy day on 16th April 1745, one day after his 25th birthday, to pack up and move his well-rested army towards Culloden Moor, north east of Inverness. It would be the last battle on British soil and it would be catastrophic.

Charles was ready for a fight but he should have listened to Commander Murray when he was told not to stop on the flat, marshy ground of Drumossie Moor, three miles south of Culloden.

Charles' original plan was to carry out a surprise night attack on the government's camp. They would set out at dusk and march to Nairn, 16 miles north of Inverness and as Murray attacked William's rear, Charles would bring up the second line. Unfortunately, there were countless delays and they only started out at 8pm, leaving Murray to lead the slow-going, tired army across the countryside in the dark.

The terrain was bad enough but it wasn't the only problem Murray was facing. His men were from Highland clans and they were basically wild, untrained ruffians fighting with pitchforks, scythes and axes. Only one-fifth of them had a sword. Even the colonels from the MacDonald clan considered their men to be uncontrollable.

By the time the leading troop reached Culraick, it was one hour before dawn and Murray decided there was not enough time to mount a surprise attack. He sent another commander to inform Charles of the change of plan, but he missed Charles in the dark.

It ended up a disorganised shambles. In the darkness, while Murray led one-third of the Jacobite forces back to camp, the other two-thirds continued towards their original objective, unaware of the change in plan. Not long after the exhausted Jacobite forces made it back to Culloden, reports came in of the advancing government troops. By then, many of the Jacobite soldiers had dispersed in search of food, while others were asleep in ditches. Meanwhile, William's army struck camp at about 5am and were well on their way to Culloden.

By 11am, both armies were within sight of each other with open moorland lying soggily between them. As the government forces steadily trudged across the moor in the driving rain, sleet blew into the faces of the already exhausted Jacobite army, hindering their progress even more.

Charles just didn't stand a chance. Within an hour, any Jacobites who had not been shot were being butchered and run through with redcoat bayonets and any survivors left standing were simply dropping their weapons and running. It was the day the Jacobite cause bled to death on the marshes of Scotland and a day they would remember losing 1500 – 2000 loyal men. In striking contrast, William is reported to have lost only 50 Englishmen with 259 wounded, although a high proportion of those wounded would most likely have died of their wounds later on.

It was a relatively short battle but the significance cannot be underestimated. The story of Culloden represents the last stand of an ancient royal dynasty that could trace its ancestry back to the Dark Ages and quite simply, it was the end of an era for Scotland.

Charles' flight has become a romantic legend with songs and poems written to tell the sad story. They tell of his escape, hiding in the moors of Scotland and criss-crossing the country for more than five months to evade capture. Many highlanders saw him and helped him, but none of them betrayed him for the £30,000 reward that had been offered, although heaven knows, they could have used the cash. The songs tell how Flora MacDonald helped Charles escape in a small boat dressed as a milkmaid over to the Isle of Skye in the hope of fleeing back to France. They also tell of a heart wrenching longing for Charles to return to them one day. In their perhaps misguided loyalty, they had worshipped him and sacrificed their lives for his cause and they were so sure he would remember that fact and return. He never did.

For her effort in saving Charles, Flora was captured and sent to the Tower to await trial for treason.

The morning after the Battle of Culloden, written orders were sent out by William *'to give no quarter'* and his men followed his orders to the word. Settlements were burnt to the ground and around 20,000 cattle, sheep and goats were confiscated from already impoverished local farms and sold at Fort Augustus where the soldiers split the profits. Some Jacobites had headed south in an attempt to escape abroad while most went north to Inverness. These were the ones William was waiting for.

William had been thinking long and hard about what to do. The orders given to his men were being carried out to the letter but the question in his mind was *'where will they run when they have nowhere else to go?'* Then, like a bolt of lightning, he knew. Most would head north to the biggest city they knew in an attempt to hide before eventually escaping to France. They'd head to Inverness.

William had thought of everything and it turned out he was absolutely correct. In no time, as more and more weary Jacobites flooded into the city, the refugees were captured and the gaols were filled. Later, they would be loaded onto prison ships and taken south to England to stand trial for high treason.

In total, 120 men were executed including one third of them from the British Army for deserting. Amongst the remaining prisoners, lots were drawn and only one out of twenty were alive to actually stand trial. With the journey taking upwards of eight months, not too many of these remainders were alive at the end of their journey anyway. Although most of those who stood trial were sentenced to death, almost all prisoners had their sentences commuted to transportation to the British colonies for life. In all, 936 men were transported, 222 were banished and another 382 obtained their freedom by being exchanged for prisoners of war in France. The high ranking 'rebel lords' were lucky enough to be simply executed on Tower Hill in London.

Following Culloden, William was rewarded with an extra £25,000 per annum for his war effort. To the Whigs, William was nothing less than the conquering hero who had saved Britain. To the Tories, well supported by Frederick who openly encouraged them, William had earned the title of 'The Butcher'. It was at this time that Frederick met Flora and eventually obtained her release during his constant unsuccessful campaigning against his father and brother.

The year 1751 should have been a bad one for George. News reached him that his son Frederick had been hit in the chest with a cricket ball although the news created barely a dent in his daily routine.

Cricket had developed into the country's most popular team sport since 1733 and by 1751, Frederick was seriously involved in the game, both as a patron and as an occasional player. On a cold day in March, a few weeks after his 44th birthday, Frederick had been playing cricket and was struck hard in the chest by a cricket ball. Days later, while walking in his garden at Kew, he caught a chill which eventually turned to pleurisy. As with all royals, the best doctors were called and three of the very best were chosen. They bled him and he seemed to be getting better but on the evening of the 20th March, confined to bed, he began to cough painfully, clutching his stomach. Within minutes, he was dead. The post mortem stated the cause of death was a burst abscess on his lung due to the cricket ball incident but the general medical opinion was that he died of pneumonia.

The news reached George when he was playing cards with a group of friends. The whole court turned expectantly to look at him, watching to see his reaction. They found that there was no reaction at all. The death of his son, the most popular member of the royal family, was received with barely a nod as the game continued.

Though George barely commiserated with his daughter-in-law, he was openly devastated in December when his favourite daughter Louisa died. No one thought he was capable of such emotion, especially since he had often stated he did not have any interest in his children, or grandchildren, at all.

Britain was turning into a nation greedy for conquests of more territories. They weren't content with the thirteen colonies in the Americas. They wanted more. But this greed was more than just a land grab. It was a war over trade routes and Global dominance, mixed in with a hatred of the French, of course. It was the start of the Seven Year War against France where George marched off to battle with his favourite lieutenant – his son William The Butcher.

The conflict broke out when Britain attacked disputed French colonies in North America and seized hundreds of French ships. It escalated further when Germany and Portugal supported Britain while Spain joined up with France. George's brother-in-law the King of Prussia who usually took sides with Austria sided with Britain instead, leaving Austria to form one of their own with France. It became even more messy and complicated when Russia who normally aligned with Austria switched sides and partnered up with Britain as well. It seemed like the whole world had gone mad and it all reflected rather badly on George.

George was out of touch with the way wars were conducted. He had a romantic vision of himself riding at the front of his army on horseback heroically leading the charge. It becomes almost comical when you remember George was 73 years old. Ever the fighter, his ministers would have had their work cut out trying to convince him that war was not won that way anymore. And it would have been up to them to suggest a replacement. Who else but the Butcher?

George may have been old and he may have been out of touch with war but he wasn't content to sit back and do nothing. There was still fire in the old man and perhaps he just needed to make his presence felt.

As you would have predicted, his anger needed someone to focus on. Frederick was dead so someone had to take the brunt. That person, strangely enough, was his son William and it was all because he signed an agreement in Hanover that George believed had totally favoured the French.

On William's return to London, he met the full force of his father's fury and he must have been in a state of shock. After all, he'd been given permission to negotiate an agreement to end the Seven Years War and that's what he'd done. But the end results of those negotiations weren't what George had wanted and he let his son know. When they met, George remarked, *"Here is my son who has ruined me and disgraced himself."*

Always the favoured son, used to praise and admiration from his father, the cruel words left a lasting impression on William. In response, he resigned all the military and public offices he held and retired into private life. In retaliation, George changed his will in favour of his eldest grandson George, the eldest of Frederick's nine children to Augusta.

George must have known his health was declining. By October 1760, he was blind in one eye and almost deaf, while his beloved wife and eight of his children were dying around him, one by one. One morning, he rose as usual at 6.00am and with a hot chocolate in his hand, he left to go to the toilet. His valet heard a loud crash and when he entered the room, he found George on the floor. He was lifted onto the bed and his daughter Amelia was quickly summoned. By the time she arrived, George was already dead. The post-mortem revealed an aortic aneurysm.

At 77 years old, George had lived longer than any of his English predecessors and had paved the way for an amazing new Britain. Britain had come through the Glorious Revolution and was about to begin the Industrial Revolution. There would be dramatic growth in the textile industry, the steel industry and iron industry as well as the invention of the steam engine, canal turnpikes and natural power.

Over the next 60 years, England would see a population explosion from 7.8 million at George II's death to 23.1 million when his grandson George III died forty years later. It was the age of George Washington and the American Revolution. It was the age of the French Revolution with Louis XVI and his wife Marie Antoinette losing their thrones and their heads. It was also the age of the Napoleonic Wars where Britain would declare war eight times and would be engaged in fighting one out of every two years. Britain would have the most colonies in the world and the largest navy in the world. She would humiliate the ancient Chinese empire and intervene in Persia and Egypt simply out of displeasure. From being a minor country somewhere on the northwest corner of Europe, Britain would become one of the greatest nations in the world.

This is what lay ahead for the 22-year-old grandson of George II. This quiet new king who succeeded his grandfather couldn't have been more different from his family. He would reject almost everything his grandfather had advocated as he tried to encourage everything his own father Frederick had never had the chance to implement.

When George III stepped up to the mark, a lot was lurking on the horizon, waiting to happen.

GEORGE III

Born 1738
Reign 1760 – 1820

From the very beginning, George was different from his Hanoverian predecessors and England welcomed him like a breath of fresh air after his previous feisty ancestors. And George wasn't about to let them down. Not only was he young enough to make a difference, he was born in Britain and English was his first language. He *felt* British. But as we all know, good intentions are sometimes not enough. Even though he was determined to improve British opinion of his family, you could say he was the one responsible for setting the most catastrophic times into motion since James II.

After a rather shaky start, born sickly and two months premature, George grew into a healthy, intelligent but shy, reserved child. No doubt, with his father, uncle and grandfather publicly ranting and raving at each other almost on a daily basis, it was best to keep a low profile. By eight years old, he could read and write in both English and German and he'd begun his extensive education in chemistry, physics, astronomy, mathematics, French, Latin, history, music, geography, commerce, agriculture and constitutional law. To round it off, he was encouraged to practice dancing, fencing and riding. All quite daunting for an eight-year-old you might think, but George took it all in his stride.

When George came to the throne in 1760, he was 22 years old, young, virile and single and finding a suitable bride for the young king became the most imperative issue on everyone's mind. After an intense search, a 17-year-old princess from Mecklenburg-Strelitz, brought up in an insignificant north German duchy and with no experience in politics, stood out from the rest for George. The fact that Charlotte could not speak English at all was a distinct advantage because George fully intended to tell her 'not to meddle' in his affairs. It was an instruction she was very happy to follow. The negotiations began and the contract was signed by both her brother and George's advisor Simon Harcourt, 1st Earl Harcourt, and nine months later, George was in the Chapel Royal at St James Palace with his future bride Charlotte of Mecklenburg-Strelitz, standing by his side, having only met her for the first time an hour before the ceremony. A fortnight later, both was crowned at Westminster Abbey and the beginning of his long and happy marriage, full of the laughter of children, began at the same time as his remarkable reign.

George had a lot on his plate from the very beginning. From what he could see, while his family had been fighting and squabbling amongst themselves, the Whig party had grown incredibly strong and it was being controlled by rich men who ran the party by bribery and nepotism. His first priority was to create a new Parliament and after a lengthy and extensive search, George found a docile Prime Minister, Lord Moore, who ran things the way George wanted them to be run. His next priority was to finish the war with France.

By this time, France's navy had been crippled by the war and both Austria and Britain were close to bankruptcy because of it. In the American colonies, Britain was also trying hard to pacify the French-Canadian population and the American Indian tribes who supported the French. The problem was that Britain was in so much debt, they were struggling to pay the costs of their new empire, more specifically the Americas, not to mention their own high court officials in Britain. The only way George could see to make ends meet was to enforce taxes on the colonies in America for revenue. As such, they became Britain's cash cow.

Before the colonies knew it, they were being told there were new taxes to be imposed on molasses and sugar, as well as paper used for playing cards, legal documents and newspapers. As new colonists in America, they were already struggling and strapped for cash. So when it finally dawned on them that Britain was intending to drain money from America indefinitely, they looked at each other in shock.

Being new to the role and inexperienced, George was still trying to play catch-up so he can be forgiven for not having a closer look at whom he was dealing with. A hundred years ago, America had been an unknown land where people in Europe and Asia had escaped from religious and social control as well as the dominance of the established monastic rulers. And when you look at the British colonists, we know they were basically rejects from Britain who'd either been sent to the Americas as punishment or arrived in the Americas to start of new life, leaving their life full of hardship and poverty behind them. But all of these people had something in common. They all wanted a fresh start in a land of their own with rules of their own and with a government of their own. So when George began enforcing more and more restrictions and taxes on them, the seed of discontent was sown.

These people had been resisting the control of rulers for many years by then and their indignation was quickly aroused. What they saw was Britain's traditional rules and infrastructure being imposed on *their* country and *their* country was nothing like Britain. As well as that, they were in an economic crisis of their own after supporting British troops with food and housing during the seven years of war. It had a snowball effect on them and the conflict soon escalated out of control.

Imposing taxes had seemed like a good idea to George at the time but problems began to pop up almost from the very beginning. America was arguing that there were constitutional issues involved, the main one being that they weren't even represented in British Parliament. The question being asked was *"why should we be forced to pay British taxes at all?"*

While everyone was pointing fingers at each other, Britain soon found they had another unforeseen problem on their hands. Even if they *wanted* to collect the taxes, there was no one to collect them anyway. By the time the taxes were fully established, most tax collectors had resigned after having seen too many men tarred and feathered by the locals. Since no one wanted to suffer the same fate, there wasn't anyone who wanted the job.

Anger was bubbling close to the surface in both Britain and the Americas and before anyone knew it, British troops in Boston open fired on an angry mob that had attacked a sentry outside a government office. One year later, the situation worsened when the Americas were told there would be a tax on tea. It was to be the final straw.

In October 1773, the colonies learnt there were seven ships bound for Boston, New York, Philadelphia and Charleston carrying 2,000 chests overflowing with 600,000 pounds of tea. The potential for a serious protest was too good to miss out on.

It was a cool dark night in December when a group of 30 to 130 men left a meeting at Old South Meeting House where Samuel Adams stood addressing 7,000 people. History says he tried desperately to reassert control as people poured out of the meeting prepared to take action of their own but there was little chance that anyone was going to listen to him. They had a plan in mind and nothing was going to stop them. They donned Native Americans clothing and stealthily crept on board three of the ships as they lay quietly moored in Boston Harbour. Over the course of three hours, they dumped all 342 chests of tea overboard into the water near the foot of Hutchison Street.

Whether or not Samuel Adams helped to plan the Boston Tea Party is still in dispute but he immediately argued that it was not an act of a lawless mob as the British insinuated but instead a principled protest and the only remaining option the people had to defend their constitutional rights.

There was a repeat performance in March the next year and similar acts such as the burning of a cargo ship, *Peggy Stewart*, in Maryland and by July 1776, the colonies had had enough. They staunchly declared they wanted their independence since the monastic government of Britain had plundered their seas, burnt their towns and destroyed their lives. They weren't about to sit back and let Britain do it any longer.

It wasn't just an unfair government or even English rule that the colonies objected to. George's determination to place himself at the heart of American politics had created a new republican movement meant to attack the rule of kings everywhere. The process of destroying the monarchy was well under way and all of a sudden, Britain knew they had a serious problem on their hands. At this stage, Britain hadn't heard of George Washington.

George Washington had been appointed Commander-in-chief in June the previous year because of his military expertise in New England. It wasn't that he was necessarily qualified to wage war on Britain because his training and experience was primarily in frontier warfare involving small numbers of soldiers. And it wasn't that he was trained in the open-field style of battle as were the commanding British generals. Unlike them, he had no practical experience manoeuvring large formations of infantry, commanding cavalry and artillery, or maintaining the flow of supplies for thousands of men in the field. But what George Washington *did* have was charisma. Add courage and determination to the recipe and you have a man who was smart enough to keep one step ahead of the enemy. After the first taste of victory in Boston, his jubilant troops moved on to New York City and set up camp, pulling down a statue of George III in the process.

Instead of taking a good hard look at the situation, George's reaction was purely Hanoverian. The colonies had to be punished and he had every intention of fighting them and crushing them into remorse. By August 1776, the British army, led by General Howe, launched a counterattack on New York City and quickly took it back.

Washington lost 2,800 of his men in the attack and it forced him to step back and rethink his manoeuvres. With his confused army in disarray, Washington ordered the remains of his army to temporarily retreat across the Delaware River into Pennsylvania while he considered options.

Perhaps General Howe was a little too confident that the war would be over in a few months. As Washington's men disappeared across the river, General Howe relaxed and decided to winter his troops at Trenton and Princeton. His mistake was leaving Washington free to attack at a time and place of his own choosing.

It was Christmas night and the air was crisp and still when Washington and his men stealthily crossed back over the Delaware River and attacked. As Washington had planned, the attack was completely unexpected and the British soldiers, who had already retired to their tents, were left scattered and confused at the suddenness of the onslaught. A few days later, evading a force that had been sent to retaliate and destroy his army, Washington attacked the British again, this time at Princeton, dealing them another humiliating blow.

General Howe's strategy had been to capture colonial cities and stop the rebellion at key economic and political centres and he never abandoned the belief that once the Americans were deprived of their major cities, the rebellion would wither and die. So in the summer of 1777, he mounted an attack on Philadelphia. Once again, Washington moved in with his army and Philadelphia fell two weeks later. Strategy after strategy backfired on Howe until finally, his entire army consisting of 6,200 men was forced to surrender.

England had always been a thorn in France's paw so this victory was a major turning point in the Seven Year's War because it encouraged France to ally itself with the American cause for independence. The alliance with France brought a large French army and a huge navy fleet at Washington's disposal and with this new assistance, he decided to attack the British General, Charles Cornwallis, at Yorktown, Virginia.

Facing the combined French and Colonial armies and a fleet of 29 French warships at his back would have been a nightmarish situation for Cornwallis and he held out for as long as he could. Three weeks to be exact. But on October 19th 1781, he could not hold out any longer and he humiliatingly surrendered. Claiming illness on the day, Cornwallis sent Brigadier General O'Hara in his place to formally surrender his sword. In turn, Washington sent his second-in-command Benjamin Lincoln to accept it.

Washington had no way of knowing that the Yorktown victory would bring the war to a close. The British still had 26,000 troops occupying New York City, Charleston, and Savannah and they still had a large fleet of warships in the harbour. But by November of the next year, Washington knew the British were finished. When they evacuated New York City and other cities, the war was essentially over and the Americans had won their independence. Peace negotiations began in April 1782 and continued through the summer led by Benjamin Franklin, John Hay, John Adams and Henry Laurens and representing Great Britain was David Hartley and Richard Oswald.

The 3rd September is a particular date that keeps returning infamously over and over in history. Oliver Cromwell began his cold-blooded, brutal attack on Drogheda on September 3rd 1649. It was the anniversary of both the Battles of Dunbar and the Battle of Worcester, one year apart from each other, and it was on 3rd September that Elizabeth, Charles I's daughter, had first contracted the cold that had turned into pneumonia and killed her. It also seems somehow befitting that Cromwell's painful death from septicaemia should come in the middle of a howling storm on September 3rd as thunder roared and lightning flashed. It was also the date when Charles II woke in the pre-dawn hours and stood at his bedroom window watching the city blazing below him as showers of hot ash filled the night skies of London. As he stared down in shock at the chaos the Great Fire of London had caused, a thought would have crossed his mind. The date was 3rd September again and all hell had broken loose once more.

On 3rd September 1783 the Treaty of Paris was finally signed although it would not have the same dreaded implications as it had in the past. It essentially put an end to the war. France was exhausted and everyone, except Spain however, wanted peace. It would be Britain's new Prime Minister Lord Shelburne who had the foresight to see the perfect opportunity to split the United States away from France permanently and make the new country a valuable economic partner.

For weeks, negotiations were held until finally, an agreement was settled. Spain was given Gibraltar, the Bahamas, Grenada and Monserrat while the United States was given their independence plus all the territories east of the Mississippi River, north of Florida and south of Canada. Britain would take control of the area north of the Ohio River, basically Canada, while France would have to settle for Tobago and Senegal with guaranteed fishing rights off Newfoundland. Dutch possessions in the East Indies captured by Britain would also be returned to the Netherlands in exchange for trading privileges.

It was a monumental treaty and George should have been ecstatic that the whole debacle had finally concluded so neatly. The end of the war was what he'd wanted in the first place and as the ink was drying on the paper, George was ruling over more of the world than any man since Genghis Khan. It was an empire five times larger than Rome and George was at the helm. But instead of being satisfied, George struggled to come to terms with the loss of the Americas, and the treaty proposed by Shelburne was at the heart of it. Finally, when the recriminations became too much for Shelburne, he stepped down from office and George was forced to find a new Prime Minister more to his liking. After a year full of resignations and changes, William Pitt the Younger was finally appointed as Prime Minister.

But the years 1782 and 1783 were bad ones for George. He was highly regarded and admired for remaining faithful to his wife, unlike his past ancestors and she in turn had given birth to fifteen children. In August

1782, Alfred, the youngest of nine sons, was inoculated for smallpox and after lengthy fevers and continuing outbreaks of spots and chest problems, the child died at not quite two years old. His parents took it badly.

Knowing this, it seems odd when six months after Alfred's death, another son Octavius and his sister Sophia were taken to Kew Palace and inoculated as well. Sophia would eventually recover but Octavius died several days later. This time, George was devastated.

George had already been showing signs of stress. The loss of Americas was ever present in his mind and he was keeping a vigilant eye on his newly appointed Prime Minister. Then there was the death of two of his beloved children to come to terms with and at the same time, he was dealing with another consuming problem: the dreadful behaviour of his eldest son, George Prince of Wales.

Young George was a man about town. He was a rather dashing, although overweight, young man and in the glorious Hanoverian tradition, the two men hated each other. The prince was wildly extravagant and spent most of his time visiting gambling clubs, drinking, womanising and renovating his home, Brighton Palace At 18, unlike his scandal-free father, the prince threw himself into life with zest. By 1783, at the age of 21, and after the death of his two young brothers, he had obtained a grant from Parliament for £60,000 (equal to £6,303,000 today) with an annual income from his father for another £50,000 (£5,252,000) to help clear his debts. But for him, the money was like a drop in the ocean. It was far too little for his needs.

Much to his father's rage, he had taken up with Maria FitzHerbert, 6 years his senior, twice widowed and worse still, a commoner. If that wasn't bad enough, she was also a Catholic. George angrily reminded his son of the Settlement Act of 1701 barring any royals, who were stupid enough to marry a Catholic, from succeeding to the throne. He also reminded him of the Royal Marriages Act from 1772 stipulating that any royals needed permission from the king before entering into a marriage. That permission, he told his son, would never be given.

Despite everything George said to his son, the prince refused to listen.

Perhaps it was the consequence of so much intense stress that finally tipped George over the edge. Everyone knew he fretted over the American disaster and the loss of his adored children. But the behaviour of his eldest son and heir apparent, well, that was something else entirely. Things started to slip off the rails a little for him. He began to complain of stomach cramps and abdominal pain, muscle pain, sleeplessness, anxiety attacks and depression. Even his urine had changed colour to a shade of purple. All very reminiscent of James I.

In history, people laugh at what is regarded as the 'Madness of King George' but at the time, it was not a laughing matter at all. England was seriously concerned by his lapses in lucidity. His symptoms began simply as talking for long lengths of time, barely stopping for breath. Sentences of 400 words and eight vowels were not unusual and he would often repeat himself over and over again. Sometimes he would talk until froth ran from his mouth.

Over the centuries, his illness has been put down to the hereditary disease porphyria that can be traced back through the Stuart dynasty to Mary Queen of Scots. We should also remember that mental illness ran in the family as far back as Henry V and his wife, Catherine of Valois. Her brother had been the King of France and had been nicknamed 'Crazy Charles'.

But as worried as his physicians were, they became very concerned when George was found wandering in his garden, trying to plant a steak. He believed that meat could be grown from trees and that by planting a juicy steak in the garden, he might perhaps grow a new breed of tree. The next incident happened when he was at Windsor Castle and he was seen shaking hands with a tree, whom he believed was his dearly departed brother-in-law Frederick of Prussia. Now his physicians were truly worried.

All of these episodes were bad enough on their own but when he began to suffer from severe seizures and fits as well, his doctors were forced to strap him into a chair to stop him from harming himself. By November 1788, his condition had worsened to such an extent, that his son was called in to help.

Medicine in the 18th century was fundamental at best. While physicians in the 1780s knew how to treat injuries and various illnesses with mildly effective medicine, they had absolutely no understanding of mental sicknesses. There was certainly no distinction between one mental condition and another and there was no real way of knowing how to treat a mental illness, if that was what it actually was, let alone curing it. In their ignorance, George III's condition was simply labelled "Madness".

In the truest sense of the word, the king was given the full Georgian medical treatment with a series of procedures that were nothing short of horrendous. The usual treatments included procedures such as bloodletting, blistering his head, sweating, restraints and scary cocktails containing arsenic. All had no effect and it was decided that something more drastic was needed.

A friend of Queen Charlotte had mentioned that a Doctor Francis Willis had successfully cured her mother and that his methods appeared effective and creditable. He was a qualified physician recommended as the best person in all England to treat the ailing king. Desperate to try anything, the royal physicians backed down and gave Willis free access to the king.

Willis's treatments were common to George's doctors. He employed many of the usual methods that other 18th century doctors were already familiar with, such as restraints and blistering, but he also spent time with the king, talking him through things, trying to understand what was going on in his head.

It was clear to Willis at least, that if the king was mad and out of control, then it was someone's duty to bring the king back again, by force if need be. Apart from regimens of therapy, restraints, exercise and plenty of exposure to fresh air, Willis also tried to make it clear to George that he had to make an effort as well to fight against his demons.

Meanwhile, and behind his back, all the other doctors snickered. Many of them thought that Willis himself was probably only just slightly less mad than George himself and that his treatments couldn't possibly work, despite the fact that Willis had significant success in treating mental illness.

Sadly they were right. Things went from bad to worse.

It was unfortunate that George's son saw this as a golden opportunity, during his father's hideous treatments, to go ahead and marry Maria Fitz-Herbert and of course, the marriage was kept quiet. To add to the disaster, the prince was well over his head in debt again and asking for more money.

Parliament had no idea what to do. They already had their hands full with trying to keep George's illness a secret so this was just one more thing they had to try and cover up. Biding for time, they took the easy way out. The Prince was given £161,000 (equal to £17,850,000 today) to pay off his fresh debts and another £60,000 (£6,303,000) for improvements to his new residence Carlton House, bought to house his growing family of illegitimate children. But Parliament knew they had to make a decision soon on what to do about his father George, who was most definitely unfit to rule.

What they had to find was a regent to take over the running of the country and the logical person to do that was the Prince of Wales. But of course, based on his recent history, not everyone agreed and heated arguments broke out between different ministers. Some of them, including the prince's younger brother Frederick, did not want to hand over so much power to his elder brother especially when he looked at the huge debts his brother was still running up. Given full rein, heaven only knew what he would do if more money was at his disposal. Others argued that he should be at least considered as the king's replacement and regent in times of illness. He *was* the king's eldest son after all and he *was* the heir apparent. And, of course, the prince was more than happy to lend a hand – if it meant increasing his income.

By February 1789, to the prince's utter delight, all aspects had been discussed and the Regency Bill, authorising George Prince of Wales to act on the king's behalf, was introduced and passed in the House of Commons. Taking every precaution, they added a codicil. While Regent, Prince George was not allowed to sell any of the king's property and he was not allowed to grant a peerage to anyone other than a child of the king.

It wasn't that George wasn't aware of what was going on around him. He was fully cognisant and communicative. It's just that most times, nothing he said made sense. So when George saw his son walk smugly into his chambers and stand grinning before him, George catapulted himself out of the chair and attacked him. After all the treatments and indignities George had endured, it was the sight of his despised and wayward son that shocked him out of his madness.

Unfortunately for George, he came to his senses just in time for the French Revolution.

When 19-year-old Louis XVI ascended the French throne in 1774, he realised he needed money desperately. His country had come out rather badly from the Seven Year's War with Britain and it was French money that had helped to fund the American Revolution. As a consequence, his country was almost bankrupt. Two decades of bad harvests, cattle disease, drought and skyrocketing bread prices had helped to inflame people's resentment towards his lifestyle, the lifestyle of the clergy and also the aristocrats. Many people were desperate for help but they could only stand by and watch as more heavy taxes were imposed on top of already unpayable ones. Demands for a change were being heard loud and clear.

Then one of Louis' generals, Charles Calonne, saw a way out of the dire situation. In France's history, aristocrats had always been excused from paying any sort of taxes. By proposing a tax reform package that included a tax by which the aristocrats would no longer be exempt, Calonne could both increase the French treasury and appease the common people.

It sounds like an entirely reasonable tax to help solve the matter but what his proposal actually did was increase the tension. With growing resentment now coming from the aristocrats as well, Louis was floundering to know what to do. Then he remembered the 'Estates-General'.

This group of delegates from three 'estates' of his kingdom – the clergy, nobility and middle class – had not been assembled for 150 years and their job had been to compile a list of grievances from all classes for the king to consider and rule on. It was regarded by most as a desperate measure since everyone knew that the aristocrats held the majority and the ruling would eventually be in their favour anyway. Louis jumped at the opportunity to put an end to the discontent and the meeting was scheduled to commence on May 5th 1789.

It was the beginning of the end for Louis. He should have realised that France's population had changed considerably since 1614 and the non-aristocratic members now represented 98% of the people. By the time the Estates-General convened in Versailles, the highly public debate had erupted into hostility between the three orders, totally eclipsing the original purpose of the meeting. By 17th June, the middle class estate was calling themselves the National Assembly as representatives of the people. They expressed a wish to include the other two estates in the debate but they made it clear that they would move forward without them if necessary. Louis at once tried to shut the National Assembly down, but by then it was way too late. They stated they had written a new constitution for France.

Things began to escalate at an alarming rate. By 12th July, angry mobs were filling the streets of Paris. By 14th, they were armed with anything they could find and they were storming the Bastille. They opened the prisons and released all of the prisoners who then stole food, muskets, pistols and swords before heading on towards Versailles. They had Louis and his hated

Austrian wife Marie Antoinette on their minds and the mob of more than 150,000 were not going to stop until they found them.

By August, the National Assembly had drawn up a declaration and by October, Louis had rejected it. Three days later, the angry mob broke into the palace of Versailles at dawn and Louis and Marie Antoinette were taken prisoner.

For two years, Louis and his family were held prisoners. But it was only a matter of time before a decision had to be made and Louis must have had a fair idea that they were never going to release him. When he was told that he was to be beheaded, he was already resigned to the fact.

He was led to the scaffold in January 1793, dignified and stoic. He began his prepared speech to declare his innocence but was cut short by a drum roll. He was pushed down onto the floor and his head unceremoniously shoved onto the block. The first strike of the guillotine severed Louis' spine but his head remained attached to his body. The second one would finish the job as the crowd ran forward to dip their handkerchiefs in his blood. Nine months later and two weeks before her 38th birthday, Marie Antoinette was undressed before her guards and dressed in a plain white dress. Her hair was hacked off, her hands were tied tightly behind her back with a rope and she was driven through Paris in an open cart to the guillotine to die as well. She'd been staring at the bare walls of the Temple Prison near the Seine for many months while sitting on a brick-tiled floor covered in slime as water trickled down the walls. Her screaming children had been wrenched from her arms and she knew her husband had been executed. I can only imagine she must have been relieved when her own time finally came on 16th October 1793.

The Reign of Terror had begun and England was in the firing line.

Between 1793 and 1794, the death toll of French aristocrats stood at 16,594 executed by guillotine after a nominal trial and another 25,000, including both aristocrats and clergy, were executed with no trial at all.

George had never liked the French but he would never have wished this on anyone. After all, Louis was the King of France just as he was the King of England. And they were related by blood. When news arrived that the royal couple had been murdered and France had declared war on England, it sent chills down his spine and dread through his heart. His wife Charlotte, already turning grey at 35 years old due to the stress of George's illness, was shocked to hear of the death of her pen friend, Marie Antoinette. Marie had sent a beseeching letter to Charlotte at the beginning of the revolution and Charlotte had already prepared apartments for the royal refugees if it became necessary.

With unrest in France still growing at an alarming rate, George watched as his son's debts continued to soar and he was continually bombarded with requests for help – which George continually refused. In his desperation to do *something*, George came up with a solution. He would pay off his son's debts, yet again, if the prince agreed to marry his first cousin, Princess Caroline of Brunswick.

Now I know you're thinking, Prince George was already married, wasn't he? And didn't he have a string of children as well? But in the eyes of both his father and Britain, the prince was still single since permission to marry had never been given and as far as George was concerned, the marriage did not exist.

After lengthy arguments and threats, the Prince of Wales eventually agreed and the couple met formally one week before the wedding. With one look at his future bride, the Prince of Wales turned and asked for a glass of very strong brandy. And it only went downhill from there. He was blind drunk at the wedding and nine months later, after Caroline gave birth to Princess Charlotte Augusta, the two were formally separated.

The distress of everything – his cousin Louis' murder, yet another French war looming, his son's reckless obstinacy and stubbornness – sent George back temporarily into the dark shadows of his mind. By the time he came back again, the French Revolution had inspired rebellion in Ireland and Napoleon Bonaparte was flexing his muscles in Italy and fast becoming France's brightest shining star. All I can think is poor George.

From the beginning, the government in Ireland had viewed Irish interest in the French Revolution with gravest suspicion. Irishmen were seeing a lot of similarities between the French and themselves. As with the French, the Irish had been suffering from bad harvests and droughts with starvation widespread throughout the country. They too were left to fend for themselves with no help whatsoever from the monarchy and they were paying taxes that they couldn't afford as well. With the outbreak of war between Britain and France and the unabashed admiration of the Irish for the

French, their suspicion deepened. It almost seemed like treason to the Irish government, basically run by the English.

The discovery of negotiations between certain Irishmen and the French government confirmed their suspicions and when a fleet of 14,000 Frenchman unsuccessfully attempted to land, only prevented due to bad weather, the government, based in Dublin Castle, stepped in.

Carnew is a village in County Wicklow just a mile from the border of Country Wexford that made its first appearance as a Norman borough during Henry III's reign. The town contained the country's largest deer park and a large iron smelting industry was established in 1619 just outside of town where Welsh families were encouraged to settle. But on 26th May 1798, Carnew turned into a battlefield.

Captain William Ryves of Rathsallagh had only been riding through Carnew on patrol when the rebels shot his horse from under him. The act was done in the heat of the moment but it had a cataclysmic effect on all of Ireland.

Captain Ryves knew how to put a stop to rebellions before they went any further and he went to work. 38 locals, including 18 married men, were rounded up and imprisoned in the dungeon of Dublin castle. The next day, they were marched to the green, lined up in front of the townspeople, including their own families, and shot by a firing squad. Before the bodies were removed, the soldiers' wives looted them of valuables. The firing squad then returned to Market House where others were flogged or hanged.

It was then the locals heard of a similar slaughter at Dunlavin.

The executions appear to have been motivated by simple revenge and intimidation but in the already tense atmosphere, the Irish had reached boiling point well before the massacres. When they heard that the men had been executed without a trial in Wicklow, they simply exploded. One hundred English soldiers were chopped to pieces before setting Carnew ablaze and as word of the uprising spread to other counties, rebels began assembling all over the southeast at an alarming rate.

George was kept informed of the outbreaks in Kildare, Carlow, Wicklow and Meath with the most successful, and unexpected, in Country Wexford. As concerned as he was with this news, when he heard that a French fleet of 1,100 men had landed in Country Mayo, he sent an order for the Irish government to do anything they could to stop them. And they did exactly that. By early September 1798, British soldiers so vastly outnumbered the French force, they simply laid down their arms and surrendered.

The French were treated as honoured prisoners of war but the Irish rebels who had supported the French would not be so lucky. Between 10,000 and 25,000 as well as 600 soldiers lay dead and large areas of the country were effectively laid waste. Two years later, a unification of British and Irish Parliaments was established when Britain passed an Act of Union in January 1801, but it had come at a huge price.

In the aftermath, as Prime Minister Pitt threatened to resign over religious issues, George's mental fragility began to resurface and he tumbled back into another mental relapse. This time, it was two years later that he would return but it was with more vigour than anyone could have expected. And he would need it because Napoleon was on the march.

After the Irish Rebellion, an invasion by Napoleon seemed imminent and it was a rejuvenated George who organised a massive volunteer movement to defend England against the French. At the height of the scare, George managed to gather 27,000 volunteers in Hyde Park, prepared to put himself at the head of the army if needed. It was a rather silly statement to make and Parliament would never have allowed it for a second, especially with George's mental deterioration still fresh in their minds. George was saved the humiliation in the nick of time by Admiral Lord Nelson's victory at the Battle of Trafalgar. But this would be no ordinary battle.

By 1805, Lord Nelson was already a national hero and the ultimate naval commander. His concept of war and his many victories assured Britain that he was the only commander-in-chief who could successfully challenge Bonaparte. If anyone possessed the practical experience and strategic flair to help Britain survive the 22-year struggle with France, it was Nelson.

After two years of waiting for the French to make a move, the temporary truce between England and France finally broke down and Napoleon's Franco-Spanish fleet left their safe haven at Toulon and set forth into the Atlantic. They found an ideal shelter at Cadiz and waited for British trading ships to appear.

It wasn't just England who was in awe of Nelson. His arrival on HMS *Victory* sent shock waves through the French fleet, already being bullied by Napoleon. Despite Nelson's unexpected arrival, the French Admiral left

Cadiz and put out to sea on 19th October hoping fervently that his fleet of 33 ships would defeat Nelson's 27 British vessels.

Nelson had anticipated his enemy's every move. At dawn on the 21st, both fleets were in visual contact of each other. With dark storm clouds brewing in the distance, he quickly formed a risky head-on approach that exposed the unarmed bows of his leading ships to the full weight of the enemy broadsides.

Nelson's first attack destroyed the enemy flagship. Knowing they would be leaderless and confused, he was sure his own captains would be able to wipe out the rest of the fleet in the few remaining hours of daylight. As they approached, he walked around his own flagship talking to the crew as they cheered him on. By then, the enemy had changed course and was heading back to Cadiz. And Nelson followed closely behind.

The French were just off Cape Trafalgar when they suddenly began firing at the *Victory*. The first shot came smashing through the bow of the ship wounding men on the upper deck and cutting John Scott, Nelson's Public Secretary, in two. The steering wheel was smashed but Nelson and his Captain, Thomas Hardy, still paced up and down as the splinters flew around them.

At 12.35pm, the *Victory* was able to return fire, shrouding the ship in smoke. She ran right under the stern of the French flagship *Bucentaure* when she fired a double shot, killing 200 men and making the ship shudder. Then through the smoke, the French *Redoutable* joined the fight. Musket fire and hand grenades showered the *Victory* and at 1.15pm, Nelson was hit by a lead ball that cut an artery in his lung and lodged in his spine.

As the muskets continued firing and the battle raged on, Nelson was carried below to the surgeon but it was clear the wound was mortal. It wasn't until 3.30pm that Captain Hardy was able to kneel beside Nelson and tell him of the victory. The French had repeatedly tried to board the *Victory* only to be driven back time and time again. It was touch and go for almost an hour but the enemy was finished. 19 of the enemy had been destroyed but not one British ship had been lost. By then, Nelson was struggling to breathe and Captain Hardy had to lean close to hear Nelson's final whispered words. Over and over, he kept repeating *"Thank God I have done my duty. Thank God I have done my duty."*

When George heard of Nelson's death, he was already struggling with the news that his youngest daughter Amelia had died. This final terrible news finished him completely.

George's last descent into complete madness nearly destroyed his family. His insanity was coming in fast waves, but try as they might, it was impossible to pull him out. Charlotte visited her husband regularly in his rooms at Windsor Castle, clearly devastated, but nothing could be done this time. It was left to his eldest son, Prince George, to take over as Regent during George's last few years, and it would be Prince George who would witness Napoleon's defeat at Waterloo.

As the years went on, George eventually became blind and deaf, just as his grandfather had. It was a blessing he was not able to understand the death of his only legitimate granddaughter, while giving birth to her stillborn son in 1817, or the death of his beloved wife one year later. It was best he remained where he was during those terrible times.

It was Prince George, Britain's least favourite prince, who ascended the throne of England at the age of 58. 'The Grand Entertainment', as he was nicknamed, was just about to step up to the mark and prove his worth.

GEORGE IV

Born 1762
Reign 1820 – 1830

By the time his father died, George felt as if he had endured a lifetime of frustration. He was unhappy in love, unhappy with his finances and by the time he finally ascended the throne, he was an ageing, 58-year-old obese playboy.

In his youth, George had certainly been one of the most gifted of the princes, but his self-absorption and self-obsession made him the butt of ridicule and a national joke by the time he came to the throne in 1820. Even his birth had caused a ripple of laughter as the Earl of Huntingdon pronounced that the newborn heir was a girl.

Maturity comes slowly to some, and more so than others, but George was slower than most. However, one thing was certain: George liked women. His first serious affair was at the age of 17 and by the time he reached 21, he was well-known as an inveterate ladies' man who would woo his targets ardently, promise them his eternal love and then brusquely drop them like hot cakes when he tired of their charms. As far as George was concerned, variety was the spice of life.

The whole structure of respectability and family values shown by his father seemed lost on George. As he grew older, George's marked preference was not for younger, libidinous lovers as you would expect, but for older, motherly mistresses who offered him a degree of sympathy and understanding for his perceived longstanding hardships. As far as George was concerned, he'd never received any of that from his own, coldly calculating mother.

Everything George did seemed out of spite towards his father and his mother. There were very few who surpassed his reputation as a scoundrel. He was a chronic gambler and without his father's permission, wilfully married a twice-widowed Catholic actress by the name of Maria FitzHerbert (nee Smythe, nee Weld) who was, not surprisingly, six years his senior.

George met Maria in the spring of 1784. She'd married her first husband, sixteen years her senior, in July 1775 but three months later, he had an unfortunate fall from his horse and died. With the marriage still in its early days, he'd failed to sign a new will and the estate went to his younger brother Thomas, leaving Maria virtually destitute with no financial support from his family. As such, she was forced to remarry as soon as she could. This time, Thomas FitzHerbert was ten years older than Maria but sadly she was widowed again, although this time she was left with an annuity of £1,000 and a town house in Park Street, Mayfair.

As we know, George loved women but in particular, he loved *older* women. Soon after they met, George became infatuated with her and pursued her endlessly until she agreed to marry him, secretly and against the law, as they were both well aware.

The marriage lasted nine years until June 1794 when George sent Maria a letter abruptly telling her that her relationship with him was over. His father was demanding that he marry a rather plain German princess by the name of Duchess Caroline of Brunswick and of course he was terribly sorry.

No one needs to be told there were better and more sensitive ways of breaking the shocking news to Maria but at the time, George was more concerned with the massive gambling hole he found himself in. It had climbed back up to the extraordinary amount of £630,000 (equivalent to £58,700,000 today) and according to his father, the only way he would clear it in full, with an additional sum of £65,000 per annum (equivalent to £6,056,000 today), was if George married Princess Caroline of Brunswick. As generous as this all sounds, it was by no means to be the last time a payout of such an astonishing amount would be necessary to pay off his debts.

Although George told his younger brother Frederick that he and Maria had 'parted amicably', I'm not sure Maria would have agreed if anyone had bothered to ask her.

Somewhat inevitably, the subsequent marriage to Princess Caroline of Brunswick was a total disaster. Admittedly, she was not the most desirable bride for a distinguished, discerning young man like George, but sometimes women blossom with the love of a patient man. Clearly, George was not that man. He took one look at Caroline and asked for a strong brandy. It went downhill from there.

Like any girl, she would have wondered what the moment would be like when she met her future husband. My guess is George was nothing like she imagined. Caroline was heard to have said, *"He is very fat and nothing like his handsome portrait."* On the other hand, George complained that she smelt and had neglected to wash or change her dirty clothes. Not exactly the makings of a Walt Disney fairy tale.

It went from bad to worse after the wedding. In a letter to a friend, the prince claimed that the couple only had sexual intercourse three times: twice the first night of the marriage, and once the second night. That was all he could stand. As for Caroline, she claimed George was so drunk that he *"passed the greatest part of his bridal night under the grate, where he fell, and where I left him"*. Nine months later however, Princess Charlotte was born and the couple officially separated with George expressing exaggerated tales of public insults perpetrated by his wife against him. As the years progressed, his complaints became increasingly more hysterical although the steady stream of mistresses never slowed down for a minute.

Women were not George's only passion. Flamboyant and extravagant costumes were another of his lifelong passions. From his earliest years he loved the feel, colour and sheer thrill of expensive and well-cut new outfits. The intricacy and classic tailoring of such outfits would soon become a distant memory, however, with George's increasing girth. By the time George and Caroline married, his weight had reached 17 stone 7 pounds (111 kg).

George knew people were talking about him behind his back. During his life as a prince and as his father's regent, he'd heard the whisperings at court about his unsuitability for the throne and the gossip varied depending on who was doing the whispering. Sure, George could be charming and witty, drunk or sober, they muttered, but it was usually when he wanted something. Most of the time, the murmurs were that he was self-indulgent, cruel and he could forget friendships in a heartbeat without a backward glance. They even went as far as saying he was self-engrossed, his judgements were harsh and he showed no regard for anyone else's feelings. And he also spent far too much money on renovating palaces, gambling, buying pictures, hosting parties, drinking alcohol and chasing mistresses, regardless of his amazing weight gain. And it was all very true. In the end, everyone was in agreeance. George was most definitely *not* king material.

George spent his early years in modest, unpretentious Surrey villas, which his father seemed to prefer to the many castles and palaces that were at his disposal. But not too far in the future, his preference for vast and elaborately decorated new homes began to emerge, which seems to have been a direct contrast to the relatively cramped and sombre surroundings chosen by his father. The astonishingly colourful, glittering and eclectic interiors he created at Brighton Pavilion, Buckingham Palace, Windsor Castle and Carlton House set new standards of lavishness and flamboyant ostentation.

George's fascinating combination of talents and insecurities can perhaps be traced back directly to his relationship with his father and what he saw as his father's stifling morality. George's collecting and building programmes seem guided by an overwhelming desire to shock his parents and to reject his father's values.

When looking at his past Hanoverian ancestors, it would seem inevitable that George would feel aggrieved at the unnecessarily strict, rigid upbringing, considering his perceived position and status. The fact that he showed no inclination in academic or military achievements seemed irrelevant to him. His overblown view of his own self-importance made it foreseeable that George would try to measure himself against the one man who really *did* dominate Europe.

Napoleon Bonaparte's unrivalled reputation was one that George was constantly trying to match and emulate although any comparison between the two rulers was laughable to all but George. While Napoleon was building his reputation as a shrewd, ambitious and skilled strategist, George was busy redecorating his palaces and sifting through brocades and silks for his coats. When Napoleon was telling his wife how passionately he loved her, George was wining and dining his mistresses, but always on the look out for the next notch on his belt. And when Napoleon became the de-facto ruler of Northern Italy and was working hard to unite his people by creating a viable constitution, George was repeatedly begging his father to pay off his massive gambling debts. Newly equipped with the financial resources of the Regency in 1811 during his father's last lapse into mental illness, George arrogantly announced that henceforth he and his court would *"quite eclipse Napoleon"*.

For 25 years, the heart-stopping sound of marching French feet had plagued the world. Born on the island of Corsica, Napoleon had rapidly risen through the ranks of the military during the French Revolution, which had changed France forever. When the crowds stormed the Bastille in 1789, Napoleon's personal revolution began. It all came to an abrupt halt when Napoleon made a colossal blunder in 1812 by trying to invade Moscow. His massive army of 600,000 had massed on the Russian border and in June, he confidently gave the order to invade.

Poland was where things started going haywire for Napoleon. The roads were soft and deeply rutted from recent rains and with the lack of food and water already a major problem, his huge army began to dissolve into a straggly mob, pillaging homes and livestock from the local peasants, while nearly 20,000 army horses died from lack of food and water. Even at this early stage, typical battlefield diseases such as dysentery began to appear. But as bad as these problems were, Napoleon's problems were just beginning.

The region was filthy beyond belief and the peasants were unwashed, with matted hair and ridden with lice and flees, while their homes were alive with cockroaches. A number of his soldiers began to develop high fevers and a red rash on their bodies. Some even developed a bluish tinge to their face before finally and painfully dying.

Surprisingly, it wasn't enemy soldiers that began to devastate Napoleon's vast army. It was Nature. His battle-hardened men, trained to tolerate the cold on fatiguing marches with the minimum of food, could not defeat a microscopic organism called typhus, spread by a scourge of lice. It wreaked havoc and began to annihilate his army.

Napoleon's army was typical for these times. They were dirty and sweaty and they lived in the same clothes for many days. It was the perfect environment for lice to feed and find a home in the seams of clothes. Once the clothes were contaminated with lice excrement, the smallest abrasion would have been enough for the germ to enter the soldiers' bodies. To compound the problem, they slept in large groups, in confined spaces for safety, and with this closeness, lice were free to jump from soldier to soldier. Within a month into the campaign, Napoleon lost 80,000 of his soldiers. His officers raised concerns and Napoleon listened to their arguments, but still he continued. By the end of August the number of deaths grew until he had lost 105,000 men.

The harsh, unforgiving Russian weather was something Napoleon had not considered either. The Russians, well aware of what a blizzard could ultimately do to an unprotected army, retreated into the interior to minimise casualties and to draw Napoleon deeper into their territory. Still Napoleon trudged on to towards Moscow. He was totally unaware that the citizens had already burned three-quarters of the city, depriving him of food and supplies. And he desperately needed both.

Add that to the worst conditions his army had ever encountered, the difficulty in finding provisions in a hostile country and you have a five-month disaster for Napoleon. By November, he had lost another 380,000 men and another 100,000 had been captured. With only 30,000 of his men fit for combat, Napoleon was forced to stop his advance and retreat. It led to his capture and a brief stay on Elba to warm up for a while as the world settled down for a well-earned break of peace and prosperity with him safely locked away.

It would be a short respite.

As always, Napoleon's mind never stopped working. He spent a full year pacing and fretting until finally, an opportunity came his way to escape and he eagerly snatched it. He saw it as his last chance to restore his fortunes.

When George and Britain's allies – Austria, Prussia and Russia – heard of the escape, they went into overdrive. This time, they promised, there would be no compromises and Napoleon would be defeated once and for all. And of course, George desperately wanted to have a major role in crushing him.

George knew that Napoleon would be preparing for war. But so was George. Even as Napoleon was gathering troops in Paris, the Prussians were assembling their own army along the French borders and the Austrians, together with Russians, were beginning the long track south to join them. Not wanting to be left behind in the rush, George was eager to get under way with his own preparations. He had already chosen his highly popular general, the Duke of Wellington, and his army was ready to join Prince Blucher of Prussia in Belgium. He could see no point in waiting, and a surprise attack was announced, set for June. It would force Napoleon to either fight or run.

It wasn't just George making plans. Napoleon had ideas of his own as well. He still wanted France to be the most powerful country in Europe and the only way he saw France getting anywhere close to the mark was by conquering other countries. In particular, Britain. He was known to be a man of action and he was going to show them all *why* he had that reputation. He had control of an army of 220,000 men and 7,000 artillery, and he knew the Allies were assembling. He also knew that they were forcing him to make a decision and he was ready to do just that.

His initial plan was to be fully assembled and ready for an initial attack in July but as it turned out, there were two things out of his control. One was he was standing on a field near Waterloo two weeks earlier than expected watching Wellington's army approach. Another, yet again, was the weather.

Summer usually brought brilliant blue skies and balmy warm nights but on the 17th June 1815, the countryside seemed to be shrouded in eerie darkness as menacing clouds rumbled in the skies above them, almost as a premonition of what was to be unleashed upon them. Both armies knew there was a thunderstorm imminent and as each huddled under makeshift shelters on either side of the valley to protect themselves, lightning flashed brilliantly across the sky, cutting it in half. Almost immediately the heavens opened up and the rain began to pour.

By the morning of the 18th, a pale, watery sun rose through the heavy clouds at dawn. Through the intermittent morning rays, Wellington's men stood on one ridge as Napoleon assembled his men on the other ridge. Both armies were drenched and the valley below them had been reduced to a quagmire.

As both armies stared at each other across the valley, nobody seemed eager to make the first move.

For Napoleon, there were some serious problems. In the muddy ground, heavy ponderous guns would be impossible to manoeuvre without sticking in the mud and cannon balls would simply sink into the ground instead of bouncing and ricocheting.

And Wellington was more than happy to wait. With every hour that passed, it brought the Prussian and Russian armies closer. He was very aware that he had an army of untrained infantry and inexperienced cavalry, but he also believed in the use of firepower. He had 156 cannons and his men had muskets fitted with a bayonet on a socket over the barrel. They would be relentless.

After the Russian fiasco and his subsequent escape from prison, Napoleon had built up his army from conscripts as well as disgruntled veterans who had been assembled at short notice. His strength lay in his artillery and cavalry and he knew they were far superior than Wellington's. Unfortunately, the unrelenting rain meant that he had to wait patiently for the ground to dry out first so the wheels of his cannons and the feet of his men did not sink into the squelching mud. He was happy to wait as well.

From his vantage point on the ridge, Wellington could see a shimmering wave of red, white and blue in the distance on a bed of deep emerald green grass. He could see the French vastly outnumbered his troops, so he knew his best plan was to stand firm until the Prussians arrived with much-needed assistance. He lined the majority of his troops up out of sight behind the ridge and garrisoned some in front of local farms.

At 11.25am, Napoleon was ready for battle and he opened fire.

By the end of the day, bodies lay piled up on top of each other in the mud. Panic-stricken men, choked by canon-fire smoke, tried to raise themselves out of the mud, only to fall back exhausted and bleeding among the bodies of their friends. Finally, the air was still and quiet and one thing was obvious in the silence. Napoleon had left his men to finish the battle while he fled.

It would be another two years before Napoleon was recaptured and sent to St Helena in exile. But by then, George was declaring himself to be Napoleon's nemesis, even though Wellington had labelled his victory as a *"damned near-run thing"*.

As 1816 dawned, Britain had reached an all time low as George struggled with the Regency and his father's health declined even further. As necessary as it had been to put Napoleon in his place, the effects of the war had seemed never-ending and disastrous. Soldiers were returning from

Europe by the thousands and none of them had any idea of how they were going to earn a living. As unemployment increased, George's appetite for luxurious furniture and pictures grew increasingly spectacular. By almost mid-year, there was a full-scale riot brewing aimed at replacing the existing government and the Duke of Wellington, who was the current Prime Minister. The only way that George could see to keep a lid on the situation was to reinstate the death penalty for printing seditious material or attending secret meetings. And there were certainly plenty of those.

Littleport was a large village in Cambridgeshire where a group of 56 residents met at The Globe Inn one night in May. Their initial purpose was to discuss the lack of work and rising grain costs but as their anger became more fuelled on by alcohol, the focus of the meeting changed menacingly to an unpopular local farmer, Henry Martin. One man ran to get a horn and started blowing it outside the inn, gathering hundreds of villagers to join the group. The situation soon got out of hand.

The rioters started by throwing stones through the windows, but it escalated when they invaded a nearby property and threw the owner's belongings into the street. Reverend John Vachell stood outside the Inn with his arms held high in the air, shouting for quiet and trying to hold them back. Rather bravely, he reminded them of the Riot Act that had been in effect since 1715 that stated unequivocally that no group of twelve men or more were allowed to assemble unlawfully under the threat of the death penalty. No one took any notice of him. The crowd screamed back at him to go home. They moved on to the nearby premises of a disabled 90-year-old, throwing his furniture into the street, before moving on to another man's house, demolishing his furniture.

It was fortunate that Reverend Vachell had taken the mob's advice and gone home. By 11pm, after ransacking the entire town, they arrived at his home. As his terrified wife and two daughters huddled together inside, he threatened to shoot anyone who entered his house. Three men rushed at him and he was quickly disarmed while his family shrieked in fear. With his house blazing behind him, he gathered his family together and fled towards Ely. When the rioters were finished with Littleport, they moved on to larger towns in Cambridgeshire.

It wasn't until June before the areas were finally cleared of trouble and all of the rioters had been captured and sent to trial. In all, there were a total of 83 people executed: the rest were transported to Australia.

It was a tense two months for George but feeling well satisfied with the result, he turned his attention back to his wife Caroline.

No one had ever called Caroline beautiful, although in her youth, she had been called 'presentable'. Britain agreed that her manners were coarse and she seemed completely unaware of her body odour and the need to wash. Her wit was crude and she took every opportunity she could to shock. For George, who was used to the mildness of society darlings, this was entirely unsatisfactory. There was no end to his stories of complaint regarding her smell and generally horrid body. He even went as far as stating that she was 'not new' as a reason to be rid of her.

Three days after the birth of his daughter Charlotte, George finally made a will stating that his wife was to have no role whatsoever in the upbringing of their child and all his worldly goods were to go to his mistress, Mrs FitzHerbert. He also acknowledged that Charlotte was his only heir since there would *certainly* be no other children to Caroline. By then, Britain was so used to the Hanoverian temper tantrums, they seemed totally unconcerned with this fresh family squabble unfolding before them. This tirade was just one of many they had endured over the years.

As it happened, they were delighted with little Charlotte although they knew she was just a pawn in the conflict between her mother and their king. She was kept on a tight rein throughout her childhood, a surprising parenting method for George to take considering he had complained endlessly about his strict childhood and the lack of affection from his father. As a parent, George had become an awful lot like his father.

Britain watched delightedly as Charlotte grew into a strong-minded young lady, fond of her grandfather George III, and seemingly unperturbed by the tense arrangement between her parents. She had turned into a beautiful, young woman who loved shocking her governess by riding recklessly through a bumpy field with the wind blowing her hair wildly around her head. She even playfully snatched the wig off her tutor and threw it into the fire. She had shown a joyous spirit that was sadly lacking in her father and the nation loved her for it.

With antics increasing daily, George began looking closely at his rebellious daughter and started seriously considering a suitable marriage for her.

His first choice was the quiet, respectable Prince William of Orange, heir apparent of the Kingdom of the Netherlands.

Charlotte had heard the palace whispers regarding her prospective marriage and she stated categorically that she did not want to marry a foreigner, especially one nicknamed 'Silly Billy'. Negotiations dragged on for several months as father and daughter clashed heatedly, but Charlotte still refused to leave England. And then, Charlotte attended a party at a hotel in London where she met Prince Leopold of Saxe-Coburg-Saalfeld and from the moment she saw him, the writing was on the wall. She was besotted.

Her father was not. He was fit to explode. Caroline, on the other hand, willing to go against George in *every* respect, was over the moon with her daughter's choice of a love match instead of a political one as hers had been. As she openly opposed the Prince of Orange, it set off a fresh round of angry words between George and Caroline who were once again at each other's throats.

Girls will be girls, no matter if they're of royal blood or common, and every one of them will do anything they can to get their own way. And if it means doing it by foul means or fair, so be it. It's results that count in the end, right?

Charlotte was no different than most, except when she had an idea in her head, most would be hard pressed to remove that idea. And Charlotte had the perfect idea.

If George had been paying attention, he would have realised that when Charlotte did an about-turn and suddenly agreed to the wedding, especially after refusing so adamantly, something was definitely up. And he would have been right. So when his daughter informed William of Orange that she would agree to the marriage, under one condition, warning bells should have been clanging loudly in George's head. Her condition to William was that Charlotte's mother would be welcome to live with them permanently in his home after the marriage.

Of course it was a bluff and the thought had never even been discussed with her mother. It was simply a condition she was sure would anger her father and be immediately rejected by William of Orange, especially when her father had been so vocal about her mother's despicable behaviour. And the bluff paid off. William refused her stipulation and Charlotte broke off any future negotiations in a pretended huff.

It was a great plan and it had worked. That is, until she received her father's response. Until she changed her mind, he stated, she was ordered to stay confined at her residence in Warwick House until she could be transferred to Windsor. While she was there, she would not be allowed to see anyone except her grandmother, his mother. Certainly not *her* mother. And most definitely *not* Prince Leopold.

When Charlotte heard her father's decision, she was horrified. Her hormones were raging and all she could imagine was being married to a short, skinny, stupid Dutchman and living her life far away from the only home she'd ever known. Apart from all that, she was in love with Leopold.

Sobbing hysterically, she raced out into the street where a passing man saw her distress and helped her to find a hackney cab, which took her to her mother's house. And of course, her mother was in full agreeance and on her side. After a heated argument with her father, she returned to his house the next day but news of her unhappy flight was already the talk of the town.

George knew he was already unpopular and this little incident didn't make things any better for him. He was well aware that keeping his 18-year-old daughter a virtual prisoner was not going to endear him to his subjects, especially when they were already at an all-time low, but that was a small price to pay for keeping Charlotte's mother out of the picture. Charlotte managed to send a letter to her uncle Augustus, George's youngest brother, and soon she had him on her side as well. Augustus stood resolutely before Parliament and stated that since Charlotte was 18, she should be free to come and go as she pleased and as an adult, she should undoubtedly be supplied with an income of her own.

When George heard what his brother had done, he was furious. It was the last time he ever spoke to his brother again.

George's main gripe with Leopold was the fact that he did not have two pennies to rub together. His dream of a match for his daughter had been one with titles and possessions where Charlotte would marry a rich man who would in turn enrich Britain. It was a wonderful dream and he clung desperately to it. Unfortunately for Leopold, he had the title but no cash to go with it.

In the end, with all of England expressing their anger over George's stubbornness, all he could do was agree to meet Leopold. Surprisingly, after several meetings, George dropped the subject of William of Orange and reluctantly agreed to the marriage.

On 2nd May 1816, the streets of London were so crowded with well wishes that it became almost impossible for the couple to continue to Charlton House for the ceremony. The only mishap was during the ceremony, when Charlotte was heard to giggle when the impoverished Leopold promised to endow her with all his worldly goods.

Months later, when Charlotte announced that she was pregnant, the wonderful news was on everyone's lips. Betting shops quickly set up to take bookings on what sex the child would be while economists calculated that the birth of a princess would raise the stock market by 2.5% and the birth of a prince would raise it by 6%. Of course, everyone hoped for a boy but in the meantime, Britain waited joyfully.

Charlotte spent her pregnancy quietly. She ate more and took less exercise and when her medical team began prenatal care in August 1817, they put her on a strict diet, hoping to reduce the size of the child at birth. The diet, and occasional bleeding, seemed to weaken Charlotte but apart from that, all progressed well.

Charlotte was due on 19th October but when the end of October came and she had still not gone into labour, people began to grow concerned. When 3rd November arrived and contractions started, everyone breathed a sigh of relief. The physician encouraged her to exercise but not to eat and later that evening, he sent for officials to witness the birth.

As the 4th became the 5th, it was clear Charlotte was in difficulty. An obstetrician was called in who advised the use of forceps, but just as quickly the idea was disregarded since the mortality rate was very high when these instruments were used. Let's not forget this procedure would have occurred without antiseptic.

At nine o'clock on 5th November, Charlotte gave birth to a large stillborn boy. All efforts to resuscitate him were used but everything was in vain and an exhausted Charlotte received the news calmly. She ate a little food and went to sleep as her equally exhausted husband went to bed in the next room.

Soon after midnight, Charlotte woke vomiting and complaining of stomach pains. Her doctor was alarmed to find her cold to the touch and she was having difficulty breathing. Worse still, she was bleeding. He placed heat compacts on her stomach but the bleeding would not stop. He ran to fetch Leopold, but by the time they both returned, she was dead.

On the whole, I'd rather take my own chances than risk the advice of doctor in 18th century England. After starving and bleeding Charlotte in the late stages of her pregnancy, the doctor warmed her up with blankets and a fire when she showed signs of haemorrhaging? I'm no doctor, but shouldn't he have used a cold compress?

It wasn't just Leopold who was inconsolable. Her mother was to hear the news from a passing courier and fainted in shock. George was so distressed; he couldn't even attend the funeral. With Charlotte's death, George's chances of producing an heir were gone and the Hanover dynasty was hanging on by a thread.

It seemed as if the whole nation went into mourning. Drapers ran out of black cloth, gambling dens closed down on the day of her funeral and businesses that had dealt in luxury items petitioned the government to shorten the mourning period for fear they would go bankrupt.

The Hanover dynasty had revolved around Charlotte and her new child and it seemed very fortunate that George's father, King George III, was not lucid enough to understand the implications. Although still the King of England, his father had no idea of what was happening and George had been acting as his regent for years. George III had produced twelve children, seven of them male, but there was not one legitimate grandchild from any of them. For a while, the nation held its breath.

The next male in line after George was his brother Frederick. Frederick was 55 years old and his wife was 51, but their marriage had been very similar to George's. He and his wife were separated and there had been no children from their marriage. Considering her age, there never would be.

After Frederick came William, unmarried but living with his mistress and ten illegitimate children. Then came 51-year-old Edward, also unmarried and living with his mistress in Brussels. Next was Ernest, happily married in Germany where his wife's family lived. But again, no children as yet. 47-year-old Augustus Frederick was next in line. But he had married in contravention of the Royal Marriages Act so his children were not eligible. Last of all brothers came Adolphus, a bachelor of 43.

Now we've all heard of panic buying and we all know what that means. This was more like panic marrying. The race was on to see which one of the overweight, late-middle-aged sons of George III could find a lawful wife who could then become the mother of his children and produce future Hanoverian monarchs. The race was definitely on.

Edward promptly left his mistress high and dry and set off to woo Leopold's sister Marie Luise Victoria, the widow of Prince Leiningen of Amorbach in Lower Franconia whom he'd never set eyes on, while William promptly ditched his mistress and ten children to search for an eligible wife elsewhere. With the limited choice of princesses available to him, William eventually proposed to Adelaide of Saxe-Meiningen, despite being 26 years older than her, but only after Parliament offered to increase his income.

By June 1818, the next year, the youngest brother Adolphus, then aged 43, led the sprint by marrying his second cousin, Princess Augusta of Hesse-Cassell, a beautiful 20-year-old who was a great-granddaughter of King George II and one month later in July, Edward and William were standing side by side at the alter with their prospective brides waiting to be married in a double wedding ceremony. Edward had only met his future wife one week earlier.

With the romance out of the way, all of a sudden the race was on to produce an heir.

Ten months later, Adolphus' wife won the race by producing a son at the end of March but within two months, his brother Edward pipped him at the post when his wife delivered a daughter they named Victoria on 24th May. As the elder brother, any of Edward's heirs were closer to the throne than Adolphus' children.

William was not to be so lucky. In Adelaide's seventh month of pregnancy, she caught pleurisy and gave birth prematurely to a baby daughter who only lived a few hours. Although he drank less, swore less and became more discreet after his marriage, there would be no children.

By the time his father King George III died in 1820, George had already begun re-inventing himself long before his coronation. He began by indulging himself in a magnificent pageant at his coronation with a seemingly inexhaustible budget. The only one not invited was his wife, Caroline. By then, their relationship had been a sham for 25 years.

By banning Caroline from the coronation, Britain had reached the climax of their hatred for George. Refused entry at both doors of Westminster Abbey, Caroline had attempted to enter via Westminster Hall where many guests were gathered before the service began. She stood fuming as bayonets were held against her chin until the Lord Chamberlain had the doors slammed in her face. She screamed hysterically that she would make him pay for her humiliation and then she left to go back to her residence, sobbing into her hands. In all the years she had stood valiantly up to George, this time she was visibly broken.

That night, Caroline fell ill. Even large doses of laudanum before going to bed did not seem to help. Over the next three weeks, she suffered more and more and whispers around the court were saying she was slowly being poisoned. Some whispers suggested she was deliberately trying to kill herself, especially after she had asked the question of her doctors, "Do you think I am poisoned?" The question was so obviously aimed at her husband that it seemed she was making sure to implicate George when she had finally accomplished the job. But would she really take vengeance that far?

Finally, she wrote a new will requesting that she be buried in her home country of Brunswick and then one scant month after George's coronation, she was dead.

It is easy to get carried away with romance, especially where history is concerned. We imagine beautiful dresses and colourful bonnets and choose to forget about the lack of hygiene during these times. Heaven only knows that Britain had never had too many nice things to say about Caroline and her sanitary habits. But when rumours began circulating that Caroline had been poisoned, all eyes turned to George and their dislike for him turned to hatred. And at the funeral procession, the crowd showed him how much they hated him.

Britain was incensed with George's lack of concern for Caroline's death. He had been on board a ship on his way to Ireland when he received the news and he reacted with barely a shrug. After all, he *did* hate her with a passion. But it was this indifference that was the final straw that served to unite the whole nation against him.

Back in London, during heavy torrential rain, the funeral procession route had been changed to the back streets when it erupted into chaos. Through the growing anger of the crowd, soldiers who had formed the guard rode with sabres drawn until finally, as people surged forward threateningly, they opened fire. Two men were shot and killed and in retaliation, people threw cobblestones and bricks at the soldiers. It was only when Caroline's body reached the docks and was placed on a ship ready to be sent off to Brunswick as she had requested that the crowd settled down.

Over the coming years, things calmed marginally but it was never the same for George. His subjects had a long memory of what his family were capable of. Ask the MacDonalds what had happened at Glencoe when the Hanoverians had stepped in.

George's heavy drinking and indulgent lifestyle were beginning to take its toll. By the late 1820s and three years before his death, his corset was made for a waist of 50 inches and he would spend whole days in bed suffering from spasms of breathlessness that would leave him half asphyxiated. He had stopped going out in public because of his immense size and his health began to worry him in more ways than he was willing to let on. He suffered from gout, arteriosclerosis, dropsy and possibly porphyria, like his father, and grandfather. He knew Britain mocked him about his size, but he was not so eager that they should know that he perhaps suffered from his father's supposed mental illness as well.

It's easy to see how his gene pool arrived at this state, regardless of porphyria or not. It had been an impossibility to marry anyone who was not of royal blood and each royal seems to have married a first cousin or close to it. But it was hard to tell with George. He had always told a story many times over if he had a favourable reaction the first time. And when he married Caroline, he was openly suspicious of her every move and claiming there were assassins everywhere, lurking in the shadows. Perhaps it was his opulent lifestyle that made his symptoms difficult to determine. Alcohol, food and opium were certainly his addictions in later life and he repeatedly bled himself. A year before his death, he was even proclaiming that he had been at the Battle of Waterloo.

In modern times, there has never been a sovereign who died so unlamented nor has a monarch retained so little respect after death. The only possibility that comes close to it is Henry VIII and the similarities between the two monarchs are more surprising than you might think.

Everyone has skeletons in their closets but Henry and George seem to have had more than their fair share. We know they both loved women. To marry Anne Boleyn, Henry had to cast aside his older Catholic wife. To marry Caroline, George had to cast aside his older Catholic wife as well, although sources indicate that the separation was more than likely mutual because Mrs FitzHerbert was no Catherine of Aragon pining away. In fact, if you look closely at George, it was a lucky escape for her.

George's account of his wedding night even echoes Henry's criticisms of Anne of Cleves, who he pointed out was flabby, smelly and probably not a virgin. Sadly both Anne and Caroline were doomed not to please their husbands.

It was George's desperation to rid himself of Caroline that he resembles Henry the most. In that respect, George and Henry were both frantic. The only thing George couldn't do was lop her head off. In youth, both had wit, humour and brains but it was their vanity that let them down. Henry truly believed he was irresistible to the opposite sex despite his festering ulcerated leg while George resembled Jabba the Hut. Their most crucial mistake was to actually believe in the image they had carefully manufactured, rather than in the less enriching reality. But no one was going to tell either of them that. Especially not their mistresses.

From love of women, we move on to love of food. We all know that Henry was immensely fat in his old age but George was even heavier than Henry when he died. Both had turned to food for comfort from their shattered love lives and ailing bodies. Both had started out in life as handsome virile young men but in old age, both just looked like fat old men.

As with Henry, there seemed to be no limit to George's wants and desires with both of them spending a personal fortune exceeding the national revenue of a third-world power during their lifetimes. Both men threw terrible temper tantrums and neither of them could dig up a friend if they tried.

Depressed by his evident failure to reinvent himself, the ailing George simply withdrew into a fantasy world of laudanum and alcohol. But by then, everyone hated him anyway and they couldn't care less. What is perhaps most astonishing about George's life is that the British monarchy survived at all.

As he grew fatter and older, he must have realised how fragile life was, with everything spiralling out of control. He daughter was dead, he had lost five siblings over recent years and his own health was failing. But it was the death of his brother Frederick, and the fact that the Hanover dynasty were dwindling away, that truly shocked him.

George had been one of four brothers born within five years of each other, although there were seven boys in total, and their dynasty looked rosy. All had been healthy, feisty young men with the world at their feet. But with Frederick dead, the next in line for the throne was 62-year-old William and he didn't have any legitimate children either. George's brother Edward, now dead, had been the only one to produce a child, Princess Victoria, but she was only ten years old. It probably wasn't what his father had envisaged with twelve young lively children running and screaming happily through the halls of his villas.

George was, by the time of his death, largely irrelevant to Britain. He undoubtedly left behind a shimmering legacy of stunning, if not eclectic, homes and collections and many of the pageants and settings he devised for his own pleasure and amusement were subsequently adapted to serve as key symbols in the 20th century monarchy. But he also bequeathed to future generations, and particularly to the sovereigns who were to follow him, a lesson in how, and how not, to conduct oneself.

By the time George died, people were thoroughly fed up with him. The thought had even crossed their minds, with all the problems the Hanovers had brought with them, "*Why not get rid of the monarchy completely?*" And then they remembered Cromwell. The fear of something possibly worse than George overshadowed their thoughts so it was pushed to the back of their minds.

George died in the early hours of 26th June 1830 of a ruptured blood vessel in his stomach and a messenger was immediately dispatched to rouse William out of bed to let him know of his brother's death. William had seen it coming for years so he was not at all surprised to hear the news. He dismissed the messenger with a curt nod and turned around, ready to return to bed, muttering to himself that he had never slept with a queen before.

WILLIAM IV

Born 1765
Reign 1830 – 1837

William never imagined he would be sitting on the throne of England. He had two older brothers who could carry that bothersome burden without any help from him and he had very little interest in politics anyway. He'd never even felt the urge to offer any opinions. Not that he had many. He'd been a soldier for most of his life, not a politician, serving in North America and the Caribbean, although even then, he hadn't seen much action. If George IV was considered the black sheep in the family, William should have been known as the dark horse.

His career in the navy was anything but sparkling or noteworthy. He did his fair share of cooking and was even arrested after a drunken brawl in Gibraltar but when it became known who he was, he was quickly released. His only claim to fame was in the Americas when George Washington approved a plan to kidnap him. Even this bit of excitement came to nothing when word leaked out who he was and he was immediately assigned guards to protect him. He was then shipped off to the West Indies under Horatio Nelson in 1788 who later became his greatest friend and promoted him to Rear Admiral the following year. The closest he ever came to action in the

Napoleonic wars was when he was watching the bombardment of Antwerp from a church steeple and a stray bullet nicked his coat. Even then, there was no real harm done, although it must have increased his heart rate for quite a time afterwards.

His political concern was equally as unimpressive. He'd only spent a small amount of time in the House of Lords where he was noted for opposing the abolition of slavery, reasoning that freedom would do the slaves little good anyway. He'd seen the standards of living among the free men in Scotland and their poverty-stricken way of life was by far worse than the slaves in the West Indies.

As a young man, he was very much like his elder brother George. They both seemed hell-bent on shocking their parents and they'd both succeeded magnificently. It was almost like they'd sat down head to head and puzzled over what was the worst thing they could possibly do. Both were nearly destitute after racking up huge gambling debts and both had chosen to take mistresses instead of marrying respectable princesses from Germany. And to make it worse, both mistresses were Irish Catholic actresses with children in tow from a couple of previous relationships. In this respect however, William surpassed his brother George. His mistress, Dorothea Jordan, had already delivered four children to two different fathers before she'd even met him.

Ireland was not the place to be starting any new career, especially acting, and Dorothea Bland had always dreamed of being a famous actress on the stage. With no prospects or jobs available in Ireland, her mother encouraged 15-year-old Dorothea to cross the Irish Sea and follow her shining star elsewhere. From all accounts, England was the place where doors opened for women of her particular talents.

When she arrived in England, things had looked enticingly hopeful for a while. She'd picked up a few acting jobs and she had a little money in her pocket for the first time in years. She even considered herself 'respectable'. That was until she was forced to change her name to the more suitable 'Mrs Jordan' to cover up an untimely pregnancy to Richard Daly, the married manager of Theatre Royal company. She delivered a little girl she named Frances Daly and moved on.

Witty, pretty and charming, there were no end of male heads turning in her direction. There was a short affair with an army lieutenant, then the owner of the Wilkinson Theatre Group in Leeds but when she met the male lead of the company, a man by the name of George Inchbald, she was in love.

If he'd asked her to marry him, she would have forsaken everything and devoted herself entirely to him. But he never asked and broken-hearted, she finally left in 1786 to begin an affair with a police magistrate by the name of Sir Richard Ford who said all the right things and *did* promise to marry her. Excitedly, she moved in with him.

This was the beginning of the Burlesque era and it was all the rage in England. It was a time when actresses sang and danced on stage while showing off their bodies in men's breeches, imitating sexually aggressive behaviour. The risqué, lewd dialogue was highly entertaining, full of laughter and innuendos, and William absolutely loved it.

Dorothea fit in perfectly, from her bawdy humour to her outrageous behaviour and to her seductive smile. Very soon, she was being credited with having the most beautiful legs on the stage and it looks like William wholeheartedly agreed. He loved them so much he asked Dorothea to live with him and be his mistress.

It was at this stage she began to weigh up her present situation. By then, she had three illegitimate children to Ford and there were still no forthcoming wedding arrangements. She would have realised it had never been his intention to marry her at all so she had a couple of choices to consider. She could stay with Ford as his mistress forever or she could leave him and set up house with the dashing and fun-loving royal, William Duke of Clarence.

She didn't think for very long. She sent for her sister Hester to come to England and care for her children and then transferred all her savings to her for the education and maintenance of them. Then she moved in with William.

Under the Royal Marriages Act of 1772, there was no chance in all of heaven that permission would be given to either him or his brother George to marry the women of their choice instead of the ones chosen by their father. But rather than listen to their adamant father's sound advice, both boys went ahead anyway and lived with their mistresses, despite what their parents thought.

William's domestic life with Dorothea was surprisingly happy for him and if the relationship had started out with her wearing the pants in the family, if you know what I mean, he must have been able to remove them at least ten times because over the years there were ten children, laughing and running wildly through the house, much to the horror and disgust of William's straight-laced parents. No expense was spared in their world full of wild extravagance and opulent parties.

The spin-off from William and Dorothea's excessive entertaining was that money was always tight. With ten hungry mouths to feed, there was never much spare cash to be seen. Add that to the fact that William had the same gambling problem as his elder brother and you begin to realise that William was more than a little desperate for a cash input.

By the time George's daughter Charlotte died in childbirth, William could not see his way out of his dire financial situation. But with her death, William was suddenly the second in line to the throne after his elder brother Frederick (who had no children and was estranged from his wife) so things improved dramatically for him almost overnight.

The decision to marry fertile princesses was not made by William or his younger brother Edward. It was Parliament who had made that decision and it was Parliament who waved the same juicy money carrot in front of them both as they had with Charles II. At this stage, their father, King George III, had retreated into his own world again and was not able to understand the death of his granddaughter Charlotte or the consequences of it. That's when Parliament stepped in to fill the gap.

The lure they offered was if the brothers could find suitable wives, and ones *they* approved of, they vowed they would pay off the bulk of their gambling debts and supply them with a good annual income. Hope blossomed for William at this unexpected windfall that would improve his lot, until he embarrassingly mentioned that he'd had limited success with women in his prime must less at this late stage of his life. As hope slowly began to evaporate, Parliament generously offered to help out by sending his youngest brother Adolphus to Europe in search of a suitable bride for him while he continued his own search in England.

At this stage, Adolphus himself was unmarried and next in line to the throne after his brothers Frederick, William, Edward, and Augustus, in that order. But you can see the obvious problem straight away. Being sixth in the line is not a very promising or realistic place to be and thoughts of finding a bride for himself, and eventually having children, had already surfaced in his mind. But before he could do that, he had to first fulfil the task given to him by Parliament and find a bride for his brother. But in the back of his mind, he had thoughts of the possibility of finding one for himself as well.

The offer from Parliament was too good for William to refuse and he grabbed it willingly.

Now a lot of you will be asking the obvious question, *"But what about Dorothea and the children?"* No matter how beautiful her legs had been in her youth, after the physical ravages on her body from producing ten children over the years, airing her breeches and returning to the stage was not going to be a viable option for Dorothea.

Luckily for her, that option was something she did not have to worry about. As part of the deal, William promised a yearly stipend to care for their daughters while he retained custody and care of the boys. To maintain that stipend, there was one stipulation: Dorothea must not return to the stage.

With everyone in agreeance, William set off to find an eligible princess.

William had never been successful with women and although he'd attempted to find a suitable wife in his youth, there was never anyone who took him up on his offer of marriage. That was well and truly before he met Dorothea. So for William, finding a bride wasn't as straightforward as his brothers' quests were. At his advanced age of 53, he knew it wasn't going to be easy especially when they found out he came with a huge gambling debt to boot. Seeing his brothers already way in front of him in the marriage race, he made repetitive hurried proposals of marriage to an heiress who in turn repeatedly refused him. He then tried a rich heiress in Brighton and when she turned him down as well, he listened to Adolphus and went down the traditional royal path of seeking a bride amongst the royal stud farms of Protestant Germany.

Adolphus' choice of a bride for William could not have been better. 26-year-old Princess Adelaide of Saxe-Meiningen was amicable, home loving and she was happy to take on William's nine remaining children, several of whom had not reached adulthood at that stage. She was also happy to take his finances in hand with the monetary gift from Parliament tucked away safely in the bank.

With the stakes so high and with prospects so low, you'd think William would have jumped at the prospect of ending the search with someone so agreeable. But there was a glitch for William. Adelaide may have been accommodating and good-natured but she was just an unassuming princess from an unimportant German state and it caused William to hesitate.

Eventually, with a limited choice of available princesses and when all other deals fell through, William took Adolphus' advice and a proposal of marriage was finally offered to Princess Adelaide. To his astonishment, she willingly accepted.

It left the way open for Adolphus, then aged 43, to offer a proposal of marriage to his second cousin, Princess Augusta of Hesse-Cassell, a beautiful 20-year-old who was a great-granddaughter of King George II, who also happily accepted.

At this stage, their brother Edward had unceremoniously dropped his mistress and was on the lookout for a suitable bride within days of the same offer.

Edward Duke of Kent had always been intended to be a soldier. But not just any soldier. He was meant to be *German* soldier, and at an early age, he was sent off to Hanover for training. Like all his brothers and ancestors before him, Edward was wild and extravagant so when he arrived in Hanover, the punishing discipline of German military life came as a rude shock to the English prince. But Edward had a surprise in store for everyone. Despite all the expected difficulties with the rigorous training and strict regime, Edward excelled.

Five years later, Edward was given his first command and posted to Gibraltar to restore discipline among the drunken troops although the command came with quite a bit of reluctance from his commanders. They understood the difference between a good soldier and a good commander and the two scenarios were totally different. Edward had excelled in his training and it had turned him into a good soldier but what the training had also done was to bring out a rather nasty, mean streak in his character.

Edward arrived with gust and bravado at his new position ready to perform his duties to the utmost. But instead of taking the time to let the troops understand his assignment, they found a tyrant who was completely and utterly severe with them.

His men detested him. He revelled in drills and inspections and the smallest infringement was met with merciless floggings. Most times, he silently watched his men stand exhaustedly on the parade ground for hours on end. It was when his commanding officers back home began receiving reports of a planned mutiny that they all agreed to relocate him elsewhere and forbid him to ever return.

But it wasn't just Edward's methods of command that was bothering his commanders. They'd heard that while Edward was stationed in Geneva during his training, he was introduced to a French colonel, Baron de Fortisson, and his beautiful, witty and clever wife Therese-Bernardine-Julie de Montgenet de Saint-Laurent. Soon afterwards, Edward and Therese-Bernardine became lovers and when Edward was transferred to Gibraltar, Therese-Bernardine left her husband and Edward smuggled her into Gibraltar so they could be together.

When his father George III was informed of the situation, brown stuff hit the fan. Instantly, he agreed with the commanders and the remote province of Quebec in Canada was suggested.

Humiliated, he refused to take the direct order from his father and angry messages were sent back and forth. It wasn't until his successor arrived five months later that he had no choice but to reluctantly accept the new posting. Three months later he left Gibraltar, steadfastly accompanied by his mistress, who he introduced as Julie de Saint-Laurent, a reputed widow.

What everyone should have realised was that being in a different country doesn't change someone's personality.

Perhaps Edward was miffed at the slur on his character by people he saw as beneath him or perhaps he just saw Canada as a barbaric country unworthy of his experience. Whatever the reason, and much to the horror of his new troops, they found the brutal Gibraltar pattern continuing. In fact, it worsened. He was even crueller to his men than he had been in Gibraltar and the barrack grounds echoed with the screams of his men being flogged daily. One French deserter was tracked down unrelentingly and when brought back was given the maximum sentence of 999 lashes. If Edward had hoped for some sort of reaction, he certainly got one. But I'm sure it wasn't the reaction he expected. As Edward stood silently watching the punishment being delivered, the deserter did not so much as whimper. When the punishment was over, he staggered up to Edward and told him that no whip could cower a Frenchman.

Had Charlotte and her baby not died, there is every chance that he and Julie would have lived happily ever after. But one morning, 28 years later, while the sun shone gloriously and while Edward was eating his breakfast,

Julie opened the mail and fished out the *Morning Chronicle*. Charlotte's death was all over the papers and the headlines jumped off the page. Princess Charlotte, heiress to the British throne, was dead.

Perhaps she had some idea that her relationship with Edward was over, because the news exploded like a bomb at the breakfast table and she fainted. And she was right to be apprehensive. After hasty messages to his brothers, Edward learned that they were doing their utmost to discard their mistresses and pursue honourable brides of childbearing age.

Edward had no intention of being left out of the baby race. Leaving Julie with no recourse but to return alone to Paris to live with friends and relatives, he packed his bags and left armed with letters of introduction to Charlotte's widower, Leopold, asking permission to woo his sister Marie Luise Victoria, the widow of Prince Leiningen of Amorbach in Lower Franconia. Ah, romance.

Marie Luise, known as Victoire, was a poverty-stricken widow with two children who lived in a country that had been impoverished since the Thirty Years War in the 17th century. Napoleon's army had left it desolate and by the time Victoire's father died, Napoleon had formally brought the region to an end and her people were starving when she became their duchess. They had never seen more wretched days.

Victoire had known the hazards of being royal where the monarchy could be reduced to ruins, or killed, at the whims of fate. The plump, rosy-cheeked woman constantly lived in a state of insecurity and had a profound sympathy for anyone else who lived the same horror. At 32 years old when she met Edward Duke of Kent, she was penniless with no prospects outside the chance of marriage and unfortunately for Edward, he was not that far in front of her. In fact, she was swapping an impoverished country to marry a virtual pauper. But taking all of this into account, she still believed she'd landed on her feet in clover.

By then, the race for a royal heir was in full swing and George III's sons were all lining up at the starting gate. William was still eyeing off the heiress in Brighton. Ernest's wife, the Duchess of Cumberland had lost her first baby minutes after his birth but was pregnant again and Adolphus was on the point of marrying Princess Augusta. It was up to his brother George, acting as regent for his ill father, to give Edward permission to marry Victoire and luckily for him all was approved. Parliament even increased his income to £6,000. With a lot of debt behind him, he had been hoping and praying for £25,000, which was what Parliament had offered his elder brother Frederick if he brought his wife back from the countryside and began producing children (which he repeatedly refused by the way). But Edward was told that times were tough and he'd have to make do with their offer. With very little time available to quibble over the money issue, Edward grudgingly agreed. All three brothers had left it nail-bitingly close.

Edward and Victoire left Britain for her native Coburg and the wedding took place in a beautiful baroque Schloss, which her brother Leopold had only just finished refurbishing. With that out of the way, they immediately turned around and headed back to England where they planned to go through another marriage ceremony according to the rites of the Church of England. At this stage, they'd only known each other a week.

Adolphus led the sprint by marrying Augusta in June and one month later in July, Edward and Victoire stood at the altar beside William and Adelaide in a double ceremony. After the ceremony all brothers parted ways.

Adolphus' wife was the first to produce a son at the end of March 1819 but within two months, his elder brother Edward pipped him at the post when Victoire delivered a daughter on 24th May they named Victoria. Her birth came in the nick of time because in just a few short months, Edward would be dead.

The family had set off on a holiday in early December, staying for a short time in Salisbury and arriving at Woolbrook Cottage in Devon on Christmas Eve. Time passed quietly, except for a rather disconcerting and ominous incident when a fortune-teller told Edward that two members of the Royal Family would soon die. Precautions were taken and Victoria was bundled up warmly and cossetted even more than usual.

As it turned out, it was Edward who caught the cold and in the weeks after Christmas, it worsened. After a fall of heavy snow, Edward and a servant took a long walk on the cliffs for some fresh air and Edward got wet. It was 15th January but there was still no cause for alarm.

By 18th January however, his condition had worsened and on the 20th, he took to his bed. Fever and delirium had set in and of course the doctors took over with their gruesome medical treatments. Blistering, bleeding and leeches were administered but not surprisingly, everything failed. During a short respite on 22nd, Edward made a hurried will making sure that his child Victoria, nicknamed Drina, would be entrusted to the care of her mother. By evening, a small group had gathered around his bed. He looked at his wife and said, *"Do not forget me"* and sank once more into delirium. After five days, on the morning of 23rd January, Edward died.

Victoire was devastated at her loss and with the help of her brother Leopold, decided to return to Kensington with her daughter.

Before the month was over, the fortune-teller was proven correct. The old King, George III, now blind and suffering from recurring madness, had spoken for 58 consecutive hours, almost without drawing breath, and had died six days after his son Edward. Victoria's Uncle George was now the king.

William was not to be as lucky as his brothers had been with his quest for children. In Adelaide's seventh month of pregnancy, on 27th March, while holidaying on the Continent, she caught pleurisy and gave birth prematurely to a baby daughter they called Charlotte who only lived a few hours.

Almost immediately, she fell pregnant again and William decided to move the household to England so his wife could rest during the pregnancy and their future heir would be born on British soil. Sadly for them both, she miscarried during the journey on 5th September. One year later, she was pregnant again and the jubilant couple produced a second daughter they named Elizabeth, born on 10th December 1820, and dropping Edward's daughter Victoria down one in the line to the throne.

Three months later in March 1821, even though Elizabeth seemed strong and healthy, she died of 'inflammation of the bowels'. One year later again, twin boys were stillborn and people were praying that Adelaide's pregnancy history was not to be the same as Queen Anne's previous horrific history of miscarriages, stillbirths and deaths.

While William and Adelaide grieved for their dead children, Edward's healthy baby girl Victoria flourished at third in the line for the throne, after her uncles Frederick and William.

After 40–odd years of living the high life, William seemed reformed by his marriage. He took to walking for hours on end, eating frugally and only drinking barley water flavoured with lemon. Both of his elder brothers were obesely overweight and unhealthy and it was only a matter of time before one of them died.

In 1827 at the age of 61, William was one step closer to the throne when his elder brother Frederick died of dropsy. If William could hold out until George died, he would certainly ascend to the throne as king of both Britain and Hanover.

And that's what happened in 1830.

With every bone in his body constantly telling him that he was 64 years old, William tried his best at ruling. He really did. After having had no interest in Parliament in the past, from the beginning of his reign he proved to be a conscientious king unlike his brother before him. Even the Duke of Wellington, still the Prime Minister after an election the previous year, stated that he had done more business with William in ten minutes than he had done with George in as many weeks. William asked questions that George had been scared to ask in case his ignorance became too evident and of the questions his brother had troubled himself to ask, he had not even bothered to wait for an answer. In all, William was a vast improvement on his brother who had growled and sulked his way through the past ten years.

William was out to bring the budget back into line and his first act was to dismiss George's French chefs and German band, replacing them both with English ones. From there, he handed over George's prized painting collection to the London museum and reduced the number of studs in his stable by half. Twice he tried to give Buckingham Palace away: once as an army barracks and secondly to Parliament when Parliament House burned down in 1834. He was so intent on penny-pinching; he almost put an end to his own coronation ceremony when he stated that simply wearing the crown was enough. He was persuaded against this by Parliament and compromised to simply cutting the budget for the ceremony to £16,000 (equivalent of around £1,500,000 by today's standards) instead of the budget his brother had used of £240,000 (almost £200,000,000).

Unlike William's previous lack of enthusiasm for politics, he began to take an active interest in Parliament and to his surprise, he found he had a knack for it. In the past, he had a reputation for tactlessness and buffoonery but he was proving that he could be shrewd and diplomatic although there were times when he had mud thrown at his carriage, and he was hissed at on more than one occasion on his way to Parliament.

Above all, William was proving to be a real thinker. He thought long and hard over every decision and always did what he felt was good for the country. He even went out of his way to flatter the American ambassador at a dinner party, announcing that George Washington was the greatest man that had ever lived. He also had the foresight to recognise that the potential construction of the Suez Canal would make good relations with Egypt.

It was when Napoleon had occupied Cairo that he had sent a team of archaeologists and scientists to investigate the remnants of an ancient waterway passage. Their findings had included detailed maps depicting an ancient canal extending northward from the Red Sea and then westward towards the Nile and Napoleon was all for opening it up again. Although construction was shelved after the preliminary survey concluded that the Red Sea was 10 metres higher than the Mediterranean, William believed somehow that the report was incorrect. It was only his wariness at stepping on French toes that held him back from sending a team of English investigators to Cairo.

Britain was not the only country taking an interest in Egypt. Archaeologists were flooding into Egypt from all over the world after Giovanni Belzoni had discovered some ancient burial sites of Egyptian pharaohs. Belzoni and his business partners had made a fortune from the antiquities they'd shipped to Europe in large amounts. Belzoni was just part of a small team where one partner made the discoveries while he and his other partner robbed the sites. It was Belzoni who had sent the head of Memnon, the trunk of Ramses and the straight left arm of an unknown pharaoh to England, all of which are in the British Museum's Egyptian section today. Despite the riches being found, if there was one thing William firmly believed in, it was that Britain should stay out of other countries' affairs. He had no want to rock anybody's boat. Especially not a French boat.

The topic of conversation on everyone's lips, either at dinner tables or in taverns, was William. They discussed his shortcomings and they discussed his insights, and eventually, they compared him to his brother George. Both had been wild boys in their youth but George had never outgrown his childishness. Some said by the looks of it, William had mellowed after marrying Adelaide and had really settled down. Some just said they were reserving their opinions until a later date. What they all agreed on though was the fact that he actually seemed to care.

William's reign was short but eventful and although he was fond of his niece, he showed open contempt for Victoria's mother, who it seems had showed William's wife some disrespect. At a banquet that included Victoria and her mother as guests, William gave a momentous speech. He said, *"I trust to God that my life may be spared for nine months longer... I should then have the satisfaction of leaving the exercise of the Royal authority to the personal authority of that young lady, heiress presumptive to the Crown, and not in the hands of a person now near me, who is surrounded by evil advisers and is herself incompetent to act with propriety in the situation in which she would be placed."*

His meaning was clear. He wanted to live long enough to see Victoria turn 18 so that her ineffectual mother would never be asked to act as regent. It left many guests open-eyed in shock and Victoria in tears.

This speech was the last he would ever give.

April of 1837 marked a sudden decline in William's already frail health. He was still close to most of his and Dorothea's children but none more so than his favourite daughter, Sophia. When she died during childbirth, the news knocked the remaining wind out of his sail. Even her death did not mend the terrible breach between William and his eldest illegitimate son, George 1st Earl of Munster. Many times over the years, there were savage quarrels between the two over money and prestige. All too familiar of the Hanoverians, William had given his son lands and titles but his son wanted more. To top it off, he had huge gambling debts he wanted his father to clear. Some things never change.

By June, William had still not been able to shake off the profound sense of loss after his daughter's death. As he fretted, his health deteriorated even more until his physicians could do little to help him. They knew he was mortally ill and Adelaide refused to leave his side. William had missed his niece's 18th birthday party the month before but he had hung on, as he had hoped and prayed he would. In the true Hanoverian tradition, William died without ever reconciling with his son.

Britain now had someone else to focus on. For the first time since Queen Elizabeth, they had a fresh young queen who was like a breath of fresh air on a hot summer's day. At 18, her life was filled with endless possibilities.

It would be a very different future from her rather melancholy childhood where she had shared a bedroom with her mother every night and been isolated from other children for most of her life.

THE VICTORIAN ERA

*W*hen looking at the Victorian era, you would be forgiven for thinking it was a highly moralistic, strait-laced time in English history with Queen Victoria's considerable influence. And basically it was. But not everything was so cut and dried.

It was a time of great reforms in technology, engineering, entertainment, medicine, sport and above all, sanitation. Britain was in a state of industrial euphoria and her people were obsessed with mechanical gadgets. But with all of this, and the growth in population, there was also an increase in poverty, prostitution and child labour.

It was a time of Charles Dickens, Arthur Conan Doyle, Charlotte Bronte and her sisters while theatre saw a series of fourteen comic operas by Gilbert and Sullivan performed. People could enjoy the sound of a brass band when strolling through parklands or they could be entertained by one of the many travelling circuses dominating the kingdom. Gentlemen went to dining clubs, and gambling establishments called casinos were wildly popular. For excitement, they could take a locomotive ride hurtling them across the country from London to Birmingham at over 30 miles per hour. By 1845, 2441 miles of railway lines had been laid and 30 million passengers were being carried every year. Gentlemen could also look forward to a relatively shorter steamship passage to America if they wanted, taking only 22 days to cross the Atlantic. By 1830, three major shipping lines had popped up and trade routes to India, South Africa and Australia were established.

It was a Golden Age when Britain was the world's most powerful nation. If you lived in this time, you would find that the Victorian era was a time of unparalleled growth where the population rose from 13.9 million in 1831 to 32.5 million by Queen Victoria's death in 1901. But while the population in England and Wales almost doubled from 16.8 million to 30.5million and Scotland saw a rise from 2.8 million to 4.4 million, Ireland's decreased rapidly to 4.5 million, less than half, mostly due to the Great Famine. This ticking time bomb had far reaching consequences as the Irish blamed the British government for the famine since Britain benefited from any new policies while they were content to sit back and let Ireland continue to suffer.

Despite 15 million emigrants leaving the United Kingdom to settle in United States, Canada, New Zealand and Australia in the hope of starting a new life, the population boomed. You could probably put this increase down to the new sanitation reforms where thousands of miles of street sewers were built to try and clean up the dirty, overflowing gutters full of human faeces and waste. You didn't have to nimbly sidestep slops being thrown out the windows anymore. Or you could put it down to the introduction of soap, which was fast becoming a main product in the relatively new phenomenon of advertising. Or perhaps it was the new sewage works that were in full swing, improving the quality of drinking water as well.

In this healthier environment, diseases were less frequent and they did not spread as easily as they once had. It was also the first century when a major epidemic did not occur although a cholera outbreak did take place in London in 1848, killing 10,000 people. If you were a woman, you were more likely to survive your childhood now as nutrition standards increased, leaving you able to produce more children. Greater prosperity allowed people to finance a marriage, which in turn meant the birth rate increased.

It was an era where upper class people could look forward to train trips to the seaside and moving around on stagecoaches and steam ships and goods could be brought in by these same methods, rapidly increasing trade and industry. Essentials and raw materials such as corn and cotton arrived from the United States as well as meat and wool from Australia. With the increase in mobility, communication between countries flourished as well.

An increase in prosperity meant longer working hours and lighting the streets for demanding businesses became imperative if you wanted to keep the lower class from waylaying you on your way home from work. Gas lighting became widespread in industry, homes and the streets and ensured your survival for another working day.

On weekends, you could watch your favourite sport. Cricket, croquet, roller-skating and horseback riding became very popular in the Victorian era as did the modern game of tennis first played at Wimbledon in London 1877. Football mania was also taking over and you could get swept up with the beginning of FA Cup fever.

If you were well off and needed an operation, chloroform was now available and the use of anaesthetic meant you did not have to be tied down to have a tooth removed anymore. More and more people were having teeth pulled, replacing them with real human teeth set into hand-carved chunks of ivory from hippopotamus or walrus jaws. If you were one of the lucky ones, you could also obtain teeth from executed criminals, victims from battlefields or even from grave robbers.

But with the increase of population came large numbers of skilled and unskilled people looking for work. This population increase kept wages down to a barely subsistence level while housing became scarce and very expensive. Seeing a potential to make a lot of money, wealthy homeowners began turning their beautiful houses into hideous flats and tenements where thirty or more people of all ages inhabited a single room. But with landlords failing to maintain the dwellings, the once beautiful homes slowly turned into slums.

In the poorer quarters of Britain's larger cities, almost one child in five born alive in the 1830s and 1840s had died by the age of five and it can be put down to polluted water and damp housing. Death rates as a whole remained obstinately above 20 per thousand until the 1880s and only dropped to 17 by the end of Victoria's reign. Of all dreaded diseases the country endured, tuberculosis still remained unconquered, claiming between 60,000 and 70,000 lives in each decade that Victoria reigned.

With finances stretched to the very limit and little work available, you could not afford to have children at school. Many could neither read nor write unless the parents taught them in their spare time, which in most instances were never. So, with work hard to find, children were expected to help towards the family budget, often working long hours in dangerous jobs for extremely low wages. Young boys were employed as chimney sweeps and small children were used to scramble under machinery to retrieve cotton bobbins. These same children also had their use in coal mines, crawling through tunnels too narrow and low for adults.

Children as young as 4 years old were put to work in the mines and a breakfast of porridge was all that was on offer at 5am in the morning. Most parents could only spare a slice of cake for the child to eat during the day, although no rest time was allotted for breaks. Generally, they died before the age of 25 after working 16-hour days for most of their lives. The lucky ones could sell flowers, matches, and work as shoe shiners and apprentices to respectable traders. Working hours were long: 64 hours a week in summer and 52 in winter while domestic servants worked 80 hours a week no matter what time of year. It was only in 1833 that a Royal Commission recommended that children aged between 11 and 18 should only work a maximum of 12 hours a day and children aged between nine and 11, a maximum of eight hours. This act, however, only applied to the textile trade, not mining.

If you were a girl and you couldn't find work as a servant, there was always prostitution and many girls between the ages of 14 and 22 had no other choice. A census in 1851 showed that the population of Great Britain was roughly 18 million and roughly 750,000 women would remain unmarried simply because there were not enough men. It was a time when men like Charles Dickens portrayed prostitutes as commodities used and then thrown away when men were finished with them. And it was a time to look out for venereal disease. It was also when Jack the Ripper stalked and prowled the streets of Whitechapel looking for his victims.

Despite all of this, Queen Victoria's reign was one of peace, prosperity and national self-confidence for Britain. Victoria had turned 18 years old on 24th May 1837 and one month later, her uncle King William IV died at the age of 71. On that day, the emotional, obstinate, straight-talking young woman became the Queen of United Kingdom.

Germany, as such, didn't exist when Victoria assumed her throne. The German people occupied a motley collection of princedoms, duchies and kingdoms, which were brought together much later primarily through the efforts of a statesman, Otto von Bismarck. He engineered the expansion of

German military, the political triumph of Prussia and the creation of the German Reich. He bequeathed to Europe a Germany that was thirsting for conquest.

Victoria's marriage to Prince Albert of Saxe-Coburg-Saalfeld would have difficult moments. Both wanted power and neither of them wanted to surrender their independence. But although there would be a thunderous clash of wills, above all, they loved each other passionately and when they weren't at loggerheads with each other, they were an amazing pair.

Like most marriages, there were times when the gears crunched. She liked to stay up late. He preferred to go to bed early. Still, they had enough shared bedtime to produce nine children, all of whom lived to adulthood at a time when child mortality rates were still appallingly high. Although she did not enjoy being perpetually pregnant, she did exactly that for about a decade and a half, and with her guidance, she and her descendants would occupy the thrones of ten major European countries. Hers was a dynastic web that guaranteed diplomacy was simply a domestic drama.

There was a very complicated German connection that ran through Victoria's veins. Through both parents and grandparents, she was German and she in turn had married a German. She even felt German. As such, it is easy to understand that Britain and Germany were the best of friends for a long time. In the future though, there would be a tragic failure for her grandchildren to understand one another. It destined these two nations to explode on the battlefields of the First World War as the biggest family squabble of all time, surpassing The War of the Roses.

How Britain came to fight alongside Russia against Germany is one of the greatest mysteries of the 20th century, especially since Germany was family, friend and a traditional ally.

Victoria had tangled connections with the kings, queens and lesser royals of Europe and hers was a dysfunctional family held tightly together largely by arranged marriages, some of which turned out to be reasonably happy and many of which did not.

With all this interbreeding, difficulties inevitably arose, such as haemophilia that was passed on to several of Victoria's family, especially her unhappy son Leopold, as well as some of her grandchildren through her daughters.

Victoria kept close tabs on all of this, as she did on almost everything.

She presided over a nation that was in a state of creative bloom and she had plenty to do with bringing it to the cusp of the modern age.

Victoria's story is one of intricate family squabbles. Their pleasures, their friendships and above all, their poisonous rivalries and jealousies, would play a key role in the realignment of Europe. It is also the story of how royalty dragged Europe into the abyss of a terrible family tragedy that would end the lives of many millions of innocent people.

Victoria did not ask to be queen. It was thrust upon her by the accident of birth and then by a succession of accidents that removed others who stood between her and the throne. She assumed it reluctantly and, at first, incompetently.

Parliament was sure she could be relied upon to leave the job of running the country to the professionals.

Couldn't she?

www.ingramcontent.com/pod-product-compliance
Lightning Source LLC
Chambersburg PA
CBHW072148070526
44585CB00015B/1044